SOMETHING IS SERIOUSLY WRONG

BASED ON A TRUE ACCOUNT OF FAMILY VIOLENCE AND SYSTEM ABUSE

DENIS BRIGHT

Cover design: Christopher Venning

Dedicated to victims of domestic violence

ABOUT THE COVER

The artwork moves around in a circumference, like a storyline, showing different ebbs and flows of each issue that appeared over the timeline of events. All the different colours and layered shapes show each phase, like a connected cycle of overlapping events. The changing colours show the different moods and emotions when passing through each phase of the system (anger, sadness, relief, connection). Although the pathway is negative in nature, its connected family closer together therefore has both negative and positive connotations, so the circular style represents the tight family, around the central issue (middle circle). An interpretation however can also be interpreted in various ways by each viewer – flower, eye, stitching, knitting. The handwritten title gives a more humanistic approach, like a letter you would pass to someone when something is seriously wrong.

INTRODUCTION

I began documenting my daughter's movements and communications to protect her – not only from her relentless abuser, Luca Savington (Sav), but from the police. Monica was required to defend two DVOs after police fell for Sav's lies. With the police doing the bidding of the abuser, Monica was arrested, interrogated and relentlessly harassed. Truth counted for nothing. Evidence seemed irrelevant. It was extraordinary that this could occur against the backdrop of a nation in crisis, where record numbers of women were being abused or killed by their partners. Through researching domestic violence, I came to understand that what was happening to Monica was not an anomaly. According to victims, this is a familiar occurrence. Wrongful identification, and the justice system's failure to protect victims of domestic violence, are disturbingly common. No wonder so many women simply give up.

The system screams dysfunction – police and courts waste hours, while the defendant takes days off work and spends thousands on legal defence against baseless claims. Meanwhile, the manipulator laughs at them all. Even when the abuser's criminal acts are unveiled, there are no real consequences.

Due to the actions of a jealous, self-centred narcissist, a child was torn from the life he knew and kept from his mother. Luca Savington weaponised his own child – an 8-year-old boy – in an attempt to exact revenge, not only against Monica, but against those who supported and protected her. By doing so, he was able to gain advantage in the Family Court, and as a result, a child was left in the care of a desperate and dangerous man. The aggressor was empowered and allowed to inflict psychological damage on the child, the outcast parent and her family.

When two detectives turned up at our home in response to serious allegations made by Luca Savington against me, I knew this story needed to be told.

Something Is Seriously Wrong is not about victimhood. It is about perseverance and unflinching determination – a mother's desperate battle to save her son. It is an important work because it exposes the procedural and institutional failures of systems designed to protect, yet which continue to endanger the lives of vulnerable women and their families. This did not happen in some foreign country under an oppressive regime. It happened in Australia, in 2024 – 25.

Hope is being able to see that there is light despite all of the darkness – Desmond Tutu

CHILD IN DANGER

'Can you please, *please* help Benji?' Steve implores Presgraves. 'We all fear for him. Just six months ago, he was a carefree, innocent boy. Now, he is in the grip of a heartless ogre, who is causing immense psychological harm in his twisted quest for power and revenge.'

When Benji was taken by his father over five months ago, he was crying and fretting for his mother. Since then, the 8-year-old has been kept in seclusion – a virtual prisoner – except for the one night he stayed with his half-sister Sienna when his father was in gaol. On that occasion, Sienna wanted to take Benji to a family barbeque, but he refused to go. When she asked him why, he told her that everyone would hate him because of the lies he'd told... lies his father forced him to tell. Meanwhile, a capable mother is left without her son, watching helplessly as he slowly suffocates.

Steve continues, his eyes practically jumping from their sockets, as he makes sure Presgraves is aware of the urgency of the situation. 'Benji is experiencing ongoing trauma. There's been numerous reports to DCJ (the Department of Communities and Justice) about this.' He sneaks a glance at his wife Narelle and contains his fury – fury she too feels. 'These are the cornerstones of your charter. Surely you can do something?'

Presgraves can't. She does not have the authority.
Presgraves is part of The Joint Child Protection Response Program, a partnership between the DCJ, NSW police (NSWPF), and NSW Health.

Narelle and Steve speak with Presgraves and her associate about the danger their family is in – not only their daughter Monica and grandson Benji, but themselves as well. They describe Luca Savington's (Sav's) escalating behaviour: stalking, vandalism, threats and relentless harassment. The hundreds of text messages, emails and phone calls at all hours of the day and night, meant to intimidate Monica. Many of them from no-ID numbers and multiple disposable phones.

What makes the situation even more volatile, they tell Presgraves, is that Sav has succeeded in deceiving police. He has portrayed Monica as a mentally unstable alcoholic – violent towards him and their son and threatening to kill him. He claims to be terrified of her. The lies have been accepted without scrutiny and as a result Sav has been emboldened. The danger has only intensified.

Although Narelle and Steve know there is little Presgraves can do, they relish the opportunity to voice their fears and frustrations to someone in authority. To be fair to Presgraves, she is not there to resolve their difficulties. Her purpose is to formally conclude her investigation into one of Luca Savington's spiteful and malicious lies.

Presgraves knows Benji was coached by his father and is almost apologetic as she explains that she is obliged to ask Steve for his response to Luca Savington's claim that he sexually abused Benji.
'How can I respond to something that didn't happen?' he says.
Nothing more is required, and the investigation is complete.

After Presgraves and her associate leave the Percy Street house, Narelle and Steve make a cup of tea and sit in the courtyard. They are relieved that this part of the saga – which has greatly affected their lives – is finally over, but they remain fearful for their daughter and grandson. And it is so frustrating.
'Surely somebody can save Benji!' Steve roars.
'Shush,' says Narelle, in a scolding tone. 'The whole neighborhood can hear you.'
Steve lowers his voice. 'For months now DCJ have known Benji is in serious danger, yet nobody does anything. Like Presgraves, they listen but do nothing.'
'You can't blame her. She's just doing her job.'
'That's the problem! Everyone is just doing their job. Presgraves's unit, DCJ, the police, the Family Court. They operate in a vacuum. Each is like an arm of a 88-armed octopus, reaching in a different direction – oblivious to what the other is doing. Nobody connects the dots. That's why psychos like Sav get away with it.'

SEVEN MONTHS EARLIER

It's a typical summer's night in suburbia. The air is thick and still. Christmas has come and gone. Sav is in a hostile mood, skulking about, ridiculing and attacking his wife, Monica. The entire household is walking on eggshells, being careful not to say or do anything that might provoke him. But Sav gets worse – erupting into a jealous rage, swearing, yelling, belittling Monica in front of the children, and accusing her of infidelity.

As she's done before when Sav 'goes ballistic,' Monica ushers the frightened children to their rooms. 'Keep your doors closed,' she whispers to each of them, before returning to face the abuse.

Monica has two sons – Benji eight and Daniel thirteen. Sav is Benji's father. Daniel is from a previous relationship. Sav has three children from a prior marriage: Leonardo (26) Sienna (23) and Marco (20). Sienna and Marco live at the house but stay out of the firing line, grateful not to be the current target of Sav's wrath.

The bullying and belittling escalate. Eventually, the humiliation becomes unbearable. In tears, Monica collects Daniel and Benji and attempts to leave the house. Sav blocks the doorway. She doesn't try to force her way past him – he's too big and the situation is too dangerous.

Defeated, Monica returns the children to their rooms and tries to escape on her own. Sav follows her outside, hurling accusations and insults. When she gets into her car, Sav stands in front of the vehicle. She can't move without running him over. A tense game of cat-and-mouse follows. The impasse breaks when Sav lunges for the passenger door, giving Monica the opportunity to flee.

Alone in the car, Monica is ridden with guilt for leaving the boys behind. But what else could she do? They will be safe, she tells herself, with Sienna and Marco there in the house. She calls her parents, Narelle and Steve. They live in Newcastle, about thirty minutes away. They tell her to come to their house.

Monica drives to her parents' house. Georgia, her sister, is up from Sydney for the weekend with baby Emma. They are all alarmed to see Monica in such a distressed state. Concerned about the children, Monica rings Daniel. While Daniel speaks with his mother, Sav can be heard muttering in the background. The conversation is short. Daniel stays calm and collected, telling his mother Benji is alright – at least for the moment. Sienna and Marco are still at the house, which gives Monica some peace of mind. She hopes they can stop Sav from doing anything stupid.

When Monica doesn't return to the family home that night, Sav derides her in front of the children, blaming her for the blow-up. 'She's left for good this time and won't be coming back. Ever. And good riddance!'

This isn't the first time this has happened. Monica had previously walked out on Luca Savington, her husband of twelve years, a year earlier, under similar circumstances. Back then, Monica, Daniel and Benji stayed with Monica's parents for a few weeks but returned to the house once school went back. A major reason for returning home was the distance the children had to travel from the Hamilton house to school. The exorbitant cost of rentals was another factor.

After Monica rests and recoups, they discuss the situation. Returning to live with Sav is not an option – it has become intolerable. Sav promises to get help, but he never follows through.

Monica calls the domestic violence hotline. She explains what has been happening but is defensive about her relationship with Sav. 'But it isn't always bad – there are good times too,' she says.
The woman on the phone is empathetic, but direct. 'What you're describing to me is the cycle of domestic violence.'
The conversation is pivotal in helping Monica accept the reality of the relationship and the seriousness of the situation.

Concerned about Benji and Daniel, Monica, accompanied by Georgia and Steve, drives to the police station to report what has occurred and ask if the police will check to ensure the children are safe.

Monica speaks with the duty officer, explaining why she fled the house and that she has concerns about Daniel and Benji's welfare. After a short wait, she is taken into a nearby room and interviewed on camera. The officer, constable

Burnside, asks a series of questions. Does she have any bruises? Was she hit? Did he threaten you?

Monica answers no to all. She tells Burnside about the shouting, insults, verbal abuse, accusations and that she was stood over. The police interview lasts about forty minutes. Afterwards, Burnside tells her that a DVO will be issued for her protection. He mentions that it's possible to apply for one online. They later find out that this information is incorrect. In fact, over the coming weeks, they come to realise that the visit to the police station was a complete waste of time.

Steve:

Reflecting on that night, I'd shake my head in dismay. If the promised DVO had been issued, countless police and court hours – as well as most of the ninety thousand dollars in legal costs – would have been spared. While the danger Luca Savington posed would still have been present, his ability to manipulate the system would have been restricted. The egregious abuse and widespread damage the man wreaked would not have occurred.

There are two types of AVOs:

An Apprehended Domestic Violence Order (ADVO or DVO) – used when there is a domestic or family relationship between the person seeking protection and the individual against whom the order is sought.

An Apprehended Personal Violence Order (APVO or AVO) – applies when the protected person and the subject of the order do not share a domestic or family relationship.

Both place conditions on the contact one person can have with another. A no-contact order forbids the defendant from contacting the protected person (in person or through electronic devices) except through a lawyer. The defendant is also prohibited from coming within a designated distance of the protected person's residence or workplace.

A provisional order is issued by the police. It becomes an interim order at the first court mention, unless revoked. If sanctioned by the court, it becomes a final order. The duration can vary, though most are set for two to five years.

The following morning, Monica, Georgia, and Steve drive back to the house. The intention is to collect Daniel and Benji as well as their essentials. They have no idea how Sav will react. When they pull up outside, Marco's car is in the driveway. The neighbourhood is eerily quiet, even for a Sunday morning. Monica uses her key to open the front door. They enter the house to see Marco sitting in the loungeroom watching television. He has a puzzled expression on his face and doesn't say much other than a subdued, 'Hello.' Sienna isn't home. Daniel and Benji are in their separate rooms, playing games on their electronic devices. They are relieved to see their mother. Sav comes into the house from the garage. He shows no emotion and says nothing, just watches on as Monica, Georgia, and Steve go about their business.

Steve:

After taking Daniel's computer to the car, I return to the house. Turning into the hallway, I see Sav standing in the bedroom doorway, his considerable bulk towering over Monica as she packs clothing into a bag. It appears he is trying to intimidate her, and when he sees me, he backs off. I find Georgia, who is in a room nearby, and ask her to stay close to Monica while I take the boys' bags out.

HARASSMENT

Monica proposes that Daniel and Benji stay with her during the week, while Sav takes them on the weekend. The arrangement makes sense, and Sav agrees. He is a plumber, and his hours are unpredictable; he often doesn't return home until after 5 pm. Monica, who works in aged care, has always handled the children's before and after school care. Furthermore, it's the school holidays, a period when Narelle and Steve usually look after the boys.

The first weekend visit seems to go smoothly. The following weekend, when Sienna arrives to pick up the boys, neither wants to go. Monica and Steve gently coax them, reminding them they'll see their beloved border collie, Roxie, and their neighbourhood friends. Monica believes it is important they maintain their relationships not just with their father, but with Sienna, Marco, and Leonardo, his children from a previous marriage. They have grown up together and share a strong bond.

This is not an easy period for Monica. Sav bombards her with an avalanche of texts and emails:

I miss coming home to you after work, giving you a cuddle and having our dinner together. Falling asleep and waking up beside you. This time we can make our marriage more beautiful than ever.

To my son Daniel, it feels like I closed my eyes for a second, and before I knew it, a young man was standing before me. I will always carry you in my heart.

You and I have so many wonderful memories, we were meant for each other. Please stop ignoring me. It's killing me softly.

Sav does not relent. He phones Monica at all hours, ignoring her pleas to leave her alone. When she doesn't respond, he tries to contact her through Benji's Facebook Messenger account, inventing flimsy excuses to check on the boys, despite having just seen them.

After their second visit, both Daniel and Benji make unusual comments. Daniel says Sav is 'overly pleasant,' which unsettles him because it is out of character. Benji says, 'Poppy (Steve) wants to be my dad.' This isn't something Benji would typically say. He's likely repeating something he's overheard – or was told. Being envious and controlling, Sav might see Steve as a threat and be trying to undermine him.

Its Sunday, mid-January. Monica indulges herself by reading her Vogue horoscope for the day. *You're tired. You're tired of the lies, the deceit, the manipulation. You want the truth, and you want it now. This is your reminder to hold space for uncomfortable conversations. Conscious uncoupling may be on the cards for some.*

The analysis hits home. Monica is depleted, exhausted by Sav's manipulations and lies. 'Conscious uncoupling' certainly seems apt. When she shows Steve, the cynic in him reminds her that the horoscope covers itself with phrases like 'maybe' and 'for some.'

Monica's phone chimes – it's another text message from Sav:
I've received a death threat. Someone told me, 'Stay away, or I'll kill you.'

Monica texts back:
Take it to the police.

Later, Monica's friend Beth calls. She had received a call from someone claiming to be her ex-boyfriend, Dave. But Beth knows it wasn't him – the voice was familiar. It was Sav's, masked behind the no-caller ID.

When the boys return that afternoon, Benji is angry and accusatory.

'Why did you have to leave Dad?'

'That's an adult matter, Benji,' says Monica. 'Between me and your father. It's not for you to worry about.'

'Everyone is saying it was you who broke up the family.' Benji stomps off towards the stairs.

Steve overheard the conversation. 'Hey Benji,' he calls.

Benji turns.

'It's not that simple. Don't go blaming your mother.'

Later that night Steve speaks privately with Narelle:

'It's not going to be easy for Monica while Sav is filling Benji's head with divisive rubbish.'

'He likes to be the one in control,' says Narelle.

'Remember when you two had that run-in, and you told him he didn't live in "old Italy"?' says Steve with a wry smile. 'He threatened to move them all to Perth.'

'He was strange with me after that – and Benji changed too,' says Narelle. I'm sure Sav was undermining me back then. He'll be doing the same with Monica now.'

WORKPLACE INTRUSION

Monica manages a dementia activity centre outside Newcastle. She's the only staff member on her floor. It's Tuesday, lunchtime, and she's with four clients. She turns around and is startled to see Sav standing in the doorway holding a bunch of flowers.

Monica's diary:
I signal for him to leave. I mouth, 'Go… Get out… Leave…' He pretends to leave. I go into the kitchen – he follows me in there. I'm trapped. I tell him to leave. I say, 'I don't want flowers. I want you to leave.' I keep asking him to go, and he eventually walks out after handing me the flowers. I feel shaken. A staff member from upstairs happens to be coming down the stairs. She notices my distress and checks if I'm okay. I let her know I don't feel safe.

Sav later texts:
I only came to tell you I love you. I won't bother you at work anymore. You looked beautiful. I thought seeing me might make you fall in love with me again. I won't bother you anymore.

Monica replies:
'Stop messaging me unless it's to do with the boys. You are not to come near my work.'

Sav texts:
'Okay I understand.'
But the messages keep coming.

Monica:
'Stop. It's over.'

Saturday is National No Phones at Home Day. The spiel promoting it declares that disconnecting from phones is like hitting the refresh button for our minds, offering a break from the digital noise of today. But Sav isn't one to disconnect. He texts Monica that he can't have the boys 'because he's going on a date.' A friend then finds a photo on Sav's Instagram of him with the supposed date.

Monica is relieved. Maybe someone new will keep him distracted.

The following Monday, Steve goes for a walk, through Gregson Park and down to Beaumont Street. When he returns, he notices something protruding from the mailbox. He opens the lid to find a torn piece of notebook paper. Scrawled in blue biro is a message:

Call me on this number 0455667354 I wanna meet Daniel – Andrew.

Andrew is Daniel's biological father. Steve is puzzled. Could Andrew have gotten wind of the separation? When Monica sees it, she says without hesitation, 'It's from Sav.'

That morning, she receives another message:
ITS DAVE IM WITH ANDREW ARE U IN LAMBTON. ANDREW WANTS TO SEE DANIEL
(Sent from a TLSPayphone).

Georgia later traces the booth to Shortland Road, about 15 minutes away.

Back before Daniel was born, Beth's then boyfriend, Dave, had been a friend of Andrew's. Monica hasn't had anything to do with either of them for over fourteen years, but weeks earlier, during the lead-up to Christmas, Monica and Sav ran into Dave at Charlestown Square. The exchange was brief, but it sparked Sav's obsessive jealousy.

That night Sav was green with envy. 'Who is he? He's your boyfriend, isn't he?' Monica tried to appease him. 'No. You know that's not true.'
'Give me your phone,' yelled Sav.
He grabbed it off her. Monica doesn't use a password – an attempt to appease him. He swore and ranted as he checked her emails and texts.
'I bet you've got another account, haven't you, ya bitch!'

Monica's diary:
Sav constantly accused me of cheating – even in front of the children. At night, my phone would vanish. He'd be going through it without my consent. If I got upset about anything Sav did, he would wake me up at night and accuse me of cheating. He'd call me the devil.
It was especially bad if I had been out with friends from work or parents from the school.

At 7:09 pm Sav texts:
I tried to stir you up… I don't have a date. I thought I'd make you jealous. But I guess you didn't come running to me.

At 8:17 pm:
I wish you gave me one more chance in our marriage. I hate what's happening. Not having you, it's like I lost a part of my heart. We had so much going for us. We were a great team, lovers, family, and best friends. Losing you is horrible. I can't imagine my life without you.

At 10:57 pm, Monica receives a threat:
IF I DON'T SEE DANIEL IM BASHING U AND YOUR MAN
When they later match the booth number to a location, they find out the text was sent from a payphone on Maitland Road, just ten-minute's drive from the Hamilton house.

Tuesday, 8:39 pm:
Just wanted to let you know you can block me, but you cannot delete our memories. You can go to the cops and get an DVO, but I know it in my heart I still love you and I forgive you. I know you are a kindhearted person, and I know in your heart you don't mean to hurt me. But please, think about what you are doing to someone who really cares and loves you.
Monica hasn't heard back about the DVO. She follows up with the police, but Officer Burnside is not on duty.

Wednesday, 4:01 pm:
I don't want to be rude… do I need to find somewhere to live? I must look for a rental soon because you want to sell the house. Please let me know, so I can organise something before I end up on the street. Please Monica, will you do that for me. It's the least you can do… thank you.

On Thursday Sav is relentless.

4:48 pm:
My heart is kind, and you know that I have not done anything because I believe you are coming back home. I don't want to sell our house.

Monica doesn't share every message. She receives over 30 a day. The intensity is staggering: Sav 2:24 pm, Sav 2:25 pm, Sav 3:12 pm (x 6), Sav 3:14 pm, Sav

3:31 pm, (x 3), Sav 3:58 pm, Sav 3:58 pm, Sav 4:03 pm, Sav 4:36 pm.

On Friday, the flurry of messages continues.

6:32 am:
Please Monica, come home, take my hand and be mine again.

6:50 am:
All I can say is I tried, with the goodness of my heart, but you completely shut me out. You abandoned me and it is painful… thank you for showing your true colours.

6:57am:
At least I know my worth. I admit my mistakes and know I'm a good person.

6:59 am:
I admit I was somewhat an idiot but never meant to hurt you. And you're hurting a decent human being… someone who would do anything for someone. I'm not going to message you. Your wish is my command.

9:06 am:
Would you like to have lunch today? I can grab a couple of pork rolls (I haven't had that for a while). I can bring it to you quickly. say hi and leave.

9:07 am:
Monica:
No, don't come here.

9:48 am, Sav (from a different number):
Ok.

9:49 am, Sav (from a different number):
I'm sorry.

9:56 am:
You don't want to talk, you don't want me to msg you, you don't want me to try and resolve our marriage. If I may ask, what do you really want? Is it really over? A yes is sufficient. If you really need time, just say so and I'll leave you alone, because this separation is doing my head in.

Monica again tells him to stop texting.

10:25 am (excerpts):

I tried 😔 and tried and tried. But it seems to me that you don't even want to try to reason and rekindle. You took the kids away from me and that ripped my heart out, you know. That really has fucked with my emotions and hurt me to the point where I can't breathe sometimes.

10:30 am:

I trust in you. I know you're not with anyone and I know what you think of me too but you are really hurting me and it's not fair... how am I going to get past this pain... talking to the therapist I know it was my past that really fucked me and now this is happening and I don't know if I can ever trust anyone else again. I'm not asking for anything but I'm really asking for your help because you are the only person that understands me, and I will do anything to make it work and never to hurt you like I did before... Please talk to me.

10:40 pm:

OK 😔 what was I thinking! No need to be scared. I'm not going to bother you anymore. I just hope you come to realise I was your knight in shining armour, your one and only.

On Saturday, Daniel and Benji go to Sav's place for the weekend. As arranged, Sienna drives them back to Newcastle on Sunday afternoon.

Later that evening, Daniel tells them that Marco and Leonardo had a fiery confrontation with their father. When he starts to explain, Benji cuts him off, saying he shouldn't talk about it. While Benji seems to have adopted the Savington code of silence, Daniel scoffs at the suggestion he should remain tight-lipped. He goes on to explain that the quarrel was about money, with Sav insisting his adult sons should contribute to the mortgage. Another point of contention was a dog Marco had brought with him. Marco wanted to leave it at the house during the week while he was away for work.

Arguments aren't uncommon with the Savingtons, but one incident that Daniel re-counted was more alarming than usual. He had been in his room playing on his iPad when, out of nowhere, Sav stormed in and demanded to know who 'Dave' was. Daniel told Sav repeatedly he didn't know anyone called Dave. But that wasn't good enough for Sav.

'Tell me. Don't lie. Who is this Dave bloke?' Sav shouted, standing over him. Eventually, Sav ran out of steam and left the room.

At 9:26 pm, Monica receives a text from TLSPayphone 0448255342:
HEY THIS DAVE U HOME?

Another message arrives at 10:03 pm:
WHERE ARE YOU YU NOT IN ADAMSTOWN?

Monica used to live in Adamstown when she first met Sav. The idea that someone would try to find her there after all these years seems implausible. Later, it's discovered both texts were sent from the phone booth just around the corner – on Reay Street Hamilton, just metres from the Hamilton house.

Georgia is determined to trace the origins of these messages. Each TLS Payphone has a number, but Telstra will not reveal the locations. She finds out the locations through the help of a friend, who puts her in touch with a Facebook group formed by women who've also experienced phonebooth harassment.

Monica becomes concerned for Roxie's safety. The boys tell her Marco's dog is being left at the house more often and has been intimidating the border collie. After Sav leaves for work, Monica goes to the house, into the backyard, and removes the dog. Roxie willingly follows her. While she is gone, Steve secures the yard in Hamilton so the dog can't escape.

LIES – DECEPTION

On Wednesday, at 5:17 pm, Monica receives another text:
Sav asked me to send you this. He was scared to ask, but I think it's good to let you know he's ok.
Attached is a photo of Sav sitting upright in a hospital bed, wearing a white gown and hooked up to monitoring equipment. The sender is unidentified. Monica doesn't believe the photo was sent by a friend of Sav's – why would they hide their identity?

At 11:51 pm, another message arrives from TLS Payphone 0249282385:
I'M GOING 2 KILL U AND YOUR MAN IF I DON'T SEE DANIEL
The message was sent from a booth on Maitland Road, about twenty minutes from Hamilton.

Excerpt from Monica's diary:
I call Sienna to talk about pick-up arrangements for Saturday. Sienna said, 'Dad will pick up Benji from his trial soccer game and then grab Daniel after Basketball.'

Sienna says her dad told her I wasn't home when he dropped the boys back last weekend. I told her Sav had asked me to make the pick-up later, at 4 pm, and then he dropped them off two hours earlier. That my dad was home, in any case. Sienna says Sav is unstable and has been blaming her and Marco for the separation. I tell Sienna it is untrue. Sienna knows that and mentions her father is grieving.

On Thursday, Sav bombards Monica with messages:
6:05 pm:
I would caress you, massage you, play with your skin smoothly and be lost in your eyes. Home is where the heart is.

6:32pm:
Sav texts Monica asking her to come home. Twelve times.

7:10 pm:
I poured my heart and soul into loving you unconditionally. Maybe that's why I'm hurting so much. But you don't care. You took my heart and squashed it.

7:32 pm:
I hope you found what you are looking for. I hope when you do, he takes good care of you. I hate the thought of someone else having you… I remember your promises. I was supposed to be your one and only.

11:34 pm (excerpts):
Why do you hate me so much?
You were the best part of me through our twelve-year marriage.
I cannot thank you enough for all the joy, love, lovemaking, and being my best friend.
I will always keep you in my heart… you were and as always will be my twin flame, my true love.

Sav's obsessive declarations stand in stark contrast to what he tells their neighbour, Darren: 'The bitch walked out and left me with the fucking mortgage. She did nothing around the place, just got pissed and went out with her friends. She has mental problems, you know. Reckon she was fucking that boyfriend all along.'
Darren is appalled. 'Hey, take it easy, man. Are we talking about the same Monica?'
When Sav continues his tirade, Darren leaves. He tells his wife, Sarah, what Sav said. She too is disgusted.

TAKEN

On Friday, the school year begins. Daniel enters Year 8 and Benji starts Year 2. What Sav does next shocks everyone.

Excerpts from Monica's diary:
Before I leave for work, I get a text from Sav. 'Would you like to have lunch today? I can grab a couple of pork rolls, bring them to you and quickly say hi and leave.'
I replied: 'No, don't come to my work.'
Later that morning I receive a voice message. 'You're gutless. It's wrong what you're doing Monica. I'm just a human being trying to sort my life with you and you're not helping me. And you've got to remember one thing. The night you bashed me, and Sienna witnessed that.

I could have left you and it's not fair, not fair at all. Pull your head in.'

It's Benji's second day back. School finishes at 3.00 pm, but Monica doesn't finish work until 4, so Narelle comes from Newcastle to collect him. She arrives early and waits at their prearranged place. The bells rings, but Benji doesn't appear. As the minutes tick by, Narelle becomes increasingly concerned. Eventually she checks with the office. The staff inform her that Sav collected Benji earlier that day, claiming his father was seriously ill.

Sav's parents live in western New South Wales, four or five hours away. Narelle immediately phones Monica, who frantically tries to contact Sav. He doesn't respond. Monica calls the police, who advise her to file a report.

When Monica gets home from work, she is distressed and fearful, aware of how unstable and unpredictable Sav can be. Although logic suggests he is on his way to his parent's place, there is no way of knowing. Steve accompanies her to the police station.

On the way, Monica rings Marco.
'Dad's not here,' Marco says. 'And I don't know where he is. He's been angry – crazy even. Pressuring us to lie for him.'
Then Marco changes tone.
'I don't know if this is the right time. But I wanted to ask… I'd like to buy your share of the house.'
Monica ignores the question.
'Bye Marco. Ring if you have any news.'
'Unbelievable,' Steve mutters.
Speaking with Marco does nothing to temper Monica's fears. Steve tries to placate her.
'If he goes to his parent's place they might talk some sense into him.'

Monica's diary:
I call Sienna who says she has no idea where her father is. I call Sav's mum. Nothing. I call Sav's sister, Elena. She is concerned and tells me Sav isn't right and once I get Benji back to keep him away from him. Elena says their dad isn't in hospital and that Sav lied. I call Sarah and Darren, our neighbours, to see if Sav's car is there. It isn't.

I speak with Marco around 6 pm. He claims to have no idea where his dad has taken Benji. He fears how his dad will react if he finds out he's talking to me. He says Sav will not listen to reason, and that he blames them (his own children) for the marriage breakup.

I go with Dad into the police station and speak with police officer Alan Trapman. Trapman says he will organise a welfare check on Benji. He takes Sav's number, numberplate and house address. He will get an officer to drop by the house and call me with an update.

Sav's sister Elena messages me just after 7pm and says that she'd spoken to Sav and that his lawyer told him he was entitled to take his son, and to live with him until court proceedings, due to no family law involvement on my side. Elena says, 'The lawyer plus the police know that you bashed Sav when you were drunk one night, and Sienna is a witness. Sav is prepared to press charges unless you come to terms with mediation and sort everything out.'
'That's not what really happened,' I reply.

Late Friday night I receive a call from the police. Sav is at his parents' place. They went to the house and made sure Benji was unharmed. Without a court order, there is nothing else they can do.

DAY 2 – SURPRISE VISIT

Not being able to speak with Benji is torturous for Monica. And she is forced to try and contact Sav. But now, he won't pick up.

When Monica comes downstairs on Sunday morning her eyes are red from crying. She is visibly distressed. Seeing her this way is upsetting for Steve and Narelle.

Narelle wants hard copies of Sav's call times, emails and texts. Steve begins printing them, but after thirty pages he realises the task is enormous. It will require a ream of paper, and a new set of ink cartridges. There are hundreds of calls and messages – many from no-caller ID numbers. This eight-minute period is an example of the intensity:

Sav 8:08 pm (x 3)
Sav 8:14 pm (x 2)
Sav 8:14 pm (x 2)
Sav 8:14 pm (x 2)

Sav 8:15 pm (x 3)
Sav 8:15 pm
Sav 8:16 pm

Sienna makes a surprise visit to the Hamilton house. She is welcomed inside. Torn between her father and Monica, she shares her concerns, reiterating what Marco had told Monica.

'Dad is going ga-ga. He blames Leonardo Marco and me for everything, including the marriage break up.'

When Monica mentions Sav is putting pressure on Sienna and Marco to lie to the police, Steve stops her mid-sentence.

'You have to think of yourself,' he warns Sienna. 'Lying to the police could get you in serious trouble.'

'I know. If I get a record, I can't become a teacher.'

Sienna had once mocked teachers, but that changed after spending time with the Keltys. Monica helped her believe in herself.

Suddenly a car approaches – one that sounds eerily like Sav's Ford.

Sienna freezes in fear.

'If Dad finds out I'm here he'll kill me.'

Monica panics too. Steve peeks out the window. A hotted-up Ford drives past the house, and parks in a driveway a few doors down.

'It's not him,' he says.

Relief floods the room. What is glaringly apparent is the extent to which both women fear the man.

Steve:

I'm beginning to comprehend the extent of the abuse Monica has endured. I wonder what she has not told us over the years. I detest the man.

Excerpt from Monica's diary:

Elena calls. She has been speaking with Lucia, her mother. Benji told Lucia he misses his mum. Lucia and Matteo were not happy with Sav snatching Benji, or that he turned up at their place with him.

Late in the afternoon, Sarah, Monica's neighbour, hears a car pull up and looks out the front window. She sees Sav get out of his vehicle. She walks outside.

'Where's Benji?' she asks.

Sav glares at her as if he'd seen a ghost. He grabs Benji, who is asleep in the car, and rushes inside. Seconds later the curtains are pulled tightly shut. Sarah rings Monica and lets her know Sav and Benji are back at the house.

DAY 4 – FALSE REPORTS

Monica's diary:
Benji went to school 9 am and was signed out by Sav at 11 am. Sarah and Darren (our neighbours) get a note in their mailbox telling them to mind their own business. They suspect it is from Sav and confront him. He claims to have also received a note.

The following day, Sarah tells Monica that the police visited Sav. She missed a large part of the conversation but overheard him criticising Monica, blaming her for the notes. Sarah couldn't help herself. She poked her head around the corner and called out.
'We all know who the abuser is in that house.'
Sienna was quick to defend her father.
'Can you not say that about my dad?'

Sarah backed off, but she tells Monica Sav put the note in her mailbox, to intimidate her because she voiced her concern about Benji's welfare the previous day. She later finds out Sav reported her and Darren to the police, claiming he lives in fear of them.

Monica receives a peculiar text from Sienna:
We are getting the blame for what kids in the street are doing.

It's unclear whether Sienna genuinely believes what she is saying or is simply echoing Sav's narrative. Monica suspects the latter. Sienna knows her father is not afraid of the neighbours.

Sav's manipulations are becoming more brazen – filing false police reports, intimidating neighbours, coercing them into silence.
Monica's diary:
I requested a welfare check on Benji and Sienna. Police call later that night and say they

sighted Benji asleep.

Monica manages to reach Officer Burnside and reminds him about the 'promised' DVO. Burnside informs her that police visited the house and spoke with Sav, his daughter Sienna, and son Marco. They downplayed the seriousness of the incident, categorising it as 'just a run of the mill argument,' and the police consequently decided not to proceed with the DVO.

'There is nothing in a DVO that isn't already illegal,' says Burnside, trying to appease Monica. In other words, who needs one?

Monica breaks down in tears while telling her sister Georgia about it.

'But the cop told us they'd give you a DVO,' Georgia says.

'I don't think it was him. He said his boss wouldn't authorise it.'

'That's pathetic. Sienna and Marco would say whatever Sav told them to.'

The decision not to issue the DVO involves multiple officers from two police stations. Given the widespread media attention around domestic violence, one would expect that a woman fleeing such a situation would be given protection – at least as a precaution.

DAY 5 – UNRAVELLING

From Monica's diary:

Received a call from Newcastle Women's Domestic Violence Advocacy Service. Probably triggered from the police report. Mentioned women's room if needed at courthouse. Contacted Benji's school just before 2 pm. He hadn't attended all day. I asked why I wasn't notified.

Called police at 3:25 pm, requesting a welfare check. They will do a welfare check as Benji wasn't at school.

Called again at 5 pm to check outcome of police check. Senior Inspect Craig Robbins said they would not be doing a welfare check. I got terribly upset as I am very worried about Benji. Robbins said he had tried to call me 15 times (no evidence of this on my phone).

I texted Sav: 'Bring Benji back.'

The saga enters a new stage. Sav continues to harass Monica, using Benji as bait. He tells Monica he will allow her to speak with Benji for a couple of minutes.

The call eventuates, but when Monica asks Benji what he has been up to, the call is disconnected. It's akin to a hostage situation. Benji is completely isolated – from his mother, his brother Daniel (whom he idolises), his friends, and Monica's family. He hasn't attended school, or his usual sporting activities. Monica is worried sick.

- **Psychological abuse** is behaviour that aims to cause emotional or mental harm (1800RESPECT).
- **In the context of family violence,** psychological abuse is when someone makes you or other people question your sanity or recollection of realty through manipulation or lying (safesteps.org.au).

Monica talks to the police but is again told they will not become involved without court orders in place. There's technically nothing illegal about what Sav has done. But if the DVO had been issued to protect Monica and the boys, his actions would have been against the law.

A call comes through to Monica from a private number. Steve answers. Sav asks to speak with Monica, despite having been told not to contact her, except about Benji. When Steve reprimands him about his appalling behaviour, Sav becomes abusive and hangs up. The call confirms what they already knew – he is using multiple phones.

More calls follow – eight attempts within the hour. Monica is conflicted and in tears. She doesn't know whether to answer – it could be Benji. Her family and friends are growing increasingly concerned. Steve notices his daughter's shallow breathing.
'Are you alright?' he asks.
'No… I'm terrible. What can I do?'
It is heart wrenching for Narelle and Steve to watch their daughter unravel.

Monica and Narelle had met with a solicitor a week after Monica left Sav, to begin mediation proceedings. The solicitor agreed to draw up the necessary documents and act on Monica's behalf. Having not heard back from the solicitor, Monica contacts the firm, only to discover nothing has been done. The secretary gives a lame excuse about a new system failing. Valuable time has been lost.

Monica then reaches out to Lisa Jones, a solicitor recommended by a friend.

Lisa refers her to her colleague Adele, a family law specialist. Adele speaks with Monica over the phone, asking for her details and the specifics of the situation. She also asks for Sav's number, and whether it's ok for her to call him immediately. Monica agrees and gives her the number.

A few minutes later, Adele calls back. She'd spoken with Sav, who launched into a tirade of abuse the moment she asked about Benji. At least now she understands what she's dealing with. An in-person appointment with Adele is booked for the following Friday.

The harassing calls and messages from Sav continue. Monica answers hoping to speak with Benji, only to be met with silence. Sav is playing mind games. Narelle answers one of the calls. This time, Sav speaks:
'I want Monica to drop off Benji's iPad and school clothes to the house.'
Narelle neither agrees nor refuses.

Monica continues contacting the police and the Department of Communities and Justice, voicing concerns about her son's safety. Somebody suggests she snatch Benji back – but it's not that simple. He's not attending school and rarely leaves the house. When he does, Sav is with him. To get him back, they'd have to physically confront Sav – a strong, intimidating man with a known capacity for violence. Even if they succeeded, they would have to hide Benji somewhere to prevent Sav from taking him again. Monica doesn't want Benji caught in a tit-for-tat custody battle. She still believes she'll get him back through legal channels.

DAY 6 – MENTAL HEALTH SPIRALS

Monica tries to carry on as usual. She continues going to work and performing her daily tasks. But Sav's cruelty is taking a toll. Her anxiety intensifies. She's constantly worried about Benji. Her thoughts are becoming jumbled. Concentration is difficult. Narelle and Steve grow increasingly concerned.

Although Monica is keeping up appearances – hoping Sav will come to his senses – she's slowly sinking into mental exhaustion.

Her boss notices that she is struggling, and she sends her home, urging her to rest and return when she's feeling better.

Monica arrives back at the Hamilton house in a daze. She tries to explain a recent conversation she had with a woman from the Newcastle Domestic Violence Resource Centre (Jenny's Place), but her words come out confused. She mixes up sentences and can't finish her thoughts.
'Slow down,' Narelle says gently.
But Monica can't. Her mind is racing. Watching her unravel is frightening. They encourage her to have a bath. She agrees but gets out after only a couple of minutes. They know the signs. Once the slide begins, it is near impossible to stop.

Monica had experienced mental health issues in her early twenties and was hospitalised at the time – not due to alcohol or drugs. For over fifteen years she has been a high-functioning adult. She's on an extremely low dose of medication, too low according to some professionals, to be effective.

DAY 7 – MISSING

Steve's account:

I remember the day as the worst in living memory. Narelle and I had been watching Monica's mental health deteriorate ever since Benji was taken. We knew she had an upcoming appointment with her doctor. We assumed the GP would increase her medication and get her back on track.

What we'd forgotten was this: while a GP can write a script, they can't adjust psychiatric doses. That requires a psychiatrist.

Narelle had an important appointment in the morning, so the plan was for her to take Monica to the Mater hospital in the afternoon. There, Monica could see a psychiatrist and get the help she needed. I was alone with Monica that morning. She was extremely restless – up and down the stairs, pacing, second-guessing herself. She thought about taking Roxie for a walk, then changed her mind. Then changed it again. Finally, she decided to go for a short walk alone.

Her phone was out of charge, so I told her to leave it behind – just go without it. I had another motive. I was worried that, in her confused and vulnerable state, if Sav rang she might give in and agree to his demands – just to see Benji. Twenty minutes passed. no sign of her. She'd gone out alone yesterday and come back, I reminded myself. Another ten minutes passed. Still nothing. It had been too long. I started to worry.

I leashed Roxie and went out to look for her. I thought, foolishly, the dog might pick up her trail. Wishful thinking. Maybe I'd watched too many police shows where the dog found the missing person. I walked to and from Gregson Park multiple times. Panic set in. Why the hell did I let her leave the house alone? I left Roxie back at the house and jumped in the car to search further. It was awful. My mind ran though all sorts of possibilities. The worst thought: that Sav had taken her. We knew he'd been lurking in the area.

I was sweating, hollow inside, shaking at the wheel. Then I had another thought. In her confused state and desperate to see Benji, what if Monica decided to hitchhike to her old house. I drove along the route she'd likely take. I called Narelle, who was now back at the house, as I drove. Monica hadn't returned, and I told her what had happened. Eventually I came home, hoping – irrationally – that she'd be there. She wasn't. Narelle was speaking on the phone. I was relieved she didn't seem upset. I heard Monica's name mentioned.

Monica had wandered into an aged-care facility a few streets away. A nurse on duty saw that she was disorientated and distressed. Monica didn't know where she was. The nurse recognised the psychotic symptoms and tried to keep her calm while phoning for an ambulance. By the time the paramedics arrived, Monica had wandered off. They searched Hamilton for half an hour, chasing her through the streets (we are so grateful for their persistence). Eventually, they caught up with her near Beaumont Street. She was taken to the Mater Hospital – a massive relief, considering what could have happened.

DAY 8 – THE AFTERMATH

Monica is admitted to hospital as a voluntary patient. Phones aren't allowed on the ward, so Narelle and Steve monitor her calls. They visit the hospital as often as possible. The nurses are outstanding. They take time to discover Monica's history, discuss her care in detail, and make an appointment for the psychiatrist to speak with Narelle and Steve directly.

Monica keeps asking about Daniel. She desperately wants to see him. She wants him to visit on the weekend.

The harassing, abusive messages from Sav continue – relentlessly.

Narelle and Steve meet with Adele, Monica's solicitor. The meeting is brief. Adele will not discuss the case, as she may need affidavits from them later.

- **An affidavit** is a written statement confirmed by oath or affirmation for use in court. It must be signed in the presence of an authorised witness, and by signing you're declaring the contents to be true. (Source: Oxford languages)

When the weekend comes, Narelle and Steve take Daniel to the hospital. By mistake, Daniel is let through the first security gate. A nurse is about to buzz him onto the ward when she asks his age. Only adults are allowed on the ward, so Narelle takes him back to the foyer. Monica is permitted to leave the ward with Steve, and they meet at the café. Daniel's presence lifts Monica's spirit. She fusses over him, full of warmth. Daniel is glad to see her – but he knows something isn't right. She isn't herself. Still, he handles the visit with a maturity beyond his years. Calm on the outside, it must be unsettling to know your mum is on a psych ward. After refreshments, they take a walk through the hospital grounds.

On Sunday morning, Steve checks Monica's phone log. Among the barrage of messages from Sav, one stands out. It was sent at 1:02 am – from a public phone on Reay Street, just around the corner from the house.

HEY ITS ANDREW WHAT HOUSE YOU AT IM COMING QUA 2 HAMILTON

The message is chaotic, barely coherent and unsettling.

Later that morning, after taking Roxie for a walk, Steve notices something. Monica's car, which has been parked directly outside the house, has a flat rear tyre. The car behind it has a flat as well.
Vandals?
Unlikely.
Narelle and Steve have lived on the street for fourteen years. There's never been trouble like this. Besides, vandals usually go for multiple cars – entire stretches of street – not just two.

Steve opens the boot to retrieve the spare tyre, but it's glued down with epoxy resin. It won't budge. It looks like it has been that way for some time.
'We should report the flat tyre to the police,' Narelle says.
'What's the point.' Steve replies. 'We can't prove anything.'
'We know it's him.'
'Yeah, and the cops will say there's no evidence.'
'Still… it adds to the profile.'
If Sav is prepared to vandalise Monica's car outside their home, what else is he capable of? They start taking extra precautions, keeping the front and back doors locked. At all times.

Tyre repair services are closed in Newcastle on Sundays, so Steve must wait until Monday to get the tyre fixed.

DAY 11 – SABOTAGE

On Monday morning, Steve contacts a nearby tyre repair centre. The puncture is small enough that he inflates the tyre with a compressor and drives the car there before it deflates again. When he returns to collect the vehicle, the repairman tells him a nail or screwdriver had been shoved into the valve. The spare tyre was almost impossible to remove – it had been glued to the boot. Eventually they pried it loose using a crowbar.

Later, Steve tells Narelle.
'Why would anybody glue a spare tyre in place?'
Narelle shakes her head. 'Only reason I can think of is he wanted Monica to be dependent on him. So he could swoop in and play the big hero if she got a flat.'

When Steve brings it up with Monica, she remembers Sav sealing the spare tyre in place. Steve wants to ask if she thought it was an odd thing to do. But he doesn't. Monica has enough on her plate. Still, the realisation unsettles him. He starts to see the subtle and disturbing ways Sav had exerted control over her.
Steve reports the tyre sabotage to the police. They take it seriously – but without solid proof, there isn't much they can do. Sav would deny it.

Georgia is furious when she hears about the tyres. She insists they install security cameras.
'Lorna and Rob just put them in after they had a break in,' she says. 'When I told them about the flat tyre business, Rob offered to install the cameras for you. He's researched it all. Knows the best ones to get.'

It's a generous offer and after a brief discussion, Narelle and Steve gratefully accept.

Later in the day, Narelle calls Benji's school. When she hangs up, she turns to Steve.
'Benji isn't at school again.'
'Sav is scared we'll try to take him,' Steve replies.
'If he keeps missing days, someone's got to notice. The Department of Education should step in.'

Neighbours confirm Benji hasn't been seen in the yard or out the front. He's been kept inside all day – cruel to any child, especially Benji. He's a kid who loves the outdoors. Normally he'd be on the trampoline, kicking a ball, or playing with the dog. When Benji was six Monica first took him to Little Athletics. He won all his races, even the long jump, which he'd never done before. The other mothers assumed he'd transferred from another club.

Steve:
When Benji was about five, we'd ride down to Gregson Park. He'd fly around the pathways, wanting to race me on his tiny bicycle. One time he asked how he and Daniel were getting back to their house. Whether they were being picked up. 'We're riding back on our bikes,' I joked. 'Ok,' he said. He was disappointed once he realised I wasn't serious. I told him it would take about four or five hours, but he wasn't deterred.

Monica receives an email from Adele. It's an affidavit from Sav's solicitors – M W McInnes & Associates. The claims are outrageous.

Sav alleges he is withholding Benji because Monica poses an unacceptable risk. He claims she drinks two bottles of wine a night – sometimes four. That she's heavily medicated and becomes aggressive when drinking. He even accuses her of smacking Benji while drunk, leaving a visible red handprint on his legs.

The document includes more:
A death threat allegedly made by Monica's partner: ***You better stay away, or I will kill you.'***
A handwritten note in his mailbox: ***Bring back my son or I will kill you.'***
That Monica assaulted him multiple times.
That police are preparing an DVO against Monica.
That Benji has nightmares going to the Hamilton house, cries hysterically, wets his bed, and has told Sav he doesn't want to return to Monica's care.
That she must be tested for drugs and alcohol, provide full medication records, and submit to hair follicle testing – at her own cost.

Sav wants Monica to have one supervised visit per month through Rekonnect, with Monica footing the bill.

Steve is livid. 'What a bastard! Surely the police don't believe those death threat claims. And the stuff about alcohol. Ridiculous! Monica has worked full-time for years – supported him when he retrained, as well as his kids and Daniel and

Benji. While he sat on his arse and played with his stupid car, Monica was volunteering at Little Athletics and soccer. Running the kids around. How can he just make up this crap?'

'Don't take it out on me,' says Narelle.

But Steve's rant continues. 'Two to four bottles a night. Come on! And even if she did, who could blame her? Living with a dickhead like him. She never yells at the boys. Sav's the one who calls her too soft. And now he's saying she bashed him. That's laughable.'

He remembers the day they returned to get the boys – Sav towering over Monica in the doorway.

'It'd be like David beating Goliath. Without the sling shot.'

'It's not just about his size,' Narelle adds. 'He trying to paint himself as the noble gentleman – the silent victim who takes it on the chin. Who would never harm a woman,'

'What a man!' Steve mutters bitterly. 'Even the heading's wrong. She's Monica Savington, not Monica Kelty. He's vindictive, delusional and dangerous.'

They decide not to show Monica the affidavit yet. It would only add more pressure. The lies themselves are disturbing, but the fact that Sav is willing to file them officially – to put them in police hands – is a serious threat.

Georgia is outraged when she hears. It tears her apart, not being able to be there to support her sister.

DAY 12 – PLEASE HELP

Steve calls the NSW Department of Communities and Justice. He reaches a caseworker named Mandy Nisbet. He explains the situation: that Sav's twenty-five-year-old daughter Sienna is acting as Benji's primary carer. She's scared of Sav, Steve says, and has been pressured into backing up his lies.

Steve has read up on the DCJ criteria for intervention. Lack of access to the child is one of the triggers. 'Benji is being withheld from his mother,' Steve tells Mandy. 'He's not at school. He's been cut from friends, family, and routine. He must be incredibly confused – he has no idea what is going on.'

Another red flag is irrational behaviour. Steve tells Mandy about the harassment, the hundreds of calls, texts and emails. The crude, menacing texts from public phone booths and creepy notes he's dropping into mailboxes. That Sav's own daughter and son are concerned about his irrational behaviour.

'Would he harm Benji?' Mandy asks.

'He already is, Steve says. 'Maybe not physically, but psychologically. He's holding Benji hostage and using the child as bait to lure Monica back. That's harm.'

He tells Mandy that Sav has been violent before – towards his eldest son, Leonardo. A DVO was issued for the incident.

Steve knows the DCJ deals with extreme cases. He knows they're stretched. But still – this one matters. 'Just because there are no bruises,' he says, 'doesn't mean the damage isn't real.'

The next day Narelle goes to work. Steve drops Daniel off at school, then heads back to Newcastle for a dental appointment. On the way, his phone rings. It's Narelle.

'Sav has turned up at the Mater Hospital,' she says. 'He has Benji with him. He wants to see Monica.'

Steve:

When I get there, the man who made all those scurrilous claims against Monica – the immoral bully who's dragged her down – is sitting in the corridor with Benji by his side. I block him out. Act as though he isn't there. I walk up to Benji, crouch beside him and say gently, 'You can see your mum if you come with me.'

Sav springs to his feet, grabs Benji by the hand and storms off down the hallway. My chest tightens. My blood boils. I watch them disappear.

Then I walk up to the reception cubicle – the staff know me by now – and say: 'That man was my daughter's abuser. I need to speak with the head of the ward.'

A short time later, the ward manger Rianna arrives. I'm still shaken. I take a few deep breaths and try to calm down. Rianna listens carefully while I explain what just happened. Rianna is appalled. She already knows Monica's breakdown has been triggered by sustained harassment and the trauma of losing Benji.

'Why would he bring a child onto a psychiatric ward? The boy should be at school.'

I speak with Monica later that day and find out that Rianna has managed to contact Sav and organise a regular time for Monica to talk with Benji each night. In the aftermath of Sav's visit, one detail remains unclear. How did Sav even know Monica was in hospital? Only a few people know. None of them would have told him. Monica has a theory. One of the nurses looks familiar. She can't place her, but she is sure she knows her from somewhere — maybe the partner of someone Sav works with. Her instincts are usually right.

Another nurse, not the one Monica suspects, floats another theory — maybe Daniel told Sav by accident. They all shake their heads. Monica, Narelle and Steve know Daniel wouldn't.

Monica finds comfort in knowing she can speak with Benji daily. The plan is straightforward: Sav initiates the call, and once the nurse hears Benji's voice, the phone is handed to Monica. But Sav can't help himself. As soon as Monica starts talking, he cuts in — taking the phone, speaking over them, controlling the conversation. He tries to lure Monica out of the hospital, promising to take her on a trip around Australia.

Rianna tightens the protocol: the phone must be on speaker, and a nurse stay beside Monica during every call. The moment Sav tries to highjack the conversation, the call is terminated. The staff are exceptional — going beyond their duties to protect Monica. But even with safeguards in place, Sav finds a way through. The next day, after Monica finishes her scheduled call with Benji, she gets another call. It's from a woman claiming to be Sav's sister Elena. Maybe Sav fakes the voice. Maybe he gets someone else to make the call. Either way, it works and he gets through. He says she won't need her medication if she's with him, that he'll take care of her. Monica is confused and emotionally drained, but she doesn't fall for his trickery.

Sav's interference proves what they already know; he doesn't care about her recovery. He doesn't want her well. He wants her reliant on him.

Back at the Hamilton house, two Ring cameras are installed — one at the front entrance, the other above the carport. With the Ring app, the house can be monitored remotely. At first, it's almost entertaining — seeing who walks past, which deliveries arrive. There's a speaker on the front-door camera, which Daniel, ever the teenager, is tempted to use for pranks. There is also a remote-triggered alarm — just in case.

At the time, they don't realise how crucial the camera footage will become.

DAY 15 – CONSTABLE LARRY

Monica is scheduled to speak with Adele via phone at 10 am. Narelle and Steve know they must show Monica the affidavit before then.

Steve:
Monica reads Sav's false claims with surprising calm. Nothing in the affidavit shocks her. It's like she expected it. Adele also knows what she is up against. Apart from copping a mouthful of abuse when she phoned him, Sav walked into her office with Benji in tow two days after she'd spoken to him. He was oblivious to the fact that Adele worked there and was trying to hire a solicitor. The receptionist recommended a solicitor nearby. Adele was appalled that he was dragging a child into legal negotiations. Using his child as leverage.

Monica finds a quiet spot near the hospital café for her talk with Adele. They talk for about thirty minutes. There's no easy fix. No short cut to bring Benji home. Unless the DCJ or the police intervene, Sav can keep him until a court rules otherwise. Adele lays out the path ahead. Monica must prepare for the long haul. She tells them what they already know. That Monica needs to lodge the evidence of Sav's harassment and coercive control – the hundreds of texts, emails and phone calls – with the police as soon as possible.

Coercive control is a pattern of controlling and manipulative behaviours, often subtle, used to dominate and install fear.

That night, there's a blackout at the hospital. The staff are ten minutes late in calling Sav for Monica's hook-up with Benji. Sav refuses to put Benji on the phone. The reason he gives is that the hospital didn't call on time.

On Saturday, Monica's leaves the hospital for the first time since being admitted. Steve picks her up, and they return to the Hamilton house and have lunch with Narelle and Daniel. Afterwards, Monica and Steve go to the police station. Monica brings her phone – filled with hundreds of harassing texts, voicemails, and missed calls from Sav.

They wait ten minutes or so before being shown into a side room. The computer is activated and the officer types away for a few seconds. But then he pauses. He frowns at something on the screen.

'What is it?' asks Steve.

The officer takes a slow breath. He leaves the room and returns with a recording device. He switches it on. Then he shows Monica a photo on-screen: a hand-written note that says:

Bring back my son or I'll kill you.

'Did you put that in Luca Savington's mailbox?' the officer asks.

Monica doesn't flinch. 'No,' she says.

With that out of the way, they move on to the purpose of the visit. The officer films the screen while scrolling through the contents of Monica's phone. The documentation is quick and methodical – emails, texts, and phone numbers, all captured as evidence. Monica describes the harassment she has endured at Mater hospital. The officer listens carefully and agrees there is more than enough here to justify a DVO.

Steve:

Police stations aren't fun places to visit. Cold lighting. Bland walls. Even when you're on the right side of the law you can feel like a suspect just being there. And for Monica – having to deny making death threats! – it rattles her. She holds it together, but by the time we leave she's drained. So am I. Still, I feel relieved. The police now have everything. The phone contents are officially recorded. I'd been so paranoid the phone would fail to work, or the files would be lost. At least that part is done.

Later that night, Narelle and Steve are sitting together in the loungeroom.

'Can you believe Monica had to defend herself over that note?' says Steve. 'And the date it happened, according to Sav's affidavit – February 2nd – was the day Sav took Benji.'

'Exactly,' Narelle says. 'He was already on his way to his parents' place. How would he have seen a note in the mailbox?'

'And Monica didn't know Benji was gone until she was on her way home from work. She was back in Hamilton fifteen minutes later. Why don't the police check these things?'

Sav continues trying to contact Monica at the hospital. He impersonates her cousin, Michael. Another time he claims to be a police officer – Constable Larry. But the hospital staff are wise to his tactics. When a nurse challenges him, he snaps, 'Fuck off.'

The team has had enough. They decide to end what has become a farce. Sav has no intention of letting Monica talk with Benji. His calls merely raise her hopes then crush them, doing more harm than good. It's a cruel game, and it's undermining her recovery.

DAY 17 – RECOVERY

Steve and Daniel drive to the hospital to visit Monica. They bring Roxie, who goes berserk when she sees Monica. Monica showers the dog with affection. They go for a walk through the backstreets near the hospital. Monica's condition is steadily improving.

Meanwhile, Sav's phone calls, texts, and emails continue nonstop. If anyone answers, the call goes dead. Narelle and Steve bring the phone into the hospital, so Monica can take care of important matters and speak with friends.
That evening, another message comes through from a public phone box.
9:43 pm:
ITS ANDREW I'M GOIN 2 COME OVER 2 FUCK U AND YOUR MAN U CUNT
The text is sent from Reay Street, the phone booth around the corner from the house. The messages are becoming more vulgar – an alarming escalation in Sav's behaviour.

On Monday, Steve visits Monica at the hospital and takes her for a long walk. Afterwards, he talks with the hospital staff, including the social worker. They agree that Sav's harassment of Monica – and the staff – should be formally recorded in Monica's release papers.

Monica calls Benji's school and is relieved to hear he is in attendance. Sav has likely figured out Monica can't retrieve Benji while she's still in hospital.

Monica is unexpectedly discharged on Wednesday. The doctor makes the decision after consulting with nurses. They don't keep patients on the ward any longer than is necessary. A release plan is in place, and her progress will be monitored by the Newcastle Mental Health team. One of the nurses quietly shares with Narelle and Steve that Monica isn't fully recovered. It's no surprise to them, but now she's stable, being at home is better than being on the ward. Rest and sleep are crucial.

Monica receives a phone call from The Newcastle Women's Domestic Violence Advocacy Services (NWDVCAS). She recounts everything – how Benji was taken from school and how Sav continues to keep her son from her.

- **The NWDVCAS** aims to provide women and children experiencing domestic violence with support, advocacy, referral and information as they negotiate the legal system and to help put an end to violence. Their goal is to assist women, so these choices may be informed.

As soon as Monica walks through the front door, her phone rings. Her face contorts – before she answers she knows it is Sav.
'He reckons his solicitor told him to ring so I could talk with Benji,' Monica mutters.
Steve signals to her, and she passes the phone over.
'You can liaise through me from now on, Sav.'
'I'll talk with Narelle, not you.'
'You can talk to me. And you can use your real identity,' Steve replies, not so subtly referencing Sav's harassing calls at the hospital.'
'You don't fucking talk to me like that.'
'Listen up Luca…'
But Before Steve can finish, Sav tells him to fuck off and hangs up.

Later, Narelle contacts Sav. He agrees to let Benji speak with his mother daily, between 5 pm and 6 pm. Monica is now certain Sav knows someone at the hospital – it's too coincidental that he rang just after her discharge.

DAY 21 – SAV IS SERVED

Sav quickly reneges on his agreement. He calls Narelle after 6 pm to say Benji is at soccer training and won't be able to talk. Benji is obsessed with soccer – but it was Monica, not Sav who nurtured his passion, ensuring he had the right gear and taking him to training and matches. Since Sav took him, he hasn't been to a training session, or any of the games.

Monica is determined to go to the oval where Benji is supposedly training. Narelle advises her against it. But Monica is desperate to see her son. Steve agrees to accompany her – on the condition they leave immediately if they see Sav or his car.

At the grounds, they don't spot Sav's red Ford. Sienna helps coach one of the teams, so they are not surprised to see her car parked on the grass near the eastern field. Benji's team often trains there, but not today. They drive to the main oval. Still no sign of Sav's car. They park in a side street. Monica waits near the entrance while Steve scouts the area. He checks the grandstand and fields, then signals the coast is clear.

They spot a group of boys huddled together near the goal posts. From a distance, it's hard to tell who's who. They walk around the outside of the oval – Monica sees him first. He's wearing a blue shirt, the only player out of uniform.

Suddenly, Sienna is hurrying towards the group from a nearby field. Her team must've been training there. She stands behind Benji, who is listening to the coach. Monica waves to Benji and he nods. Then Sienna taps his shoulder, and the two make a beeline for the grandstand. Monica and Steve leave the grounds. Monica is heartened to have seen her son. But disturbed he is the only one out of uniform. Sienna once said Sav coerced her into lying to the police. Her behaviour tonight suggests it might be true.

On Friday, Bianca, a social worker from the hospital, calls Monica to check on her wellbeing. She also lets Monica know that she'd contacted the police days earlier, insisting they issue a DVO for Monica's protection. Monica thanks her but remains cautious – she's been let down before.

Later in the day, the police call to confirm the DVO was issued two days ago. It's been twenty-two-days since Benji was taken and more than fifty since Monica first went to the police station seeking help. Whether the police would have acted without Bianca's advocacy is anyone's guess. Hopefully, this order will finally stop the harassment.

Monica and Narelle head to the police station to collect the DVO and report the latest wave of abusive calls, emails, and texts from Sav.

An email arrives from the Mater hospital, containing the social worker's report. It's detailed – three pages outlining the harassment Monica and the hospital staff endured, and the role Sav played in her deteriorating mental health.
'The report is damning of Sav's behaviour,' says Steve to Monica and Narelle. 'I'm glad it mentions Sav pretending to be a cop. Luca Savington, hereinafter known as (legal terminology borrowed from Sav's affidavit) Constable Larry.'

Monica hears from her solicitor, Adele. A date has been set for the first return hearing in the Family Court. It is a month away. It offers hope.

DAY 23 – TRICKERY

Sav contacts Narelle and says he'll call so Monica can speak to Benji. He nominates 12:30 pm. At 12:23, a no-caller ID call comes through. The caller hangs up. Seconds later, another call comes through – this time, Sav's name appears as the caller. What's likely happened is that Sav made the first call with the no-caller ID on by mistake.
Monica is overjoyed to hear Benji's voice. She tells him how much she misses and loves him.
'It's Dad's birthday party,' says Benji. 'Can you come to Dad's birthday party?' It's clearly a trap.
'That will be good for your dad and you. It's nice to have a party. It was good to see you at soccer.' There is a long silence.
'You scared me,' Benji eventually says. 'Because you were trying to get me.'

'No, I only wanted to see you. Just to say hello. I wanted to give you a cuddle.'
'Are you coming home?'
'That's not for you to worry about, Benji. I can still see you without coming home. I'd love to take you to the movies, or we can go to a park. Maybe go shopping.'
Benji starts to cry. 'Can I have my iPad?'
'You can have it when you come back here. All your things are here.'
Monica changes the subject. 'I wish I could take you to the gala day tomorrow in Port Macquarie. So you can play with your team.'
She had booked accommodation for the gala day months ago. The phone goes dead.
'The gala day talk was too much for Constable Larry,' Steve quips.

Monica's diary:
Family trip to Sydney to visit sister Georgia. 1 get calls from Sav's new number. Eighteen private calls.
And a text about divorce from Sav that didn't make sense.
Cst Hutchinson messaged. My DVO against Sav has been served.
Spoke to mental health team. They are always available for support, which I really appreciate.

Narelle texts Sav to organise a phone call between Benji and Monica. Sav had previously said 'after 5, maybe 5:30' but now insists on 4:45. Narelle agrees.
'What have you been up to?' asks Monica.
'Having fun,' says Benji.
'Having fun doing what?'
'Soccer.'
'Oh… you played soccer,' Monica responds.
Sav interjects. 'Been to gala day. Four games.'
'I'm here to speak to Benji,' Monica says firmly.
Benji is put back on the line.
Monica speaks, 'We missed you today, Benji. We went to Sydney.'
Sav cuts the call.
A minute later he rings back. There is a brief exchange between Monica and Benji that lasts about 30 seconds, until Benji says he has to go.

Steve's diary:
Narelle and I would always look after Daniel and Benji during their school holiday break. Sometimes I'd take my bike up to their place and we'd go riding. Benji. still on his tiny bicycle, would pedal like mad, expecting to keep up with Daniel. It was impossible — but it didn't

stop him trying. Benji could be explosive from a standing start. Sometimes he'd leave me in his wake, and I'd have to ride hard to catch up. We'd sometimes go into the bush off the main road where there were makeshift jumps. Benji pushed it to the limit.

Daniel said to him. 'You're going to be one of those kids who shows off and gets himself injured.'

DAY 25 – UNDER DURESS

Monica's diary:

Phoned school. Benji's not there. After lunch there was a message from police officer Tess Fleming advising me to attend the police station for an interview to avoid arrest. Police showed me three letters. I confirmed I did not write threats to Sav or attend Sav's address and bang on his door. Mum, Dad and I provided CCTV from the Hamilton address – evidence I was not near the house when Sav accused me of doing this.

Phone call from Celeste (mental health team). I advised about the police station visit and the added stress involved re false allegations from Sav.

When Monica is told she must attend the police station to avoid arrest, Narelle and Steve are stunned. Monica has only just come out of hospital. She's far from recovered. They do not know what the accusations are. The three of them go together. They report at the desk and, shortly after, a male sergeant and a female officer come into the lobby. They are from the Domestic Abuse Team. The fact that it is the Domestic Abuse Team who have threatened to arrest Monica – one might think it was their role to protect a domestic violence victim – makes the whole situation even more surreal. Then it gets worse. Sav reported to the police that the previous night, at around 8:30, he heard a loud banging on the front door. He went outside and found a note stuck to the screen door: **Sav, you bring Benji back to me or I will kill you. I'll get Dave to grab Benji and you won't see him anymore.**

He claimed the man he referenced – Dave – is someone they encountered while shopping at Charlestown Square before Christmas. According to Sav, Monica orchestrated the death threats.

As Narelle hunts down CCTV footage from their house, Steve insists the sergeant read the social worker's report from Mater hospital, so he knows that Sav is the one doing the harassing. To his credit, the officer skims the report for nearly a minute.

The footage from Narelle's phone shows Monica never left the house that night. They had returned from Sydney at 4:20 pm, and Monica spoke with Benji on the phone shortly after. Monica didn't leave the house for the entire evening, and her car was parked out the front. Officer Jess accepts this and shows the sergeant. Despite this, they still want Monica for further questioning.

Steve and Narelle are furious that the police are putting Monica through this while she is still fragile. Whether or not they would have arrested her if she had refused to be interviewed is unclear. Maybe they should have demanded a solicitor be present – but the evidence of her innocence is compelling, and Monica wants the matter resolved. She agrees to go through with the interview.

After twenty minutes, one of the officers returns and informs them that a support person can accompany Monica. Steve volunteers. Inside the station, Steve is surprised by the number of officers working behind computer screens. He and the officer walk through to the rear of the station where suspects are taken. The space is drab and lifeless. There are three officers present: the two they spoke with in the foyer and a supervising sergeant. Steve's name is run through the system.
'Not even a speeding fine,' jokes Jess.
Steve notices the officer misspells his name as 'Steven' (it's Stephen) but lets it slide.

Monica is formally interviewed by the police:

On January 14, 2024:
Sav claims he received a threatening call at 2:00 am: ***You better stay away, or I will kill you.***
He alleges it was Monica's current partner (Monica has no current partner) and that he recognised the voice. He says a similar call came in at 4 pm.

February 2, 2024:
Sav claims to have found a note in his mailbox: ***Bring back my son or I will kill you.***

This is the same claim he made when Monica and Steve previously reported his harassment to the police. Why is it being brought up again?

February 13, 2024:
Sav says that at 8 pm while he was showering after work, Sienna saw a man exit a black car and place something in the mailbox. The man fitted the description of 'Dave' from Charlestown. The note read: *I love you I hate you Bring back Benji to me or I will kill U.*

Monica calmly tells police she was at the Mater Hospital on February 13, on a locked ward. When she left it was only briefly, and she was accompanied by staff or family.

Steve is not sure what Monica has told them already but makes sure they understand that Monica was in an abusive relationship. That she came to the police for help over fifty days ago. That she doesn't have a partner. That she cared for Benji until Sav took him from school. That he has withheld him ever since. That he has harassed her non-stop – including at the hospital. And that only now is there a DVO in place against him.
'The guy sounds like a nasty piece of work,' says the supervising sergeant.
Monica asks why the incidents weren't caught on Sav's own security camera.
'It wasn't working,' she's told.
Convenient.
Monica is taken into a nearby interview room. Steve is allowed to accompany her. He's worried the pressure will push her over the edge – but she surprises him. Calm, composed, unshaken. She refutes every absurd accusation one by one.

Monica is not charged. Yet the police took Sav's lies seriously enough to formally interview her.

Steve's reflection:
The language used in those threatening notes is crude. The grammar's wrong. It's not Monica's style. Anyone who's spent five minutes with her would know that. If they checked their own records, they'd see Sav's full of it. One of his texts to Monica on February 2 contradicts his own 'boyfriend story.' He literally says, 'I know you're not with anyone.' So why are they dragging Monica into the police station?

Monica's diary:

Phone call to Women's Domestic Violence Corrective Services at 9:12 am. Spoke for over 30 minutes. We talked about how to stay safe and protect our family from Sav. We discussed the DVO already in place, and the one Sav supposedly has against me but is yet to be served.

Benji wasn't at school again today. I had a parent-teacher interview with Benji's teacher and also spoke with the school principal. They say Benji is doing well academically – but his attendance and classroom engagement are major concerns.

Later, I had a phone appointment with Dr. Lett. He's written a supporting medical letter, confirming that after ten years of monitoring, I've always been a high-functioning member of the community. A reliable mother – not only to Daniel and Benji, but to Sav's three children as well. That I have always worked and achieved an Associate Degree in Integrated Care in Aging while parenting five children.

No harassment today.

DAY 29 – MISIDENTIFICATION

Sav breaches his DVO twice by phoning Monica, showing his impulsivity and disregard for the law.

Although AVOs and DVOs are a civil order, breaching them can result in criminal prosecution. The maximum penalty for breaching them is a $5500 fine, or two years imprisonment.

Steve:

Around this time, Daniel comes across Sav's affidavit sitting on top of the piano. He reads the absurd and degrading claims Sav made about his mother. I watch on. It is impossible – and unhealthy – to protect a 14-year-old from the truth. Daniel notices me.

'This is so wrong,' he says, firmly.

It is only right that Daniel knows what a base, inhumane, and dangerous individual Luca Savington really is. For his own protection.

Monica's lawyer advises her to obtain a hair follicle test. Though Monica rarely drinks, this will help refute Sav's preposterous claims that she is an alcoholic who is violent toward Benji and himself. The cost? Over $600. After some hesitation, Monica agrees. It will serve as hard evidence of both her temperance and Sav's lies.

On a sunny Friday morning, Monica and Steve drive to Mayfield for the test. She expected a clinic, but instead they are to meet a woman in a white Winnebago near Kennards Hire at 10 am. She receives the first call as they pass through Islington – the woman is running late. They wait in the car park. Monica is not to approach the Winnebago until she receives another call, which means the follicle test is ready to proceed.

Monica has a solicitor appointment at 12 pm, and Chantel is meeting her in Hamilton at 11 am so they can go together. They are relieved when at last, a white Winnebago comes chugging down the hill and parks nearby. A short time later, Monica gets the call. Steve walks her to the van. After the technician confirms her identity, she enters alone. Only a small hair sample is needed. Most of the time is spent confirming details. The technician explains the hair will be sent to a Melbourne lab. Her work usually involves drug testing in custody disputes. Alcohol testing is rarer. It strikes Monica how easily a baseless accusation can become a costly burden. Forty minutes later, she exits the van feeling relieved. On their way home, Monica receives a text – Chantel is almost at the house. They arrive at roughly the same time.

Monica and Chantel spend nearly three hours with Adele, the solicitor. Adele plays devil's advocate and digs deep into Monica's medical history. Chantel is impressed by Monica's composure. Due to Sav's damning claims, they always seem to be on the defensive. Adele recommends Monica report Sav's DVO breaches to police. Though exhausted, they follow her advice.

That evening, Monica is emotionally drained. Her eyes are puffy, clearly from crying. Her parents' fear she may spiral again. After dinner, she takes her medication at 8:00 pm and heads to bed early.

Twenty minutes later, while Steve watches a movie, Narelle reads, and Daniel is on his computer. The doorbell rings. Concerned it may wake Monica, Steve hurries to answer. Two police officers – a male and a female – stand at the door. Senior Constable Bancroft, the female officer, insists they speak with Monica. Steve explains Monica is asleep, but Bancroft demands she be woken. Narelle joins him at the door. Daniel watches from his room. Monica, after hearing her name, gets dressed and comes downstairs. Roxie makes a commotion in the background, so they step outside.

Bancroft announces that a note with a bullet and a death threat was placed in Sav's mailbox earlier that day. She then shows Monica another note, allegedly received earlier: *I love you I hate you bring Benji back to me or I will kill you.*

Monica explains she was questioned about this note previously, and her account was accepted. Bancroft isn't satisfied. She holds the note against a birthday card from years ago.
'It looks like your handwriting,' Bancroft says.
'It's not,' Monica replies firmly.

Narelle tries to explain that Sav snatched Benji and refuses Monica access.
'That's legal,' Bancroft interrupts. 'There isn't a court order.'
Steve can't help himself, 'And you're sure about that?'
'I think I'd know. I've been in this job for over ten years,' Bancroft brags.
Steve refrains from making a rude remark about her job capabilities.
The front light is on a timer and turns off every few minutes and must be reengaged. This adds a chaotic ambience to proceedings. When Steve mentions the ongoing harassment Monica has endured, and that Sav has been in the area, Bancroft retorts Sav has every right to drive down their street. Her attitude is grating on Steve who can barely contain his outrage. He gets some satisfaction watching her being pestered by mosquitoes that are targeting her more than the others. Bancroft then serves Monica with two DVOs. The first, from Western NSW, claims Monica assaulted Sav in December. The second, from Bancroft's own station, alleges Monica placed the threatening note in Sav's mailbox on February 13.

They are stunned. Monica was hospitalised on February 13.
'This is absolutely ridiculous,' says Steve.
'I might insist on a DNA test,' Bancroft says.
Steve snaps: 'Are you serious? Monica's DNA is everywhere in the house – she lived there for six years. Narelle urges Steve to calm down and listen to what Bancroft has to say. But Steve's heard enough. As he turns to go back into the house, the male officer asks, 'Do you have a gun?'
The question startles Steve. 'Haven't touched one since school cadets,' he replies in a droll tone.

The officer chuckles.

Monica and Narelle try to prove Monica's alibi. Surveillance footage confirms Monica was at home, at the solicitor's, and later at a basketball game. Bancroft refuses to view the footage. Monica knows from what the police told her the previous day that Sav's entrance camera isn't working, so she pushes the point with Bancroft who admits as much.

'With all these threats, you'd think he'd have it fixed,' Narelle says.

'We can order him to,' Bancroft replies. But that never happens.

Eventually, Bancroft becomes less combative. She says Monica has every right to collect her belongings. This too proves to be not that simple. They later discover she must apply to the court.

After the police leave, they are at their wits end. Now they must contend with this on top of yesterday's accusations. It is perplexing. Despite Sav's relentless harassment of Monica, along with his behaviour toward hospital staff – all recorded in police files – Monica is the one served with two DVOs. Why was she questioned again on a matter she had already addressed to police satisfaction the previous day?

They read through the details of the DVOs served by Bancroft. Both contain blatant fabrications. Regarding the first, Sav claims he didn't report the alleged injuries at the time because his wife suffers from a mental illness. He alleges the defendant had been drinking prior to the supposed assault. Despite there being not a skerrick of evidence, the police claim they have safety concerns for Sav due to the delay in reporting and a fear of escalating violence. But Monica fled the house at the end of December. How can the police fear an escalation of violence from someone who no longer lives there?

Narelle, Steve, Daniel, Monica's friends and family, as well as her neighbours, all saw Sav socially after December 9, 2023, during the lead-up to Christmas. They can attest that there were no bruises to his left eye or face, as described.

The second DVO is even more astounding. It's based on a note allegedly placed in Sav's mailbox on February 13 that reads: *I love you I hate you bring Benji back to me or I will kill you.* But on that date, Monica was a patient at the Mater Hospital. She was confined to a locked psychiatric ward and did not leave the grounds until the following Saturday – and then only briefly, in the company of her father. A simple five-minute call to hospital administration could have confirmed this.

As with the first DVO, the second also contains allegations of alcohol abuse. It claims Monica has mental health issues that impact her parenting – assertions repeated twice, based entirely on Sav's hearsay. Perhaps the term 'mental illness' serves as a red flag to certain officers.

The second DVO states there are concerns due to 'the escalating behaviour of the defendant.' The first DVO noted Sav's fear of 'escalating violence.' This is precisely what happened when Sav fabricated notes and lied to police – a self-fulfilling prophecy.

When examined from the perspective of proper police process and administrative management, both DVOs fail dismally. The first states that the relationship ended in late November, yet the alleged assault took place in the bedroom of the family home in December. How could Monica have attacked Sav if she wasn't living there? Daniel is listed in Sav's DVO, even though he lives with Monica and is included in her DVO against Sav. Benji's date of birth is listed incorrectly as May 15 instead of May 17. Daniel's is wrong too. He was born in January, not November. Furthermore, the documents make no mention of Sav's prior DVOs, which surely are relevant.

The issuing of these two DVOs highlights the treatment domestic violence victims sometimes receive from police. Monica fled the family home in late December out of fear for her safety. She was interviewed by police that night but denied a DVO. She only received protective intervention after the Mater Hospital social worker intervened on her behalf. Meanwhile, her abuser was granted two DVOs, based on multiple lies, culminating in the false claim that he fears Monica's violence – despite his documented history of aggression, and despite Monica never having displayed violent behaviour.

The police might have considered Sav's known tactic of placing intimidating notes in mailboxes. His neighbours have reported such behaviour. So have Monica and Steve, when they found a threatening note in the Hamilton house mailbox.

Monica's treatment reflects a complete failure of evidence-based policing. Monica's rights are trampled while Sav's fabrications are treated as fact.

Steve:

Do the police even undertake a basic fact-checking exercise? They don't appear to collate the information they already have. Again, I'm reminded of an 88-armed octopus, with each arm oblivious to what the others are doing. It is preposterous that a perpetrator can turn up at two different police stations, fabricate stories, and obtain not one but two DVOs against the actual victim.

Sav told the police he knew the threatening note came from Monica because it was written on a notepad headed 'The Naughty Dog School' where he claimed (wrongly) Monica once worked. Constable Larry did the so-called detective work and produced a note Monica had written years earlier. 'Look, officer. Caught her red-handed. And as you can see, the writing matches.'

Apart from the fact that Monica was in a locked ward and was not anywhere near Sav's house when Sav received the death threat, do the police think the ambulance made a detour on the way to the Mater Hospital so Monica could pick up a notepad?

The notepad bearing 'The Naughty Dog School' caption clearly came from inside Sav's residence. Bancroft's assertion that the handwriting matched an earlier sample from Monica is incorrect. The imitator made a fair attempt, but some of the letters clearly do not match. The police swallowed Battered Sav's lies hook, line, and sinker. I have serious concerns about the escalating gullibility of some police officers – believing such absolute claptrap. Highly damaging claptrap.

It may be coincidence, but it's interesting to note that both officers who believed Sav and issued the DVOs are female. Add the fired-up Bancroft to the mix, and it seems Sav knows how to manipulate women into thinking he is the victim – that he has been maligned by a spiteful woman. The authorising officers were male, but it's unlikely they ever saw or spoke to Sav. Meanwhile, another victim – 8-year-old Benji – has been left in the care of a dangerous, manipulative, mentally unhinged man.

Excerpts from Monica's diary:

I think of his threats – that if I didn't go back to him, he would tell the police about the night he says I assaulted him. I had been out with a group of friends and was tired. When I got home, Sav ignored me. He always carried on when I'd been out with friends. I went to bed. Sav came into the room and woke me up. I asked him several times to let me sleep and that we could talk in the morning.
He kept screaming. I said, 'You're going to wake everyone up.'
'Who is he? Who is he?' Sav shouted.
There's no-one but you. I've only been out with friends – friends you know,' I said.

Sav grabbed my phone and kept raising his voice. I said, 'Give me my phone back. I just want to go to sleep.' I got up and tried to take it back. He called me a bitch and refused to return it or let me sleep. I tried again. He pushed me back several times. I pushed him back and said, 'Give me my phone. Give me my phone.'

Sav called out for Sienna.
Sienna told him, 'Give her back her phone.'
He refused and said to Sienna, 'Help, she's attacking me.'
I said, 'I can't take it anymore.'
Sienna said she would call the police.
Sav told her not to.

ABC journalist Hayley Gleeson reported on March 31, 2022, that, 'Police are still misjudging domestic violence, and the victims are suffering the consequences.' The following paragraph was appropriated from Hayley Gleeson's article:

For years, experts have been warning of a victim misidentification crisis emerging alongside a steady increase in the number of women being named as respondents on domestic violence protection orders. The consequences can be life-altering and, in extreme cases, life-threatening. A 2017 analysis of twenty-seven domestic homicides in Queensland (based on statistics from Queensland courts) found that half the women who were killed had previously been identified by police as the perpetrator on a protection order. Shockingly, nearly every one of the Aboriginal women killed had been identified as a perpetrator. A 2018 review by Women's Legal (Monash University, July 2018) found that one in ten women were being misidentified as the aggressor in police applications for family violence intervention orders.

Monica is one of thousands of misidentified victims. Many women accept the conditions of the protection order because they feel ashamed and humiliated. After years of abuse, they are emotionally unprepared to face court. But these incorrect identifications carry serious ramifications. They can limit access to children, restrict housing, employment, and services, and further traumatise victims who were already fighting to survive.

When the sheer volume of DVOs issued by police is considered, the scale of the problem becomes even more staggering. According to the NSW Bureau of Crime Statistics and Research, 48,814 DVOs were commenced in New South Wales in 2023/24 – a 32% increase from 37,099 domestic AVOs in 2019/20. That's tens of thousands of women and children directly affected by a system that, too often, gets it wrong.

DAY 30 – FAMILY UNDER SIEGE

Steve bristles with anger every time he thinks of Senior Constable Bancroft – how confidently she accused Monica of putting a bullet in Sav's mailbox. He calls his sister Chantel to tell her what happened. She is livid. Outraged that police would believe such an absurd claim, Chantel immediately writes a statement and emails it to Bancroft, including her full contact details.

Chantel:
Good afternoon,
I am writing regarding your visit to Monica Savington (nee Kelty) at 148 Percy St Hamilton NSW on Friday night 1/3/2024 at approximately 9 pm. I spoke with Monica's parents who reside at the property, and they told me of your visit. They advised that on this visit you served Monica with two DVOs and that her ex-husband Luca Savington has made an accusation that she has put a note/letter and bullet in his mailbox. I am Monica's Aunty and was with Monica from 9 am yesterday until approximately 4:50 pm. Our timeline is below.

I am very concerned that Sav would make this accusation and somehow have this bullet in his possession. I have no doubt that Monica would never do such a thing. I urge you to consider seriously that he has in his procession not only a bullet but also possibly a gun. He continues to project his anger and abuse at Monica, making accusations that can be shown to be false. Monica is terrified of him. He lied and verbally abused staff at the Mater Hospital and even impersonated a police officer to get to her. THIS IS ON POLICE RECORD. See social worker's report. I believe Monica is very much at risk and urge you to please take this seriously. This is a list of our movements yesterday, Friday 1st of March 2024, to highlight to you that Monica was not anywhere near the location that the bullet and note were left:

- *7:55 am – I drove from my residence at 67 Borne Avenue, Swansea, to Percy Street, Hamilton. I arrived at 9:00 am. Monica and her father, Steve, met me at the door. This is confirmed by home surveillance footage.*
- *9:15 am – Monica and I drove directly to her solicitor's office. We arrived at 10:00 am and stayed for 2 hours and 10 minutes. Adele, her solicitor, can verify this. Footage shows us leaving the house.*
- *12:47 pm – We walked into the police station and spoke with Constable Oliveri at the front desk, to report a breach of the DVO, as directed by the solicitor.*

Police should have this on record.

- *1:00 pm – We were taken into an interview room to formally report the breach.*
- *2:00 pm – We left the station, returned to my car, and drove directly back to 148 Percy Street. Again, the return is confirmed by the home camera.*
- *4:40 pm – Steve and I left to collect his car from a mechanic nearby, returning within 10 minutes.*

Monica remained at home with her mother, Narelle, and her son, Daniel. She did not leave the house at any point that evening. The camera confirms this.
Kind regards,
Chantel.

The past few days have taken a visible toll on everyone.
'How can Monica recover, with the constant harassment from Sav – and now the police?' says Steve.
Narelle convinces Monica to take a break and to go stay at her sister Georgia's place in Sydney.
'At least she'll be out of the firing line for a few days.'
'What about Daniel?' Steve asks.
'He wants to stay here,' Narelle replies. 'Monica is going to take him to the Newcastle Show on Saturday morning. I'll drive her to Sydney in the afternoon.'
'I'll go to the show with them,' Steve adds. 'I don't want just the two of them there.'

They've all tried to maintain some normalcy for Daniel – but it's slipping away. The trauma of the past two months is catching up with him. His father discarded him and took his brother. He's watched his mother collapse, get admitted to hospital, then be accused – falsely and publicly – by police, right on their doorstep.

The Newcastle Show is just a ten-minute walk from the Hamilton house, and the top of the Ferris wheel is visible from the backyard. Monica is still not functioning at her best, but she is determined that she and Daniel enjoy themselves. Narelle drops the three of them off at the gate. The plan is to walk home afterwards.

When they enter the showgrounds, they're pleased to see it's not too crowded. They decide to go on the rides first, before it gets too busy. Steve is well and truly over the thrill rides but agrees to go with them on the Ferris wheel. The view is spectacular – seeing the city from up high, with the mountains stretching to the west.

Monica and Daniel then go on the Cup and Saucer while Steve watches. He feels on edge. It's difficult watching Monica struggle, but it's more than that. He has a strange feeling that Sav is at the show. He knows it's not logical, but he can't shake it.

Daniel goes on a ride alone – one that's far too daunting for Steve or Monica. The apparatus rises about forty metres into the air. Ten arms with seats dangle and spin around an elongated tower high above the ground. Daniel enjoys himself. They take some photos. The carnival atmosphere is contagious. After playing a few games, they have lunch then visit the animal nursery. Daniel loves being able to handle the animals, and it's gratifying for Monica to see a smile on his face.

On the way home, Monica checks her phone. She notices a text message she missed – received at 11:00 am:

MONICA IT ME DAVE TOLD SAV WE HAD GRATE FUCK THAT NIGHT HNW U LOVED TO FUCK ME SEE U 2 MORROW

Monica keeps it to herself, not wanting to alarm Daniel or Steve. The message was sent from a public phone booth on Maitland Road, near the TAFE, just a kilometre away.

Later that afternoon, Narelle drives Monica to Sydney. Monica stays the night, wanting to spend time with her sister Georgia, baby Emma, and Matt. But without Benji, she feels the need to return to Newcastle the next morning and stay close to Daniel. At least she had one night away.

Narelle meets Georgia halfway and brings Monica back. That afternoon, Steve takes Daniel to basketball practice at the blue courts in the city, near Marketown.

DAY 32 – BACK TO WORK

Monica receives a call from an unidentifiable number. Steve answers. It's from a psychologist's office – the caller wants to speak to Monica in relation to a doctor's referral for Benji. Steve assumes he's speaking with the psychologist and begins to explain Benji's predicament – how he was taken by his father and kept in isolation, and how Monica hasn't laid eyes on her son for well over a month. The woman on the line becomes upset. Her voice shakes. She agrees it's horrid and sounds as though she might cry.
'Are you OK?' asks Steve.
'I've only been working here two weeks,' replies the woman.
Steve realises, to his embarrassment, that he's speaking with the receptionist – not the psychologist. Although he and Narelle laugh about it later, the moment says a lot about Steve's state of mind. The frustration. The helplessness. The need to unload.

Later, Monica contacts the office of the referring doctor, Dr Phan. She explains to the receptionist that Benji's father does not have full responsibility for the child's care, and as the mother, she wants to understand why her son is being referred to a psychologist. An appointment is made for a phone consultation. The earliest available time is the following Thursday.

Monica is pushing herself to return to work. Her boss has been understanding and doesn't want to lose her – but she also needs someone in the role. They agree on a temporary arrangement; Monica will return part-time, working just two days a week to ease back into it. Even though it doesn't seem like much, the emotional weight of Benji's situation – and the fact that Monica hasn't fully recovered – makes it uncertain whether she'll be able to cope. The work is demanding. Clients and families require energy. Focus. Emotional strength.

Safety is also a concern. Monica's boss has seen Sav's car nearby in recent weeks. Monica is often alone at the office, and Sav has already turned up when told to stay away. The downstairs entrance must remain unlocked so the public can access the upstairs services.

Monica and Steve work out a survival plan. Steve often plays music for the clients – they're used to his presence. They love hearing the old standards: *Moon River*, *Alexander's Ragtime Band*. Until Monica finds her feet again, they decide Steve will play in the mornings and return after lunch. In the hours between, he'll pass the time at the shopping centre nearby, working on music mixes on his laptop. It eases Monica's burden and ensures she's not always alone.

The following day, Monica has her phone appointment with Dr Phan. When the doctor calls, she explains the situation and the extenuating circumstances. He mentions something about her dropping off documents at the office. Monica clarifies – it wasn't her. In fact, she's only just learned about Benji's referral to the psychologist. When she asks about the reason for the referral, the doctor goes quiet. Monica explains that full responsibility for Benji has not been granted to Sav, and as the child's mother, she has the right to be informed. Without explanation, the doctor cuts the call. He doesn't ring back. The abrupt end makes her suspicious.

Benji remains in seclusion. Sav has dragged him into adult matters, taking him into solicitors' offices, police stations, and exposing him to a litany of lies. He even tried to bring him onto a mental health ward. If Sav is taking Benji to see a psychologist, Monica doubts it's for the child's benefit. She suspects an ulterior motive. But they are powerless to do anything about it.

Benji is still not attending school or participating in any of his usual sporting or recreational activities. Despite repeated attempts by concerned family and friends to alert the Department of Communities and Justice, the authorities do not consider the case serious enough to intervene.

DAY 36 – EMERALD BEACH

Narelle has plans to travel north to Woolgoolga for the weekend. She's meant to care for baby Emma while Georgia and Matt attend a wedding. But with the recent upheaval, she's unsure what to do. After talking it over, they decide they'll all go. Narelle books a cabin at a caravan park in nearby Emerald Beach. Daniel isn't keen on a long drive, but he lights up at the mention of the Big Banana – toboggan rides, arcade games, and waterslides. The Big Banana becomes the carrot that lures him from the comfort of his computer.

But just when everyone's set for a change of scenery, baby Emma gets sick. Georgia and Matt cancel their plans. Narelle, Steve, Monica, and Daniel decide to go anyway. The accommodation is non-refundable, and they all need the break.

They leave early. The mood is light – for a while. But tension creeps in as Monica raises the issue of her follicle test. A test she undertook to disprove Sav's preposterous claim that she was an alcoholic. It's been a week since she gave her hair sample. Still no result. She waits until after 9:00 am and calls the lab in Melbourne. A technician answers but can't locate the sample.
'That's unbelievable,' says Steve. 'After paying a fortune for those tests?'
'Yeah…
 the woman who took the sample said we'd have results in a few days.'
'Can you get onto her?' asks Narelle.
'I tried earlier. I'll try again in a minute.'
Daniel, headphones on, is deep in his game. He's oblivious to the rising anxiety around him.
'You might have to give another sample,' Steve says.
'I can't," Monica replies. 'I've dyed my hair. They'll only take untreated hair.'
'Okay… I'm sure they'll find it,' Steve says, masking his concern.

No-one says aloud what they're all thinking: the Judicial Registrar is hearing the case next Thursday. Monica's solicitor needs the follicle test to refute Sav's false allegations of alcohol abuse.

They pull off the highway for lunch. Still no news. Monica is told the lab is 'frantically searching.'

As they rejoin the Pacific Highway, Monica receives an email from her solicitor, Adele. Attached are five documents from Sav's solicitor – hundreds of pages, most of it a repeat of the first affidavit.

But it's more than repetition. It's escalation.

Sav insists that because of Monica's supposed alcohol abuse and mental instability, the case must bypass mediation and go straight to court. He claims the child is in danger. He alleges that Steve – Benji's grandfather – tried to push Benji down the stairs. He says Monica used to smack Benji regularly. He states he's too frightened to attend court in person.

And he has weaponised the DVOs.

Reading it is distressing. It changes the tone in the car.
'How can solicitors send out such rubbish?' says Steve. 'They must know the claims are false.'
'They just follow their client's directions,' says Narelle.
'If they knowingly send false information, they should be held accountable.'
'It's just the same old lies,' Monica says quietly.
'We're always on the back foot,' adds Narelle.
'I'm glad Sav is applying to have the case heard urgently,' Steve says. 'He has no evidence. Surely The Registrar will see that.'

Monica eventually reaches the woman who collected the hair sample in the Winnebago. The collector confirms she sent the sample to the lab last Friday – the day it was taken.
'Sometimes it takes a while,' she says. 'But the results should be back by now. I'll contact the lab.'
Nobody speaks for a while. The highway hums beneath them.
'At least the lady in the Winnebago wasn't a fraudster,' Steve says.

Late that afternoon, Monica gets another call. The sample has been found. Relief.
But the analysis hasn't been done.
'Nothing will happen over the weekend,' Monica says. 'But they've promised to prioritise it next week.'

'At over $600 a pop, you'd bloody well hope so,' says Steve.

It's nearly sunset when they arrive at Emerald Beach Caravan Park. Their cabin sits near the bush, a short trail leading to the ocean. It's a beautiful spot. Daniel and Steve head to the beach for a quick dip before dark. The waves are gentle. They laugh, splash around. It feels like a long-overdue release.

The next morning, Narelle buys Daniel a bodyboard in town. He's excited to try it. Soon, he's riding waves like he's done it for years. Steve joins him, bodysurfing beside him. Daniel wants to stay in the water until sunset. He doesn't realise that his seventy-two-year-old Pop can't keep up with a fit 14-year-old. But he agrees to return in the morning for one last surf before heading home.

Buying the board turns out to be a great idea. Surfing becomes a lifeline for Daniel – a joyful distraction from everything swirling around him.

On the drive back down the coast, Daniel downloads the Surf Watch app to track beach conditions. He checks the swell in Newcastle – Bar Beach, Merewether. He and Steve make plans to surf together the following week after school.

DAY 39 – STYMIED

Monica has an easy day at the Centre, with just two clients attending. She knows they both love dogs, so she brings Roxie along. As expected, the border collie is a big hit. Roxie laps up the attention, and her presence lifts everyone's spirits, making Monica's job easier. She even sits quietly through morning tea. Monica snaps a few photos and posts them to Facebook. For once, the morning feels light.

While Monica works, Sav continues to call. So much for the DVO putting the brakes on his communications.

After the clients leave, Monica answers one of his calls – concerned something might be wrong with Benji. But Sav tells her Benji is fine. Monica cuts the call. Moments later, more messages arrive. Crude and abusive. Sent under the guise of being from Monica's 'boyfriend.'

Steve is furious. It seems nothing will stop Luca Savington. He calls the local police station – where Monica was previously interrogated – and asks to speak with someone from the domestic violence unit. He's eventually put through to an officer named Laurens, a name he doesn't recognise.

Steve explains that Sav continues to harass Monica, all while using the DVOs issued against her to damage her reputation and push for sole custody of Benji. Laurens listens. She doesn't have a solution but says Sav's behaviour will eventually count against him. Steve pushes further. He tells Laurens that the DVOs Sav obtained are fabricated and easily disproved. Laurens says Monica will have to wait until they are addressed in court.

After the call, Steve feels defeated. Maybe Laurens is right – Sav's lies will catch up with him in the long-term. But meanwhile, he's still isolating Benji, still manipulating the system, and still tarnishing Monica's name. He's already poisoned her reputation at Benji's soccer club. And at the Medical Centre where Benji is a patient. Judging by the coolness of the school principal, he's been doing the same at the school. With the DVOs in place, Sav now has legal documents to support his false narrative that Monica sends death threats, mistreats her child, and is unfit to be a mother. Steve is exasperated – staggered by how easily the system is manipulated.

He vents to Narelle over dinner. 'No-one sees the full picture. That plays straight into Sav's hands.'
'So far, yes,' says Narelle. 'Let's hope the lies start catching up with him.'
'The police department is so damn compartmentalised – and slow. I think the 88-armed octopus is now on sedatives. If just one intelligent officer took three or four hours, picked up the phone, cross-checked a few facts – they'd realise none of Sav's claims add up.'
'He knows how to play the victim,' Narelle says. 'I'll give him that.'
'He knows how to play the police too. But you saw through him the first time you met him. You knew the type. You were worried about what Monica was getting into.'

As the day closes, there's still no news about Monica's follicle test results.

DAY 40 – IN FROM THE COLD

Monica drops Daniel at school before heading to work. Mid-morning, Adele calls. The follicle test results are in – and they're negative. It's no surprise, but the relief is immense. If that sample had been lost, it could have been disastrous. Instead, they now have hard proof: Monica doesn't drink two or sometimes four bottles of wine a night. By implication, Luca Savington's claim was pure fabrication.

People experienced in family law keep telling them the same thing – once the case reaches court, the truth will surface. Narelle digs a little deeper and discovers that the judicial officer assigned to the first return hearing is a former police prosecutor, with years of experience leading teams in Western Sydney. It's a small but welcome comfort. Someone with that background won't be easily taken in by the likes of Sav.

Meanwhile, Daniel has been saving up for a small waterproof camera. He buys one online and mounts it to the front of his bodyboard. He can't wait to film himself riding waves.
The moment he gets home from school, he's ready to hit the beach. The Surf Watch app shows the swell is nothing special, but it doesn't matter. They drive to Bar Beach. Daniel paddles out, laughing, recording each ride. Later, he's back on shore, scrolling through the clips on his phone, replaying his best waves.

Events take an unexpected and monumental turn. Sienna contacts Georgia.

It's a shock for everyone – like a scene from a spy film when a key agent defects. Something must have changed, because at Benji's soccer training Sienna was doing her father's bidding. Apart from that occasion, this is the first contact – from her or any of the Savingtons – since the Sunday before Benji was taken, six weeks earlier when Sienna dropped by the Hamilton house.

Text from Sienna to Georgia – 6:45 pm
Can I give you a call in a tick? I've had some hesitation about this for a while… don't alert anyone. I'm in a situation that if Dad's solicitor finds out and then tells Dad, I'm in very, very muddy waters… in fact, we all will be.

So, can I give you a call in 10 min?

When Sienna doesn't call back, Georgia sends a message:
Hi Sienna – I just called Mum, and Beckie has offered her house for you to stay in if you need. Your dog can go there too.

Sienna:
Thank you for offering me a place to stay, but I'll stay with my friend for a few days, so Dad doesn't come looking for me.

Later, Sienna phones Georgia. She says she's been talking to friends who encouraged her to tell the truth. She plans to contact both the police and the university crisis hotline that night. Then, to Georgia's surprise, she says she'll collect Benji early from school the next afternoon and bring him to Monica.

Sienna to Georgia:
These are some of the texts my dad sent from the public phone box to manipulate me.

To Sienna from the phone booth:
Is this Sienna? I got your number from Beth. Your mum has been sleeping with my boyfriend Dave. Does your dad know? She's been sleeping with him for some time. Dog act. You better tell your mum to keep away from him, or I'll smash her head in.

Are you up? YOU better tell your dad what's going on. And you tell Monica to stay away or I'm going to rip her face out.

Sienna reveals to Georgia that she and Marco were fooled by Sav at first, believing the calls and threats were from a disturbed, vengeful Monica. But then they began to notice patterns. The messages always came during the night – when Sav wasn't in the house.

When Sav claimed to find a bullet in the mailbox, it confirmed Sienna's suspicions. That day, she saw him slip out the back, circle around the side of the house, then return inside before heading to the front. He gathered everyone in the loungeroom before opening the letter – making sure Benji was present. Sav wanted his son to believe the bullet and the death threats came from his mother. Sienna's account lays bare Sav's willingness to sacrifice his own child on the altar of his own vengeful ego.

As tempting as it is, Monica can't take Sienna up on the offer to bring Benji to her. The risk is too high. With two DVOs in place – both naming Benji as a person in need of protection – such an action would be a breach. Police would return Benji to Sav, and the incident could harm Monica's case in the Family Court. Monica checks with her solicitor, who advises firmly against it.

Sienna insists she wants to set the record straight. She's prepared to sign an affidavit retracting the false statements Sav forced her to make to police. But there's a condition: the affidavit can't be used until she's collected her belongings and is safely away from him. She fears Sav – and for good reason. He knows her friend's address. Both she and her friend are terrified he'll turn up.

Statistics show women take an average of twelve attempts to finally leave an abusive partner. Lack of money and safe accommodation is often the reason. If Sienna has nowhere to go, she may well return to Sav's house – facing the same invidious choice: live with a cruel abuser or be homeless.

Adele advises Monica to avoid direct contact with Sienna and to communicate through a third party. Sienna is welcome to attend her office on Friday to make a statement. When Georgia relays this, Sienna agrees. She says she has already told police her father coerced her into making false statements.

When Sienna tells Benji she might move out, his reply takes her by surprise: 'If you leave, the notes in the mailbox will start again.'
Benji is a smart boy. Despite all the deception, he knows his father is the author of the threats. The thought of him alone with an unhinged father is deeply troubling. What a grim life for a child.

That evening, Monica returns home from work and tells Narelle and Steve that Sav called seventy times during the day. She speaks with a woman from the Domestic Violence Advocacy Service and discovers she is at the top of the list of women considered at risk of serious harm.

DAY 41 – BRING BACK BENJI

Monica is about to leave to take Daniel to school when she sees a police car pull up outside. Two officers step out, walk up the driveway, and knock. She feels a flicker of hope. Maybe – with Sienna's defection – Sav's lies have finally caught up with him. Maybe they're here to say Benji will be returned. But instead, to the astonishment of Narelle, Steve, and Monica, the officers accuse her of placing another letter in Sav's mailbox – this one allegedly on February 6, 2024. The note reads: ***Bring back my son or I will kill you.***

The officers are polite. They leave after Monica denies the allegation. But the repeated visits and accusations are wearing everyone down – especially Monica.

They are frustrated – and puzzled. That alleged incident happened five weeks ago. Why bring it up now? And something else sticks out. After Monica leaves with Daniel, Steve and Narelle rifle through the piles of paperwork.
'Narelle, have a look at this. Sav originally told police that the note – ***Bring back my son or I will kill you*** – was put in his mailbox on Friday, February 2. That's on his affidavit. But now he says it happened on Tuesday, February 6. I reckon he changed the date because he found out Monica had an alibi for February 2. Or it dawned on him he was on his way to see his parents that day. Surely the police can see something so obvious?'
'Don't count on it.'
'This is becoming farcical,' Steve mutters.

Their faith in the police and the justice system slips further.

Later, Monica answers a call from Sav's number. She's startled – and thrilled – to hear Benji's voice.
'Will you come over and have dinner with Dad and me?'
Sav is using Benji as bait again. Monica tells him she'd love to, but it's not that simple. Before she can explain, the line goes silent – and then Sav's voice cuts in.
'Hello, Monica.'
'What is it you want, Sav?' she says pleasantly.
Narelle and Steve can't hear his reply, but Monica sounds as if she's trying to

negotiate. When the call ends, Steve looks at her in disbelief.

'He cannot be reasoned with,' Steve says, voice tight. 'He wants to get you arrested.'

'I get it. It's just… you and Mum would save a lot of money if we reached an agreement.'

'It's gone way past that,' says Narelle. 'He's claiming you're an alcoholic who bashes her children.'

'He's prepared to put you – and Benji – through hell.' Steve adds.

'I know… I know,' Monica says quietly.

She takes her medication and goes upstairs early.

Monica's diary:

I feel in tatters tonight. The police at the door, again. Yet Sav was the one who breached his DVO. It's not right that Daniel has to go through this. I'm pleased that Sienna has left the house, but poor Benji is now stuck there alone with Sav. I can't stop crying. I'm counting on getting him back Thursday week. That's what is keeping me going. I so desperately want to hold him. To give him a hug.

DAY 42 – ALL LEGAL

Monica is reluctant to report Sav's breaches. Every time she does, the police turn up at the door with a fresh accusation. She feels uneasy at home and at work, wondering not just what Sav has planned next, but what the police might have in store for her. Steve is in the kitchen with Narelle, talking to Georgia on speakerphone.

'How would a woman escaping domestic violence survive if she didn't have a family to help her get through it?' Georgia says. 'Monica's lucky she has you guys.'

'I'm just glad she didn't get that rental back in January,' Steve replies. 'She would've been a sitting duck for a sick bastard like Sav.'

'She'd probably be locked up by now,' says Narelle. 'Without witnesses to back her up.'

'Thank heavens we got the camera,' Steve says.

'I put in a report to DCJ,' Georgia tells them. 'Said Benji's being kept prisoner. Not allowed to see Monica. How confused and lonely must he be through all this? Probably told by the abuser that his mother's deserted him. He'd be so upset, utterly lost.'

'All legal,' Steve adds bitterly, repeating Senior Constable Bancroft's words when she said Sav had every right to keep Benji and accused Monica of putting a bullet in Sav's mailbox. 'DCJ doesn't seem to want to do anything. This is just how the system works… or more to the point, doesn't work.'

Narelle shakes her head in irritation. 'What a massive waste of community resources this has been so far. And if the experts are right, Sav will up the ante. No wonder domestic violence takes up sixty percent of police time. There are so many people and organisations working to help victims, yet Monica's case – top of the list of women considered at risk of serious harm – means nothing for her or Benji's situation. If police can't tell the abuser from the abused, you can throw all the money in the world at the problem, but nothing will change. The system needs a total overhaul.'

'Sav must be laughing to himself – two DVOs in his favour, the police doing his dirty work harassing Monica. Just imagine how successful Sav would be if he could control his impulses.' Steve makes a tight fist, resisting the impulsion to thump the table. 'But the police! Do they truly believe Luca Savington he is a man who lives in fear of his ex-wife?'

Monica's safety is a constant concern. It's not possible for someone to be with her every minute. The wealthy might hire a bodyguard.

That afternoon, Steve takes Daniel to Bar Beach for a surf after school. Meanwhile, Narelle and Monica meet with Beckie, Narelle's sister, to prepare documents for Monica's solicitor appointment on Friday morning, ahead of the Family Court hearing the following week.

DAY 43 – FIRST RETURN

Monica meets with Adele to discuss Benji's case for the first return hearing. The first return is an introductory session where parties appear before a registrar. The objective is to identify key issues in a dispute and establish a framework for future hearings.

- **Case management** – the court assesses the case's status, the filing of documents, and timelines.
- **Interim orders** – these can be issued, providing temporary solutions until a final decision is made.
- **Dispute resolution** – there is a strong emphasis on resolving disputes through mediation or negotiation.
- **Next steps** – the court outlines the next procedural steps.

The registrar has the power to make interim orders. Monica's solicitor is confident the registrar will see through Sav's unsubstantiated lies and order that the child be returned to the mother.

Marco's dog is still at Sav's house. It's a young male husky. It has somehow become Sienna's responsibility, but she is at a loss to know what to do with it. She worries her father won't feed it if it is left there. Beckie agrees to take it for a couple of days until something is sorted.

Sienna fronts up at the solicitor's office as she said she would. What she writes in her statement to the solicitor is private, but Adele considers it of value to Monica's case. The statement can be withdrawn if she so desires, but the fact that she has gone to that much trouble means the truth is thicker than blood, and that Sienna's days of being controlled by Luca Savington have come to an end.

Sienna has moved from her father's house because of her desire to be free of Sav's coercive control. She has been used by Sav. In his affidavit, he claims Sienna saw Monica's non-existent boyfriend drive up to the house and place a note in the mailbox. Sienna was named as a witness on Sav's first DVO (where

Sav claims Monica bashed him). There are additional reasons.

Sienna tells Georgia she doesn't want to live a dishonest life. She wants Benji to be back with his mother, knowing the harm Sav has caused to her and her brothers. It concerns her that Benji might turn out like her brother Leonardo. And, as Sienna has pointed out previously, if she were found to be lying in court, she would not pass the Working for Children check, thereby ruining her chances of becoming a teacher.

But there is another reason for Sienna removing herself from her father's influence and control. Sienna would have been about ten when her mother, Sav's first wife, separated from him. She was an Indigenous woman in her twenties. Sav accused her of being a drug addict and an alcoholic. He was successful in framing her as an unfit mother, and Sienna could now see that Sav was repeating a pattern of behaviour she witnessed as a child in his quest to destroy Monica.

Monica is hanging her hopes on the Court hearing next week. Sav has refused to give an inch and is still standing by his wild, malicious accusations and lies: two bottles of wine a night then bashes the children; four bottles of wine in a two-hour binge; that Monica has an untreated mental illness.

'Lucky there are angels' says Monica.

Georgia and baby Emma come up from Sydney for a visit. As usual, this lifts everyone's spirits. Emma has been in hospital with serious respiratory issues, as well as influenza, and still isn't fully recovered. Now she is at pre-school and mixing with other children, she is more prone to catching viruses. They go with Monica to watch Daniel play basketball. Monica can't go anywhere alone. If those with experience in the field of domestic violence are correct, there is more to come from Luca Savington. But it's not just the risk Sav poses; Monica needs to be able to prove her whereabouts, and to have witnesses, as safeguards against further police accusations.

DAY 44 – MENTION

Georgia is staying at Grandma's house, which is nearby. She leaves Emma with Narelle while she accompanies Monica into the police station to report Sav's latest batch of DVO breaches: seventy calls in one day and crude text messages. When Monica expresses some sympathy for Sav, Georgia gives her a reality check, reminding her that Sav is trying to get her charged by the police and that he has taken Benji. It's possible Sav's declarations of love combined with his attempts to make Monica feel responsible for breaking up the family have had some effect.

Later in the day, Monica visits her friends, Beth and Carol. Narelle drops her off and picks her up an hour or so later. The time of their comings and goings are recorded on camera and saved.

Sav texts Monica, saying he will allow her to talk with Benji. Georgia rings Sav and tells him not to interject, because the conversation will be recorded. Sav hangs up. Once again, he uses Benji as bait and to show he in control. The poor child must be in a confused, mixed-up state by now. More so without Sienna there to care for him.

On Tuesday, Sav's and Monica's two DVOs will be mentioned in court.

- **The first time a case goes to court** it is called a 'mention.' The defendant or legal representative must appear before a magistrate. The purpose of a mention is to determine whether the accused will plead guilty or not guilty.

Monica must either defend herself (unwise) or pay for a barrister.
Steve takes Daniel to Bar Beach for a surf. Afterwards, Narelle, Monica, and Daniel set off to K-mart. Daniel has outgrown his clothes.

The next day, Narelle's family meet at the Wetlands for lunch. Georgia and baby Emma join them. Narelle's ninety-three-year-old mother, Irene, is absolutely disgusted with Sav's behaviour and shocked at Monica's treatment by the police. The affidavit Monica's solicitor will file for Thursday's Family Court hearing arrives Sunday night. Monica and Narelle make a few minor corrections before returning the document. The affidavit is scathing of Sav's actions and recounts his behaviour before and after he took Benji. It criticises him for exposing Benji to adult issues, something Adele has witnessed first-hand. It proposes a return to the parenting plan in place before Sav withheld Benji from his mother. Urgent mediation is proposed, with a mediator's name put forward.

On Monday morning the clouds are spitting rain, the weather noticeably cooler. Steve and Monica visit the solicitor's office to drop off the affidavit. Adele intends to send the documentation to Sav's solicitor just inside the 48-hour deadline, to give him the least amount of time as possible to respond. After dropping Monica at work, Steve drives back to Hamilton only to discover the police have again been to the house.

'What! You must be joking. What the hell did they want this time?' he asks Narelle.

'They wanted to know what car she drives. Said they'd be back to see her after she gets home from work.'

'Seriously? After all the investigations into Monica about these fake letters and the bullet, the police now want to know what car she drives? Why don't they bloody well look up her registration? It's under M for motor vehicle,' says an irate Steve. 'I wonder what bullshit Sav has told them this time... Yes, Constable Larry, this is the Gullible Police Department. How can we be of service? Another note, is it? Or did she bash you up again? What a bitch! You want another DVO? Yes, Sir. Be right onto it. It's no damn wonder people take the law into their own hands.'

Georgia drops by with baby Emma. She too is shattered by the injustice of it all. For anyone who knows Monica, her treatment by the police is difficult to comprehend.

DAY 47 – COURTHOUSE

It is peculiar that Monica's DVOs and Sav's breaches are heard in court at different locations on the same day. Narelle goes to Monica's hearing, where they are expecting common sense to prevail and the DVOs served on Monica to be withdrawn. The others attend Sav's.

When Monica, Steve and Georgia arrive at the courthouse they see Luca Savington standing alone near the bottom of the escalator. They go through security, where Chantel is waiting for them. Sav has moved on.
'The bastard said hello to me,' exclaims Chantel. 'Is the guy serious?'
They take the escalator up to the next level. The courtroom for the DVO hearings is on the second floor. When they get to level one, they walk across to the stairwell. They see Sav in a queue up ahead. He doesn't realise it yet, but he is in the wrong place, lining up for jury duty. They continue up the stairs to Level 2, where the local courtrooms are located. Monica and Georgia go down a passageway to the right and into the women's safe room.

Sav steps out of the lift and is recognised by a court official. He is told to stay down the far end of the room, well away from Chantel and Steve. Around 9:20 am the court doors open and people begin filing through. Chantel and Steve find a seat, and a short time later Phillip, who has been parking the car, joins them.

Steve's phone buzzes. It is a text from Georgia. There is some confusion with the police as to whether Monica should be at the other courthouse where her case is to be mentioned.
Steve leaves the courtroom and meets up with Georgia in the foyer, where she tells him the matter has now been sorted. Monica is not required to appear in person because she has a barrister representing her.

When Steve re-enters the courtroom, Luca Savington is sitting in front of Chantel and Phillip. Steve returns to his seat, which is directly behind Sav. The courtroom attendees stand when the magistrate comes in through the side door. After a few minutes of discussion between court officials and the solicitors, the proceedings begin. The cases where defendants are represented by solicitors or barristers are given priority. The first case is postponed. The magistrate, in conjunction with the lawyer and prosecutor, agree on a suitable date for the case to return to court and the participants leave the courtroom. The next case is announced. The defendant, a wretched teenager, deemed to have to have a mental age of five (they say this in front of him) is represented by a different solicitor from when he previously appeared before the court. The youth's facial features indicate he could be afflicted with fetal alcohol syndrome. The magistrate defers the hearing.

Next to appear is Luca Savington. Sav's solicitor, a man in his late twenties, gets to his feet. He is the man Steve had seen ingratiating himself to a young female solicitor earlier, while waiting for court to begin. Sav's solicitor advises the court his client is pleading guilty to breaking the DVO but disagrees with some of the facts surrounding the breach.
'Of course he does,' whispers Chantel to Steve. 'It's all about power and control.' The matter is adjourned and will return to court in four weeks.

After giving Sav time to clear out, the three of them leave the courtroom. They wait in the foyer for Georgia and Monica. They all leave the building together. As they are walking down the steps of the building, Chantel says, 'There was a guy sitting on the steps before. He was a dead ringer for Warren.'
Warren was their sibling, who passed away a year earlier.
'Was he on his phone?' Steve replies. Chantel gives him a funny look. 'Ringer, on his phone,' says Steve drolly.
'I understand...' Chantel replies. 'But it's not funny.'
Warren was part gangster, part musician. He would be disgusted by what has happened. If he were alive, he would have likely confronted Sav over his disgusting deeds towards Monica, and the outcome would not have been pretty.

Narelle rings from the courthouse. The DVOs were mentioned and will be heard at another time. They are all disappointed. They'd hoped the police prosecutor would see through Sav's lies and withdraw the DVOs against Monica.

Later in the day, after Daniel returns from basketball practice, Monica and Steve take Roxie for a walk to Gregson Park. A few cockatoos fly past and Monica says, 'That's Granddad, giving his support.' Granddad, Narelle's father, is no longer with them. Because of the presence of the white cockatoo at his funeral, the family associate him with the bird. He too would be disgusted with Sav, the court process, and the police.

The long-anticipated Family Court hearing is just two days away. Apparently, the term 'custody' is no longer used. It has been replaced by the word 'care.' 'Be prepared for a long day,' warns Adele. Adele is confident. 'You'll have your son back in two days. Sav's lies should be blown to bits, exposed by the lack of actual evidence.'

Monica is desperate to see Benji. It is imperative for her mental health that this hearing goes her way. And it is imperative for Benji's wellbeing that it goes her way. Benji must be feeling increasingly abandoned and alone.

DAY 49 – DESOLATION

Monica and Narelle set off for the hearing in a positive mood. It has been a long time coming. They meet Adele at her office in town, then walk together to the Children's Court. Adele had warned Monica to be prepared for a long day – but what happens is soul-destroying.

They learn that the experienced registrar originally listed to hear the case has been replaced by a junior registrar. Rather than listen to the evidence and adjudicate, the registrar leaves it to the solicitors to negotiate a solution. Sav refuses to give an inch. He has the child – so tough luck. After an hour, nothing is resolved.

Then comes the real blow. In the only arrangement Sav will agree to, Monica is granted minimal access: two hours a fortnight through ReKonnect, a privately owned children's contact service. To see her son, she must pay over two hundred dollars for each supervised visit – plus four hundred for the initial registration – or she will have no contact at all. As absurd as it is, if she doesn't agree, she walks away with nothing.

Monica and Narelle leave, inconsolable. Benji will remain with Sav until the interim hearing in nearly three months – a lifetime away. The cost of preparing and attending the hearing with a solicitor is substantial, yet nothing meaningful has been achieved.

When they return home, Monica retreats upstairs, wanting to be alone. Narelle is distraught.
'He'll get everything,' she tells Steve. 'Benji, the house – you name it. Whatever he wants.'

The misery spreads through the family and friends.
'What sort of human gets his kicks from stopping a mother and her 8-year-old boy from seeing each other?' Steve says to Georgia later that night. Then he answers his own question. 'I'll tell you. A real arsehole – a person devoid of humanity. And now his behaviour is sanctioned by the court. What a system!'

Adele salvages one small concession: Sav must undergo a psychological assessment and attend a men's behavioural change program. Which program will depend on availability.

On the night Monica fled her home due to Sav's abuse, he told Daniel and Benji that their mother wasn't coming back – that she had walked out on the family. One can only imagine what he has since told the now-isolated 8-year-old. Benji must be bewildered and feeling abandoned, dragged around town listening to Sav pour abuse on his mother. Imagine the state the boy will be in by the time the interim hearing finally comes.

Sav's tactic of taking Benji and denying access has worked. No wonder women stay in abusive relationships. Monica's only 'crime' was wanting a life free of manipulation and intimidation – for herself and her children.

Sav has already broken his DVO by trying to contact Monica and seems incapable of controlling his impulses. Friends and family are incredulous. In the wider community, Monica has the support of women's advocacy groups, domestic violence organisations, and mental health professionals. At the monthly inter-agency meeting of police and domestic violence groups, her case is given top priority. Monica Savington is classified as high risk and in danger of becoming another statistic. Yet it means nothing.

Monica was told that in the long run the truth will come out and Sav will be exposed. To her, it feels like a very, very, very long run – seven weeks until the interim hearing. The lack of urgency is baffling. Benji is the forgotten child.

Monica is grief-stricken by the court's inaction. The registrar's non-decision has validated Sav's actions and lies.

Late that afternoon, Monica and Narelle attend Benji's soccer training. Monica desperately needs to see her son – even if only from a distance. Sav is not there; likely he dropped Benji off and left. It is no surprise. In the past, when Sav attended soccer, he was always on his phone and never interested in the game. Now he has nothing to worry about – legally, he has sole parental responsibility.

Monica waves to Benji and he smiles. *What the hell is going on?* the boy must be thinking.

DAY 50 – HOPE FLICKERS

Monica receives another email from Sav's solicitor. This time he claims she yelled at him during soccer training, calling out for Benji to come over. Sav wasn't even there. But truth seems irrelevant in his world – accusations stick whether they're real or not. In the same email, Sav announces he'd like to see Daniel on the weekend.

Narelle and Steve are slouched on the lounge at home. 'Daniel doesn't want to see him,' says Narelle flatly.
'The guy lives in Ga Ga Land. He's delusional,' says Steve. 'Sure, Battered Sav, swing by the house and pick him up. We'll have a beer together first. Then maybe head to a movie… or a psych ward.'

When Daniel is warned Sav might turn up without notice, he barely reacts.
'I can easily outrun Constable Larry,' he says.
Daniel hides it well, but the truth must sting – knowing the man who was his stepfather for twelve years is nothing but a despicable miscreant. He's been home when the police came knocking. Must have overheard parts of the conversation. At 14, he's mature, insightful, and intuitive. He doesn't need the sugar-coated version

Steve's phone rings. It's Billy Holden, one of Sydney's leading family law barristers. His sister Janet, a close family friend, has told him everything. Billy listens, the weight in his voice confirming the seriousness of what they're up against. Without hesitation, he offers his services for the June hearing. He asks the name of the judicial officer from the First Return. He doesn't recognise it and is surprised the case wasn't given priority. Steve arranges for him to speak with Adele on Monday. For the first time in days, hope flickers. Billy's call is a shot of oxygen to their suffocating morale.

Monica needs to go to the chemist, so she and Steve decide to take Roxie and walk to Beaumont Street. Steve waits with Roxie while Monica goes into the shop. A few minutes later, Monica comes out in tears. The chemist will not dispense the medication without Monica having a blood test. This is normal procedure for the medication she is on, and not the chemist's fault. Monica had hoped the chemist would bend the rules, as they do at the pharmacy where she usually goes. It's not a major problem as she still has a few days' supply of medication and should have time to get a blood test before work on Monday. This type of set-back would not normally bother Monica, but with the court decision, the police visits, and the constant worry about Benji, she has gradually become more vulnerable, often close to tears over small things and life's constant pressures.

On Saturday, Narelle and Steve go to watch Benji play soccer. Monica decides to stay home – she's worried Sav might twist her attendance into an excuse to cancel her upcoming visit, and she can't take that risk. Seeing Benji is too important.

The game is already underway when Narelle and Steve arrive at the oval. Narelle spots Sav first – standing near the grandstand, phone to his ear, scanning the field as if he owns the place. They keep well away from him. Benji is in good form, scoring twice, and when he spots his Nan and Pop on the sidelines, his face lights up. That moment matters – he knows the family hasn't given up.

When the match ends, Narelle and Steve head for the car. The quickest route takes them back past the oval, along a narrow footpath running close to the fence. Sav has moved – now leaning casually against the inside fence. If they keep walking, they'll pass within a few metres of him.
'Let's cross the road,' says Narelle. 'Or he'll say we harassed him.'
'Just pretend he isn't there,' Steve replies, his eyes fixed ahead.
Sav doesn't react, but he must have known they were there.

DAY 52 – TRUTH COUNTS FOR NOTHING

Monica and Narelle front up to the police station with Monica's friend Beth. The faint smell of stale coffee hangs in the air. There is a line of people inching forward toward the single officer on the desk. Both Adele and Lisa have stressed the importance of lodging Sav's breaches, and Monica is determined to do it. Beth finds it intimidating but stays strong and reports her strange call from Sav, where he pretended to be her ex-boyfriend from many years ago. Monica is told the police are investigating all three DVOs, which sounds positive! Considering Sav has breached his DVO on multiple occasions, the conclusion regarding this should be simple. Investigating the two DVO issued against Monica should also be straightforward. The first DVO issued against Monica has zero evidence and the second is based on a physical impossibility.

What happens next leaves Monica and Narelle flabbergasted. The police officer who logged Sav's latest breaches into the system refers to the phone call from Sav that Monica answered. According to the officer, this could be construed as encouragement. The fact that Sav took Benji, and is using him to entice Monica, is overlooked. Answering one phone call, out of concern for her son's health, is surely insubstantial compared to the hundreds of harassing calls, emails, and texts from Sav. Narelle thinks the police officer might have been playing devil's advocate, warning Monica what to expect from Sav's solicitor.

The following day Monica receives an email from Sav's solicitor, forwarded by Adele. Sav demands that Monica and her grandparents stop attending Benji's soccer training sessions and games, claiming it is upsetting the child and not in the spirit of the agreement reached at the judicial hearing. The email is filled with the usual lies – Sav insists Monica attended the last game (she didn't) and invents an incident that supposedly occurred at training the previous Friday.

Adele dismisses the claim as nonsense – they are fully entitled to attend Benji's soccer. She replies to Sav's solicitor that if any more bogus allegations are sent for her to read and respond to, Sav will be billed for the costs. Then she asks the question on everyone's mind: how is Sav paying for all of this? Nobody knows. Adele also decides to act to prevent Sav from selling off their shared assets. A partner can be stopped from selling assets by having a lawyer put them on notice that they cannot do so without consent – or by filing an urgent application for an injunction. Adele will put him on notice and see if that works.

At least Monica has always worked, kept her own bank account, and been part of financial decisions. The mortgage and the title to the house are in both names. But financial control is a classic tool in domestic abuse. It appears in 99% of domestic violence cases – one of the most effective ways to trap a survivor and strip away their ability to stay safe after leaving an abuser (*nndv.org*).

Some of Monica's old neighbours have been keeping an eye out for Benji. It does give Monica some peace of mind, but sometimes knowing can be worse than being kept in the dark. She finds out Benji is walking home from school alone and spending hours inside the house alone. Sav doesn't get home until nearly 6:00 pm, so that's nearly three hours. This is immensely disturbing for Monica. She wants to meet Benji after school and walk him home, yet legally, even though she is his mother, Monica is forbidden by the Family Court from doing so.

Then the mail arrives: Monica is required to defend the two DVOs served against her. So much for the investigation. The system screams dysfunction – police and courts waste hours, while the defendant takes days off work and spends thousands on legal defence against baseless claims. Meanwhile, the manipulator laughs at them all. Truth counts for nothing. Evidence seems irrelevant. The police continue to do the bidding of Sav, the abuser. According to victims, this is a familiar occurrence. No wonder so many women simply give up.

Excerpt from Monica's diary:
I remember Sav throwing my phone at the wall and smashing it to pieces in 2022. I remember arguments between Sav and Sienna at the old house. Sienna said Sav dragged her by the hair, called her names like slut, bitch. When they argued, Sienna would say that Sav had hit her. Sav would deny it. Sav pulled Sienna by the wrist, and I took Sienna to the hospital to be checked over as Sienna was concerned there was damage. Sienna had her head slammed into the door by Sav and had a bruise. Neighbours heard Sav scream at Sienna from next door. They were very concerned and willing to make statements. Sienna would go and stay with my parents when she and Sav were fighting.

Steve contacts DCJ again. His complaint is simple: Sav, in Sienna's absence, is incapable of caring for Benji. An 8-year-old boy is in danger, either stuck in a house alone or in the company of an irrational, delusional, and unpredictable brute. Why? Because a woman left an abusive relationship and wanted a better life for herself and her children.

It's Narelle's birthday. Steve walks to the nearby florist and returns with a colourful mixed bunch, a few crimson roses tucked in among the blooms. Narelle would have preferred chocolates – but the top of the piano is already a mountain of Easter eggs, and Easter isn't until the weekend.

Later, Billy Holden calls Steve. He's spoken with Adele who reassures him that she knows her stuff – they're in good hands. They talk about the family law system. Billy says Sav's antics will count against him eventually and describes the senior registrar listed for the interim hearing as the Rod Marsh (legendary Australian wicketkeeper) of magistrates – experienced, sharp, and missing nothing. Steve ends the call feeling optimistic. Monica isn't convinced. She's really missing Benji and, like everyone else, feels as though nothing is going her way. Sav still hasn't responded to the proposed two-hour fortnightly visits.

That night, Monica, Daniel, Narelle, and Steve head into town for Narelle's birthday dinner. Their booking is at Light Years, an Asian fusion restaurant – fitting, because the Interim Hearing feels like light years away. The food is delicious and reasonably priced. Daniel is in a playful mood, cracking jokes and keeping them entertained.

The following day, Benji is absent from school again. A police officer calls Monica with a request: remove no-ID calls from the DVO that restrains Sav. Monica rejects it outright. Without that restriction, the harassment would continue unchecked.

When she tells Narelle and Steve, they are baffled. Why would the police even consider such a thing? Steve rings the local police station again and asks to be put through to someone from the domestic violence unit. A female officer picks up. Steve explains Monica's situation, and the problems removing the no-ID calls would cause. The officer tells Steve he isn't making sense, as the police have the means to trace the source of no-ID calls. It is done through I ASK.

After the call, Steve is fuming. If they can trace Sav's calls, why haven't they done it? Monica has endured over two months of harassment by this method.

Steve:

A domestic violence worker tells Monica she is still on the list of women at serious risk in the community – her case again discussed at the monthly inter-agency meetings attended by police – but still, nothing changes. The arms of the 88-armed octopus never connect.

There is a story on the news about Kelly Wilkinson. In 2021 she was burnt alive by her jealous ex-husband. Leading up to her murder, she constantly went to police. Kelly was accused of 'cop shopping' by the Queensland police.

DAY 56 – MOTHER'S PROMISE

News comes through from Monica's neighbour that police have visited Sav's house – yesterday and again today. It could be about breaching his DVO. It's unlikely Sav's receiving a citizenship award. For Benji, these interactions with police must seem normal. Since the day Sav took him from Monica in early February, he's been dragged into police stations by his father.

Back then, according to Sav's sister, their father Matteo reprimanded Sav for badmouthing Monica in front of Benji. That first weekend, when Sav's mother asked Benji if he was feeling okay, he replied, 'I miss my mum.' Imagine what he must be feeling now, two months later. Benji may have sensed what was coming. Perhaps he overheard Sav's plans, because the last time Monica saw him, he said, 'You will always take care of me, won't you, Mum?'
'Of course I will,' she'd replied.

Those words – and her promise – have haunted Monica ever since. She had no idea what lay ahead, that the combined actions of Sav, the police, and the Family Court would make it impossible for her to keep that promise. And Benji is too young to understand why.

Nobody has heard from Sienna for several days. She may be lying low, fearful of her father's reaction. Or perhaps she simply can't afford to move. The bond alone for a rental is substantial, and four weeks' rent is usually required in advance.

Georgia Kelty writes a letter to Luca Savington:

Luca,
During the past seven weeks while you've kept Benji from his mother who loves him, a family
who adore him, and a life he knew and thrived in, Benji has missed out on so much.
Benji has missed seeing his baby cousin begin to crawl, which I know would have brought that
big smile to his face. Benji, the little boy who every single week knew what size fruit or veggie
Emma was inside my belly, the boy who asked excitedly every time we spoke if Emma was
talking yet, will be missing seeing his baby cousin Emma grow outside my belly.

Benji has missed his great grandma's 93rd birthday.
Benji has missed numerous family catchups, which he always loved attending.
He's missed giving his Nana, who has always looked after Benji on weekends, school holidays
and after school, a big, big, hug for her birthday.
Benji will be upset that he's missed his own mother's birthday and picking out a present for
her, watching her blow out the candles of her birthday cake.

Benji has missed bike riding with his Poppy, seeing who can ride the fastest down at the park
on a beautiful bike that Nana and Poppy bought for him. Benji is going to miss the annual
Easter egg hunt with all his cousins, racing around Aunty Beckie's yard to find the most
Easter Eggs, then eating so much chocolate his tummy hurts.
Benji has missed kicking the soccer ball down at Gregson Park with Uncle Matt, who loves
teaching him new tricks that Benji then goes home to practise for hours on end.

The biggest thing Benji is missing is growing up next to his brother, Daniel. Daniel is missing
Benji so much he has Benji as his screensaver on his computer. These boys are missing out on
brotherly bickering about meaningless things, taking their dog Roxie for walks, jumping
through the waves at Merewether beach together, racing on their bikes, all things that should
be a rite of passage for two young boys who have spent their whole lives together.

This is what Benji has missed in just the 7 weeks since you took him from school and withheld
him from his mother and brother.

What you are doing to Benji, is not fair.
What you are doing to Daniel, is not fair.
What you are doing to Sienna, Marco, and Leonardo, is not fair.
What you are doing to Monica, is not fair.

What you are doing to my family and me, is not fair.

Benji is 8 years old, and he will be missing his family and all the love that comes with us. You are making up lies to the police, solicitors, and to your son who is an 8-year-old boy, because your ego was hurt when my sister left the abusive home you foster. You are acting out of pure selfishness and cruelty and there seems to be no other intent.

Benji doesn't understand that you're making up lies right now, he is young and trusting. But the innocence you are taking away from him will affect him psychologically for the rest of his life, as with your older children, and that is disgusting.

You are doing this for yourself and with no care for how you're hurting Benji and what you have taken from the poor boy. You should be ashamed of yourself.

My sister never kept Benji from you; she let you see him every weekend. You have had no reason to behave the way you have towards Benji, Daniel and my sister. You have taken our Benji from us, from a family who loves him so dearly, but what is worse is what you have taken from him.

In truth,
From a very distressed and loving aunt,
Georgia Kelty

DAY 57 – BROTHERS

Monica and Steve take Roxie for a walk in town, near the fisherman's co-op. As they cross the Carrington Bridge, Monica tells Steve something funny. 'I thought I was the main character,' Daniel had said. And he was – until Sav snatched his brother.

Daniel is upset by Benji's solitary confinement, as anyone would be. He has Benji's photo as the screensaver on his laptop. Daniel plays his cards close to his chest, but it can't be easy. The only father he knew trashed the relationship. He hasn't heard a word from Marco or Leonardo, both of whom have been part of his life since he was a toddler. Leonardo might be a rogue, but he treated

Daniel decently, and Daniel looked up to him as a younger brother would. Although Daniel was having second thoughts about staying at Sav's place on weekends, he had every intention of staying in contact.

On Saturday, Monica goes to Beth and Carol's for lunch while Steve takes Daniel for a surf at Bar Beach. The day begins uneventfully. It has been an abnormally quiet period – but that is about to change.

Late in the afternoon, Georgia calls Monica. Gabby, Sav's sister, has contacted her out of the blue – a complete surprise. Apart from Sienna, there has been no contact between the families since Benji was taken. Gabby has been talking with Marco, Sav's 23-year-old son. Marco and Sav had a screaming match over money – likely Sav demanding rent for the two nights a week Marco stays at the house. No doubt Sav is learning that solicitors don't work for free. Marco told Gabby that Benji cried out for his mother during the argument – a distressing detail for Monica to hear. According to Gabby, Marco packed his belongings and left to stay with a friend. Without Sienna and now Marco (who had been staying on weekends), Benji is further isolated – and more vulnerable.

The school holidays are approaching. According to Gabby, Sav first asked their mother to come and care for Benji; she refused. He then asked Gabby, who lives on the Central Coast, to take Benji for the first week. She was reluctant but agreed for Benji's sake.

But what will happen for the second week of the holidays? Will Benji stay at the house? If so, it will be a lonely week for the boy, alone in the house until around 6 pm each night when Sav gets home and not allowed contact with friends or neighbours. Normally, Benji and Daniel would be cared for by Narelle and Steve. It would usually be a fun time: bike rides, swimming in the summer months, kayaking, bush walks, and movies. In the past they have gone to Canberra, Sydney, or as they did over the Christmas break, rented a house near the beach.

Gabby suggested she might bring Benji straight back to Monica. How she could actually manage that is anyone's guess – more a thought bubble than a practical plan. As was pointed out when Sienna wanted to bring Benji to Monica from school, the DVOs in place make it impossible. Now there is also a Family Court order in Sav's favour.

Georgia tells Gabby that if she wants to help, the best thing to do is to contact the DCJ. Gabby promises to do so. Then Georgia suggests they meet up for a day. Monica is forbidden from having contact with her son, but Narelle could drive down from Newcastle and Georgia come up from Sydney with baby Emma and see Benji at Gabby's place. They decide to do it on the Wednesday.

At 10:15 pm, there's a knock at the door of the Hamilton house. Everyone is in bed. Steve and Narelle answer to find two police officers on the steps. They've had a report of fighting and shouting from the Percy Street house. Sav still has enough hate in him at the end of the day to make a nuisance call, likely projecting whatever happened at his place onto Monica. The officers say the call was anonymous. The coward strikes again. They are apologetic but obliged to check.

At 11 pm, a crashing sound breaks the quiet. Moments later, Monica's agitated voice calls out – Narelle has collapsed at the foot of the stairs. Steve gets out of bed to find Daniel and Monica helping her up. She falls again. Her breathing is normal, and she is conscious and aware, but unable to stand. Daniel rings 000, Monica fetches a pillow, and Steve dresses to accompany her to hospital.

The paramedics arrive within ten minutes. They check her blood pressure, pulse, and for any signs of stroke – nothing symptomatic, to everyone's relief. A portable ECG shows a steady heartbeat, though her blood pressure is slightly low. Narelle begins to feel better and manages to stand. The decision is whether to take her to hospital for overnight monitoring and blood tests or wait until morning for her GP. She chooses to stay home. The male paramedic, a country boy, takes a liking to Roxie. He teases her with high-pitched whistles that send her into a frenzy. The moment lightens the mood.

DAY 59 – EASTER EGGS

The family spends Easter at Beckie's, and the highlight for the young ones is the Easter egg hunt. Benji is sorely missed, but Monica stays positive, putting an assortment of chocolate eggs aside for him. She hopes to see him next weekend. Sav once told her that after he and his previous wife had separated, she'd brought chocolate eggs for the children during a scheduled visit. When they were returned to Sav, he had tossed the gifts into the bin in front of them. 'Let him do it,' Narelle says. 'Benji won't be happy if he does.'
To think a father could do such a thing to a vulnerable mother and his three children speaks of cruelty and a lack of decency. His parents and siblings never call out his atrocious behaviour. Sienna is the exception – but whether she can stay strong remains to be seen. Her car hasn't been spotted by Sav's neighbours, which is a positive sign. According to them, Leonardo is back at the house. Typical Luca Savington – losing one son but luring back another. The pattern of a manipulator.

Monica once said to Benji, 'If you treat people well, they will treat you well.'
'That's not true Mum,' he replied. 'People can be mean no matter how you treat them.'
When Benji was first at school, there was a timid girl in the class. Without being asked, he took on the role of protecting her from bullies. Not only did he empathise with her predicament, but he also found out that some bullies don't stop easily. That they can be relentless. Benji is astute and he doesn't miss much.

It's Christmas Day 2022, and Benji is seven. He points to a picture of himself with Santa, held to the refrigerator with a magnet. The photo was taken a couple of weeks earlier, when Monica had taken him to see Santa.
'That man's a liar,' he declares. His tone is full of vitriol, unusual for a seven-year-old, though Benji can be dramatic.
'What! Why are you saying that Benji?' asks Mum.
'I asked Santa for a Squishy. He promised I'd get one, and he didn't bring it.'
He hadn't told her about the request.

Benji might see through Santa, but he it is unlikely he sees his father for what he really is at his age. Benji probably feels sympathy for the man, who is skilled at playing victim. Even if he does see through the charade, he is only nine, and incapable of challenging a brute like his father.

Daniel has wanted a part-time job for a while. He's applied at McDonalds and Kentucky Fried, both just down the road from the house, but hasn't heard back. Narelle remembers seeing a job advertisement at the Wetlands Centre near Shortland when she was there recently with the family. Daniel is keen, so Monica and Steve drive out there with him. Unfortunately, the Centre is closed. They'll try again on Monday.

DAY 60 – APRIL'S FOOL

It is April Fool's Day. Luca Savington marked the occasion early by calling the police to Percy Street the night before. The screaming and yelling between him and Marco was likely the trigger – but today, the joke is on him. Steve drops by the police station to report the suspicious noise complaint. He explains there was no excessive noise and that he is almost certain Sav made the call. It can't be proven, but it's exactly his style – and it fits the pattern.

Monica contacts the Wetlands about a job for Daniel. Alan, the boss, also manages the café at Charlestown Golf Club. He wants to meet Daniel in person – no résumé required. Old school, he prefers to size people up face-to-face. The meeting goes well, and he offers Daniel a trial shift the following Sunday.

On Tuesday, Narelle catches the train to Sydney. She is to look after baby Emma, while Georgia and Matt attend a wedding down the south coast. Her intention is to stay until Thursday, when Georgia starts a new job in HR with a Swiss-based robotics company. While Narelle is away, Steve replaces the weathered logs on the raised garden bed in the yard. At night he records some music. It's the first time in months he has felt motivated.

Two calls from no-ID numbers come through to Monica's phone.

On Wednesday, Daniel receives a text from a no-ID number:
Just wanted to say hi and I miss you so much. Hope you are well.

Daniel replies:
Who is this?
There is no answer. Steve is home, and Daniel shows him the message. Steve praises him for being cautious.

Steve:
Perhaps Luca Savington lives in a parallel universe – does he really think Daniel is oblivious to what's been happening? The sheer audacity of the man.

Excerpt from Monica's diary:
Sav and Leonardo were screaming and fighting in the loungeroom. Sav hurled his keys at Leonardo, then swung punches at him. Daniel went to his room. I tried to calm everyone down. Benji – still just a baby – was crying.

Four days pass. The weather is atrocious with flash flood warnings in place. Daniel wants to stay home from school, but Monica refuses. 'You're not a good parent,' he mutters. 'Why are you making me go to school on a day like this?'
Near the school, traffic crawls. Parents pull over as close as possible to the undercover area. Monica glances at Daniel.
'Look at all the terrible parents making their children go to school in atrocious weather,' she says.

Back home, she rings the bank. She can't access her online account and wants to check the mortgage payments – and make sure Sav can't touch the overdraft. A break in the rain gives Steve a chance to take Roxie for a walk. When he returns half an hour later, Monica is still in the queue for customer service. So much for online banking. At least in a branch you can see who's in front of you.

An hour later when she finally gets through, she jokes, 'Anyone working today?' The call centre operator isn't amused, but Steve is glad to see Monica hasn't lost her sense of humour.

Afterwards, Steve presses her to report the recent no-ID calls, along with Daniel's text message, to the police. She's reluctant. There is the likelihood of Sav retaliating, but it's not just that. It's coming away feeling like she's the problem. Steve insists and goes with her. Her instincts prove right. When Monica tells the officer she's concerned Sav is trying to contact her son, the officer shrugs.
'Saying you missed someone and asking how they are isn't harassment.'

Steve bites his tongue, resisting the urge to ask if the same would apply if the caller was serial killer, Ivan Milat.

When Monica shows the officer the call log, he claims there's nothing they can do. Monica stands firm.

'Can you log them, please? My lawyer says it must be done.'

The officer reluctantly complies. As he types, Monica and Steve step back from the counter to sit down. What happens next would seem too far-fetched in fiction.

Monica receives an email from Sav's solicitor via her solicitor, Adele. She expects the usual late-Friday rubbish, but this is far more serious. Weeks earlier, after the psychologist's office called, she had guessed Sav's next move. She and Narelle had even speculated on the likely target. Still, the reality stuns her.

Luca Savington is accusing Steve of sexually abusing Benji. Of interfering with him. It's a stark reminder of how dangerous he is – willing to put his own son through such an ordeal, to plant those thoughts in a child's head, to school him in lies for the authorities. The letter says it has already been reported to the DCJ and the police.

If past actions of the police are an indication, the authorities will take Sav's allegations seriously. This escalation would not have been possible if the police had acted four months earlier, in late December, when Monica walked into the police station and bared her soul on camera. Back then, police visited Sav's home, spoke to him, Sienna, and Leonardo, and decided a DVO wasn't necessary. Not only did the police refuse Monica but they issued two DVOs on Sav's behalf. Monica did eventually get a DVO, but that was only after the hospital social worker took up her case with the police. If the officers involved in issuing the two DVOs against Monica had done a basic fact or background check, Sav's history of lies and manipulations would have been exposed. Were these officers aware that Monica had fled an abusive relationship? It is on police files. It seems no-one connects the dots.

Millions are spent on domestic violence education and prevention, but if frontline responders act in this manner, nothing will change. If Monica had been given protection when she first reported the abuse, events would have unfolded very differently. Sav might have still caused trouble, but he wouldn't have been able to manipulate the system the way he has. The police, by targeting Monica, have emboldened him. That he can breach his DVO repeatedly yet still gain traction with baseless claims is hard to comprehend.

Many women downplay the violence at home – blaming themselves, feeling ashamed for putting up with it, or even sympathising with their abuser. Monica didn't. She reported ongoing coercive control and psychological abuse. If more astute questions had been asked, physical abuse would have also been in the equation.

The officers – two police stations were involved – who refused Monica's DVO request, showed little understanding of domestic violence. The mindset of the officers who granted and served Sav's two DVOs is difficult to fathom. Police culture varies station to station, and officers carry their own biases. For whatever reasons, in Monica's case the police have favoured the abuser and punished the abused.

The DCJ has failed Benji. Despite multiple reports from family and friends, they've refused to intervene without evidence of serious physical harm. They've failed to recognise that psychological abuse can be just as damaging – sometimes more so.

Sav's coercion of Benji to accuse Steve shocks and angers the family and friends who know of Sav's manipulations. Steve's sister, Chantel, drives up from the Central Coast to support him. Outrage doesn't change the reality: once the accusation is lodged, the wheels are in motion.

'He watches me in the shower.'
'How often?'
'All the time.'

According to the affidavit, when Benji is asked the same question later in the interview, he holds up two fingers to indicate this happened twice. It's a contradiction. Surely the DCJ will see through it. But what other lies has Sav drilled into him? Even though Monica saw this coming, it still hits her hard. She shared twelve years of her life with him. As Chantel tells her, 'Your decency has been his shield.'

Monica's solicitor warns her that she and Daniel might not be able to stay in the same house as Steve during the investigation. Steve decides that if it comes to that, he will leave.

That night is Daniel's basketball semi-final. Minutes before he leaves, his teammate Spencer calls, describing blurred vision, headaches, and slurred speech. Daniel insists he call 000 immediately. The symptoms sound like a stroke, but Spencer is only 14. Daniel's team wins the semi and qualifies for the final at Broadmeadow Stadium next Friday. He's quiet afterwards, worried about Spencer, but relieved when he learns the hospital has diagnosed a rare migraine that mimics stroke symptoms. Steve is impressed by Daniel's composure – just like when Narelle collapsed, he stayed calm and knew exactly what to do. Steve finds solace knowing Daniel will be an asset if he is to leave the house.

When night falls, Narelle and Steve lie in bed, unable to sleep. The latest accusation has escalated things to a dangerous level. In the past, Sav's reports to the police have been followed by late-night visits. Steve tries to reassure her. 'The truth will come out.'

DAY 65 – PRESSURE

Monica and Steve drive to the Carrington waterfront with Roxie. They are both still seething over Sav's malicious accusations – there seems to be no limit to what the man will do to get back at Monica – but they refuse to let it beat them. They even manage to see the humorous side of the previous day's shock allegations: the two of them in the police station, Steve wearing a Holter monitor to record his heart rhythms after a suspected TIA in December; Monica despondent, frustrated at the blasé attitude of the police officer she'd spoken with. And then, at that moment, Monica receives the email from Sav's solicitor accusing Steve of sexually abusing Benji.

News comes through that Sienna's affidavit has been served on Sav. As was said earlier, it is a matter between her and the solicitor. Exactly what it contains is unknown. Through Georgia's contact with Sav's sister, Gabby, they learn that Sav is pressuring Sienna to withdraw her affidavit. Sav makes numerous calls in the space of half an hour.

Initially, he is angry. 'I've tried, Sienna, but you've turned on me, your father... your own flesh and blood. I'm disgusted with you.'

'Don't you care about my career? I want to be a teacher – I need to pass the Working with Children Check,' replies Sienna.

Sav hangs up.

He rings back a few minutes later. This time he is charming. 'All I can say to you, my beautiful Sienna, is that I love you with all the goodness of my heart. I'm so sorry that I hurt you. I know I can be an idiot sometimes.'

Sienna is blunt. 'I know what you're trying to do. I'm not withdrawing the affidavit.'

'Won't you give me a chance to make it up to you?'

'It's too late for that.'

Sav hangs up.

A few minutes later he calls again, this time expressing disappointment. 'My own daughter has abandoned me. After all I've done for you. All I can say is, I tried. I'm just so disappointed in you. Everyone is. The whole family. Nona and Papa. Your aunties.'

'I'm not going to keep lying for you,' says Sienna.

Sav hangs up.

Then comes disownment. 'I can't have you treat me like this… your own father. It's not right. I disown you, Sienna. I don't want anything more to do with you. You are a disgrace to the family. You…'

Sienna hangs up.

His behaviour is erratic. The next time she answers, Sav pleads. 'Please, Sienna. Come on… do you want to see me go to gaol? Give me just one more chance. I promise I'll make it up to you.'

When more attempts fail, he turns to Marco, asking him to talk her round.

According to Sienna, when Luca Savington first tried to obtain a DVO claiming Monica had bashed him, he told police it happened in October. They turned him away, saying it was too far in the past. He then went to another station and claimed it happened on December 9 – and that did the trick. There seems to be no limit to the lengths to which he is prepared to go. Speaking with her parents, Monica recalls an ugly altercation between Sav and Leonardo she witnessed a year or so ago. After a barrage of abuse from Sav, Leonardo fired back, 'You've done far worse things than I've ever done.' And 'continues to do,' can now be added to that proclamation.

Steve:

Will a DCJ social worker know that Sav has filled Benji's head with lies? Will Benji keep repeating them, knowing he'll be in trouble if he disobeys his father? He has been held captive for more than two months and, in his reality, his monster of a father owns him. Two months is a long time in the life of an 8-year-old boy. Recent experiences with police and the courts do little to inspire confidence in the system.

But the tactic could backfire and reveal Sav for the insidious manipulator he is. Expose him as a person willing to use and destroy a child's innocence to attain his own ends.

One of Monica's friends saw on a dating app that Sav had hooked up with a woman over for the weekend. 'Lucky woman,' says Monica sarcastically.

DAY 66 – SOCCER

In the afternoon Narelle, Monica, Steve, Narelle's sister Beckie, Narelle's mother Irene (Benji's ninety-three-year-old great grandmother) travel to Speers Point to watch Benji play soccer. Again, they want Benji to know the family hasn't given up on him. The presence of witnesses becomes useful as events unfold.

Steve spots Sav first. He is sitting alone in the second of two stands furthest from the entrance. He quietly warns Monica. She and Narelle take seats in the stand closest to the exit, keeping well away from him. Irene seems oblivious to the tension – she just wants shade and a better view – and continues past both stands, Beckie and Steve close behind. She settles in a shaded spot beyond the stands where she can watch the game.

At half-time, Monica and Narelle decide to join the others. To avoid Sav, they circle behind the stands, not realising Sav has left his seat and is already back there, talking on his phone.

Steve:

From a distance, I can almost hear the 'Jaws' theme playing. By the time Monica and Narelle spot him, it's too late. They turn sharply and head back the way they came – but Sav has seen them and is on the move. He raises his phone, filming, and shouts over and over, 'Excuse me, excuse me – you can't be here!'

I close the distance quickly, telling Sav to stop harassing them and to leave. He ignores me, still filming and following us. By the time we reach Grandma, curious spectators are watching. Sav hangs back but lingers nearby. Beckie confronts him, saying she can go wherever she wants. He jabs a finger in Monica's direction, 'She can't, she can't.'

Eventually, Sav moves away, stopping in front of the grandstand where he half-hides behind a post. When Benji is subbed off, Sav goes straight to the coach. Moments later, Benji leaves the team bench and walks with Sav towards the pavilion. We wait until the game ends, wary of another encounter. As we make our way to the cars, we keep close to Irene – the last thing she needs at her age is to be dragged into one of Sav's confrontations.

In the afternoon, Daniel works his shift at the golf club. He's given real responsibility and even cooks his own burger for lunch. Most of the shift is running food to the driving range next to the clubhouse. His boss treats him well, and Daniel comes home pleased – especially with cash in his pocket from his first day's pay.

DAY 67 – THE PENNY DROPS

Steve goes to the police station to report the soccer incident. The desk officer tells him that if he wants the report included in Monica's file, she must be present. He hates the idea of adding to her stress, but there's no alternative. They agree to go together after Monica finishes work.

At the station, the officer takes time to familiarise herself with the ongoing saga. Monica gives her account, but Steve can't help interjecting with his own points. The officer warns him to stop or be removed from the room. He bites his tongue, simmering. His daughter has been harassed for over three months, and the police seem powerless to stop it. At one point, the officer comments that it 'looks like tit for tat.' The remark rankles Steve – as if the blame were equal.

Still, the officer is thorough, videoing Monica's statement and taking a detailed one from Steve.

But it's never straightforward. They're told Sav has already complained about their 'behaviour' at soccer, alleging Monica made a death threat – with Benji as his witness. What is peculiar regarding Sav's report, is he claims the altercation occurred at 10 am. Yet the game didn't commence until 3 pm. Monica and Steve are not perturbed. They have five witnesses who will back up their version of what transpired. Narelle, Beckie, and Grandma's contact details are passed on to the officer.

Steve points out that Sav followed and filmed Monica. 'If she harassed him, it'll be on his phone,' he says.
'There's nothing on the files,' replies the officer.

Then comes another twist. Sav has accused Monica of threatening him on Facebook Messenger; he's almost certainly using a fake account in her name. Monica still has to deny it on camera. But then comes the turning point: the officer says police do not believe Luca Savington – neither his Facebook Messenger claims nor his soccer-ground story.

Steve:
In my head, a giant penny drops from the sky and crashes through the police station roof, shaking the place to its foundations. Finally!

I file another report with the DCJ. At least I get his birthdate correct; more than his father could do in his fabricated DVO. I tell the DCJ the child has not had contact with mother, brother, or any of the Kelty family for over two months. He has been held in captivity since he was snatched from school by the father, Luca Savington, in early February. That the father has been schooling him to lie for over two months now. The man has zero impulse control and has been charged with breaching his DVO but is yet to face court. The child is alone for hours on end day after day. That his sibling, Sienna, had been caring for him, but she has now fled the house in fear of her father.

For Sav, it's a reality check. By approaching and harassing Monica, he's breached his DVO – again. But Monica knows that if he'll breach it once, he'll breach it again. And there's Benji, caught in the middle – forced to lie for his father, against his Pop, against his own mother.

DAY 69 – DUCKS LINED UP

It's National Siblings Day. It's also Chantel's birthday. Hip, hip, hooray, but not today – celebrations are on hold as Chantel is unwell. Nothing too serious, but she in no state to venture outside of her home.

Monica drives into town for her mental health appointment. Her blood tests are fine, and she's functioning normally. Sav's supposed to have had a psych assessment by now, but Monica's solicitor has heard nothing.

Sienna has been asked to meet with Benji's soccer coach. Monica sends the coach a message, stating that as Benji's mother, she should be contacted if the meeting concerns her son. No reply.

Narelle offers to accompany Sienna, but she insists on going alone. It raises the question: will Sav be there? And does this link back to his recent stunt at Benji's match? Likely – poisoning others against Monica is his standard tactic.

Friends and family reach out, worried for Benji. Gabby, Sav's sister, says she's filed a DCJ report as promised – anonymously, out of fear of her brother's backlash.

Monica speaks with DCJ triage and gets a boost: 'You have all your ducks lined up,' she's told. Meagan from the women's support group is also optimistic. It's encouraging that those who work in the field see through Sav's manipulations. Their reactions suggest the kind of injustice Monica is suffering is far from rare. But the real test will be the Interim Hearing. The fear is that the highly regarded Senior Registrar Mansfield – praised by Billy Holden for his thoroughness – might be replaced by an inexperienced junior, as happened before.

Steve has heard nothing further about Sav's sexual abuse allegations against him, but the claim is never far from his mind. Except for the soccer incident, police have acted on all Sav's accusations.

DAY 70 – HAPPY BIRTHDAY

It's Monica's birthday. The four of them go out for dinner at the Verde Luna, an Italian restaurant down the road. On occasions like this, Daniel must miss Leonardo and Marco. He's known them since he was three or four – they were his family, even if not by blood. And he hasn't seen Benji for more than two months. Steve tries to reassure him, telling him this will blow over one day – at least most of it. But who will forgive Luca Savington for his crimes?

They've barely arrived home from the restaurant when Monica's phone rings. Another no-ID call. 'Happy birthday,' the voice says. Monica hangs up. They're all floored. It's bizarre and creepy – the man has denied her access to her son, chased her at Benji's soccer, tried to have her arrested with fabricated death threats – and then decides to call with birthday wishes. The call unsettles Monica. Another trip to the police station looms. Will the officer on duty see it for what it is – or will the reaction be, 'What a thoughtful man! How considerate.' It all depends on who's on duty.

Excerpt from Monica's diary:
One night when we were living at Jalna Pde, I went for dinner with some of the mums from Daniel's school. Sav came and picked me up when I hadn't asked for a lift home. One of the mum's, Zoe, asked to be dropped home too. Sav was driving over the speed limit. After Zoe had been dropped off, Sav screamed at me accusing me of cheating on him. I said I wasn't, that I had just gone for dinner. Sav threw my handbag out the car window down the road from our house. I asked Sav to pull over. I got out and Sav took off. I collected my things from the side of the road and walked home. When I got home, Sav wouldn't let me inside.

In her award-winning book *See What You Made Me Do*, Jess Hill explains in 'Notes on My Methods' why she replaces the term 'domestic violence' with 'domestic abuse.' She quotes from an article in *Women's Agenda* by Yasmin Khan: *Many women that we support assure me there has been no domestic violence – 'he's never laid a hand on me' – but on deeper questioning and reflection, realise they have been abused for many years, in ways that have been more subtle but just as damaging and potent.*

Daniel is booked for two shifts at Charlestown Golf Club the coming weekend. He's happy.

DAY 71 – SWITCH

Reporting to the police is like going to the dentist – draining and always tempting to put off. Monica and Steve steel themselves. They have to stay in the fight. The officer Monica reports to reviews the history and immediately recognises the passive aggression in the birthday call. She deems it a breach of the DVO and, like others before her, expresses surprise that Benji remains in his father's care.

Georgia calls. She's been speaking to Sav's sister, Gabby. Plans for Benji's school holiday visit have changed – he's no longer staying with her for the first week, just one night. Sav will collect him on Tuesday. He tells Gabby Benji has an appointment with a child solicitor on Thursday. The story doesn't add up – child solicitors are appointed by the court, and Monica, as Benji's mother, would have been informed.

Georgia tries to arrange a video call between Benji and baby Emma, but Gabby refuses. Something has shifted – likely Sav caught wind of their plan to meet.

Georgia:
Savingtons will turn. They switch and they ditch.

Sienna is the exception. She's stood her ground despite being shunned by the Savington clan. She has been welcomed by Monica's extended family.

That evening, Daniel plays his basketball final. Tip-off is at 5:30 and the stadium is packed to capacity. Monica and Steve slip into seats at the end of the players' section. The team loses, but Daniel plays one of his best games of the season. Basketball has been a bright spot for him – a focus, a distraction from the chaos swirling around his family.

DAY 72 – REKONNECT

Monica receives three no-ID calls in a row. Sav can't control himself. The impulse to call must be overwhelming. He probably thinks he'll get away with it, and he will unless the police investigate the no-ID calls.

Sienna fills Monica in on her meeting with Benji's soccer coach. The coach is worried the police might turn up at games, disrupting the team. Sav had threatened to call them the previous Sunday. The coach is also concerned that Benji isn't attending training. Monica phones Sav but, as before, he doesn't return her call.

Monica's neighbour Sarah rings. Sav's car isn't at the house; instead, Marco, Leonardo, and a friend are there with Benji. Sarah wonders if Sav has been arrested.

On Sunday, Benji's game is at a field near Swansea. There's a big turnout again – Narelle, Beckie, Grandma, Chantel, Steve, and Phillip. If Sav tries another stunt, witnesses won't be in short supply. As at Speers Point, Monica stays away, not wanting to give Sav a reason to cancel her visit with Benji later that day.

But Benji doesn't turn up to the game. They wait until the final whistle, then Narelle, Beckie, and Steve speak to the coach. Sav is trying to blame Benji's lack of enthusiasm on their attendance, but the coach says Benji's performance on the field hasn't suffered. The real issue is that Benji has only attended about thirty percent of the training sessions. They explain briefly that Sav has been withholding Benji from school and social activities. The coach adds that in his meeting with Sienna, she sided more with Monica than her father.

That afternoon, Steve drives Monica to Stockton for her long-awaited reunion with Benji. The weather is pleasant, with a light breeze. They park, scanning for Benji and the ReKonnect supervisor. After a tense couple of minutes, Monica's phone rings – they're at the east end of the park. Steve stays by the car while Monica walks over. Benji is on the flying fox, not running to greet his mother but continuing to play as though she isn't there. 'Get off the damned thing and give your mum a hug,' Steve wants to yell.

The supervisor chats openly. Before Monica arrived, Sav had been coaching Benji in front of her, telling him what to say and warning him not to mention Pop. Monica notices Benji is not only standoffish but hyper-vigilant. She's brought presents, but he's reluctant to engage and says he wants to go home. Monica persists.

They walk to a nearby café for lunch. Benji begins to relax – until the supervisor spots a car. Sav is parked on the corner. Benji sees him, shuts down, and turns away from his mother. The supervisor calls Sav, telling him he's breaking the rules and must leave. Benji repeats that he wants to go home, but Monica holds her ground.

After they eat, Monica pulls out a colouring book and pencils. It's something Benji has always enjoyed. Gradually, he thaws, chatting about Daniel and Roxie. When it's time to go, he wants to stay longer. It's painful for Monica to leave, but at least she's seen her son. For Steve, the idea of a paid, supervised visit is bitter – his daughter is a capable mother, and the arrangement seems absurd.

Later, a police officer calls Monica. Sav denies making the birthday call. The officer says they are determined to get to the bottom of the no-ID calls – welcome news, though Monica has heard it all before. She stays polite with the officer, but the harassment has dragged on for more than three months without effective intervention.

DAY 75 – SIDESHOW

Monica's two DVOs and Sav's breaches are back in court. With a barrister appearing on her behalf, Monica doesn't have to attend. She heads to work, wanting updates on the outcome. Both DVOs – riddled with mistakes, lies, and impossibilities – must still be defended. Again, the hope is they'll be withdrawn or tossed out by the magistrate.

Sav's breaches are to be heard in Newcastle. When Steve, Chantel, and Phillip arrive, they catch Sav unawares. He's smug, joking with his barrister, until he spots them watching. Then the laughter stops, and he switches to serious.

Once proceedings start, they don't wait long for Sav's matter. Two of the first three cases are adjourned; the third is over quickly when the accused pleads guilty. Sav's barrister tells the court the police prosecutor is on holidays and didn't get back to him on an important matter. Because of that, Sav's breaches aren't heard. The can is kicked down the road.

The DVOs have become the sideshow to the custody battle. Monica receives some positive news. Her second DVO, detailing how she supposedly placed a death threat in Sav's mailbox from a locked hospital ward, is withdrawn. But the first DVO, in which Monica is accused of bashing Sav, is not. It is to be heard at a later date.

DVOs are a gravy train – money, money, money. A bonanza for 'men fluffing around in suits' as Narelle described the behaviour of the barristers and solicitors at the courthouse.

Monica's expenses to defend herself are already over twenty thousand dollars, and she's done nothing wrong. It's like a high-stakes poker game where you must borrow thousands just to stay in. She might have the best hand, but no-one knows what's coming. The matter Sav's solicitor was waiting on may well be the no-ID calls he won't admit to. He'll be pushing to have them excluded.

At around 8.30 pm there's a knock at the door. It's the same two police officers who came looking for Monica the previous Sunday. They ask if she assaulted Luca Savington on 20 September 2023. From their wording, it sounds like they're investigating the same accusation behind the first DVO – only with a new date. Why do police countenance such rubbish? Monica denies it on camera.

Steve is wondering what on earth is going on. 'Have you seen this guy, Luca Savington?' he asks.
'Once,' says one of the officers.
'It would take two of you to hold him. Yet my daughter bashed him up?'
They get it.
'When will all this stop?' Steve asks.
'Soon,' says the younger officer.
Maybe he knows something we don't, Steve thinks.

Steve:

I don't know whether to laugh or cry at this latest stitch-up. Sav doesn't even need to harass Monica directly – he's worked the system, so police do it for him. The officers who sign off on these orders not only embolden men like Sav to keep going but become accomplices in intimidating the victim.

Monica will stay strong. So will her family. They won't rest until Benji is safe. She has a wide network of friends and family standing behind her. But what about women without such support? Or without funds to fight? Not every woman is as determined or resolute as Monica.

Steve's sister Chantel gets a call from Senior Constable Bancroft – the same officer who served Monica's DVOs, insisted the death threat was in Monica's handwriting, and accused her of mailing Sav a bullet. Chantel had already told Bancroft that Monica was with her the entire day, making it impossible. Now, police want Chantel to make an official statement. Justice may yet prevail.

DAY 77 – CHILD ABUSE

Steve is at Charlestown Square attending a health appointment when the surveillance camera at the house pings an alert. A minute later, his phone rings. He'd meant to switch it off but forgot. Instantly, he senses his life is about to change and runs through the possible ways it might.

Twenty minutes later, he leaves the centre and checks his phone. The Ring app shows two detectives at the front door. The missed call is from Daniel. When Steve calls back, Daniel tells him the detectives said they'd return in a couple of hours. Narelle views the footage from her app at Georgia's unit in Camperdown. Steve does some shopping before heading home.

Two hours later, they return. A male, Senior Police Officer Russell Dreiser, and a female, Detective Lizbeth Bauer. Bauer does the talking. She says she has interviewed Benji, who claims Poppy has sexually interfered with him. Steve is served with a DVO – the usual a, b, c conditions, plus a ban on coming within 200 metres of Benji. He must appear in court at the end of April.

'You can't go to his soccer games,' Bauer adds. The comment seems trivial in light of the accusations.

The DVO states: *Offences disclosed amount to sexual touching which are currently subject to further investigation.*

Steve asks where and when this supposedly happened. Bauer says the Hamilton house in December, after Monica fled with Daniel and Benji but before Sav took Benji.

Steve gives his account – how Monica left Sav, the harassment, the breaches, the litany of lies. How Sienna is hiding from her father's wrath. How Sav is coaching Benji to lie. How, fourteen years ago, Sav accused an uncle of sexually assaulting his eldest son, Leonardo. Steve talks for forty minutes, even showing them where Benji stayed upstairs with his mother in a small bed-sitter/bathroom setting. Bauer mentions she's going on holidays and will be back in three weeks to take his statement.

When Steve tells Monica and Narelle, they chide him for trusting the detectives. After Monica's recent police and court experiences, faith in the system is thin. Steve understands, but at seventy-two, he's determined to defend his name. He sensed the detectives weren't ambitious career cops chasing another notch on their belts, but still…

Steve needs legal advice, and with only two working days to find a lawyer before court on Tuesday, Steve feels wrong-footed. Later in the day, Narelle returns from Sydney, and they contact Lisa Jones. She promises to organise a barrister and sets a Monday meeting. It gives Steve some solace.

Sav has manipulated police; now he's doing it with the Child Abuse Squad. To use Benji like this is beyond the pale.

Steve:
I'm horrified – agitated, angry, sad, incredulous this is happening. I'm extremely anxious about court. Will I have to stand there while the filth on the DVO is read out? Steve Kelty: accused of interfering with a child – in my eyes, the most heinous crime imaginable. In many people's eyes. I'd rather be accused of murder.

DAY 78 – SLASHED TYRES

The lengths to which Sav is willing to go to punish Monica for leaving him are extreme. What sort of person puts a child through such an ordeal, without a thought for the damage it will cause? Monica has always called out lies. It is not the way Benji was brought up – until now. Steve recalls something Lizbeth Bauer said, 'Children do not understand the seriousness of what they are saying.' Does that mean Bauer knows Benji is fabricating the allegations? Or was it just a passing comment?

Benji will be both scared and scarred. He has been lied to, told his mother deserted him. He will live in fear of Sav, wary of triggering his anger, believing there is no escape and that he must do as his father says.

Monica's neighbours see Benji at the mailbox. He used to play with their son, and they were once good friends. Since Sav took him, that friendship has been cut off. Benji now lives in seclusion. The boy who once loved the outdoors now lives in a tomb.

Steve contacts Turnbull Hill solicitors and begins a conversation. Do Monica and him have enough documented information to sue Luca Savington for defamation?

It rains on Saturday morning, leaving no chance to take Roxie for a walk. Last night, Daniel quit his job after being rostered three long shifts in a row at a different venue under a new boss. He met the man – gruff and abrasive – and took an instant dislike to him. With everything going on, work has become too much for him.

Just before 4:30, Monica leaves for a party at her friend Alisha's place, an hour away. There's an element of risk if Sav fabricates another allegation and she happens to be nearby.

She returns home around 8:30, unsettled. Almost home, she had spotted Sav's distinctive red Ford approaching. It turned sharply down a side street, then accelerated away. Steve goes out the front to check but sees no sign of the car.

Monica has received six more no-ID phone calls.

On Sunday morning Monica finds her car with two flat tyres, slashed on the side nearest the road. This time Steve can't inflate them with the compressor. Reviewing camera footage, they see that at 5:54 pm the previous evening, a man with a build like Sav's walked past the house. Dressed in black and white sport shoes, he kept his head turned away from the camera, looking at his phone.

Steve cancels plans to drive to Wingham with Narelle to see her sister – he doesn't want to leave Monica alone. Besides, the vandalism needs to be reported. The tyres will have to wait. As Steve knows from previous experience, it's impossible to get tyres on a Sunday.

At the police station, Steve insists Monica speak with someone familiar with her case. The desk officer, shaking his head in exasperation, says, 'Everyone knows about it,' as he takes the report. At first Steve thinks the frustration is directed at them, but it's not – the officer recognises the pattern in Sav's behaviour. Steve realises it's the same officer who, the previous Tuesday, investigated Sav's claim that Monica bashed him the year before.

While Monica is in the interview room, Steve chats with a woman. She suggests the station could do with some artwork. 'They aren't designed to encourage you to stay,' Steve replies. She laughs. He adds, 'This is one of the better stations.' She says she's never been in one before. As they leave, Steve overhears her reporting an abandoned car in Carrington. He longs for simpler times.

Later, Beckie and Narelle's mum, Irene, drop by the police station to give their account of the soccer incident. They are surprised to be turned away – the police say the matter is closed and they have their details if statements are needed. Beckie is annoyed, but it's likely they have what they need. Monica and Steve were told earlier the police do not believe Sav's version of events.

DAY 81 – BARRISTER

Monica borrows Grandma's car so she can get to work. Steve rings a mobile tyre service based in Mayfield, and the technician turns up within the hour, switches a tyre, and fits two new ones on the front. Cost: $380. Add it to Sav's bill. It's a tight fit, but from this point on, both vehicles are parked in the carport. If Sav tries anything again, he will be caught on camera.

In the afternoon, Narelle and Steve set off for their appointment with Lisa. Held up in traffic, they arrive half an hour late. After a short conversation, Lisa introduces them to a barrister, James Exxon – an ex-police prosecutor. What he has to say is disconcerting: there is no longer a presumption of innocence with child sex allegations. These are times, he explains, where to be male and accused is to be presumed guilty. There is a belief that children don't lie. Steve is shattered.

James reads the DVO issued against Steve. In his opinion, they have two options. The first: don't fight the DVO. It's the cheapest option, and the police are unlikely to act because the evidence appears flimsy. The problem is that Steve would be barred from contact with Benji while the DVO is in place – typically two years.

The second option: fight it. Steve tells James that Detective Bauer, the one who did the talking, said she would return for a statement in three weeks. 'Oh… that changes everything,' James says. 'If they want a statement, they intend to arrest you. Which means we'll have to fight the accusations.'

Steve is speechless. If arrested, according to James, he will almost certainly be charged. He can't understand why the Child Abuse Squad would choose that course without speaking to other occupants of the house. The prospect of being charged with sexual abuse is bad enough, but what James says next is even more disturbing.

'What the detective has accused you of, Steve, is barely grounds for a DVO. Which means they must have more evidence.'
Steve stares at the barrister, gobsmacked.

'They hold back evidence, so they have more ammunition when they interview you.'

James cites a previous case where this happened, but Steve barely hears him. He is too busy wondering what other lies Sav has coerced Benji into telling. After more than two months, the indoctrination could be deep. James warns that if repeated often enough, Benji may come to believe the lies himself – something that's not uncommon. James advises them to keep a detailed daily record. Over time, dates can become vital in court to challenge inconsistencies in a child's account. Time, James says, is Steve's ally. If the case proceeds to the district court, however, legal costs could reach $70,000.

Afterwards, Steve and Narelle are devastated. 'James's advice is to get the DVO hearing delayed for six weeks or so,' Steve says, 'but the problem is Monica's custody hearing is around that time. And the court won't allow Benji to return to a house where there is an alleged sex offender.'

Steve exhales, overwhelmed. 'It feels surreal. I cannot believe it is happening – that he could do this… not just to me, but to his own son.' He takes a deep breath. 'I'm in serious trouble, according to the barrister. He was pretty sure Benji reported more than is on the DVO. So, it seems in a few weeks I'll be taken to the police station, asked to make a statement, and then be charged with interfering with a child.'
'Let's wait and see. It could change if Monica gets Benji back in June.'
'James's analysis is too terrifying to contemplate. But I can't pretend it's not happening; he's not some novice barrister. And if the police can serve a DVO on Monica for bashing up Sav, anything is possible.'

There is one positive from the meeting: James is on friendly terms with a police prosecutor. 'This guy's trouble,' he told James recently. 'This guy' being Luca Savington. It's another sign the police may finally be waking up to Sav. But will that help Steve? Just when the police are becoming aware of Sav's true nature, he changes his tactics, manipulating detectives and DCJ investigators from the Child Abuse Squad.

Again, Narelle and Steve barely sleep a wink. They talk about the close relationship they both once had with their grandson Benji – swimming, bike riding, music, soccer, the jokes they shared. It is all so sad and debilitating. Family and friends insist the truth will eventually come out. But will it? Child abuse cases are murky. Steve could find himself bogged deep in the quagmire.

Steve:

I'm feeling frustrated and angry, distraught at the prospect of this dragging on long-term — that I could never again be alone, not just with my grandson Benji, but with my other grandchildren, Daniel and Emma. Or any other child. Could I live with that? Benji must have been convincing, or Detective Bauer would not have issued the DVO. Imagine how Benji must be feeling — abandoned by everyone, knowing he must make up lies to frame his Poppy in a police interview just to placate his malevolent father.

It is to be investigated further by Bauer. But how? Will Sav have coerced another witness besides Benji to back up his claims? In three weeks, when Bauer returns from her holiday, I will be arrested. It felt cruel — the detective talking about holidays while accusing me of sexually abusing my own grandchild. If the case proceeds to the district court, the $70,000 it will cost is money we cannot afford. It will be reported in the media. I will be placed on the sexual predator's register. My life will not be worth living.

Where do the rest of the Savingtons stand on this? They know Sav has been involved in a child abuse case before with Leonardo, because Sav's sister Elena was close friends with his first wife. Will they step up, or are they cowardly, devoid of a moral compass? Maybe they are afraid of Luca Savington.

Up until now, Steve and Narelle have been Monica's main protectors. Without Steve around, Monica will be easier to target. The lengths to which Luca Savington is willing to go are still unknown.

DAY 83 – SCORN AND HATE

'Childcare worker and mother, Molly Ticehurst, was found dead in a regional New South Wales home on Monday morning. The Forbes local was 28 years old, the 25th woman to die from gender-based violence in Australia his year, according to data interpreted from Counting Dead Women.' (ABC News, Wednesday April 24, 2024, by political reporter Georgia Roberts). At this time last year, 14 women had died. In 2022, the number was 17 – up from 14 in 2021 and 2020.

Comments made on Facebook:

Steve Kelty:

The support for abused and at-risk women seems to come from other women. The decent men seem to shy away; not my business. They need to come to the fore, call out violent, abusive men.

Silvia Jacobs:

The legal system is broken. It protects/supports the perpetrators.

Calvin Stevens:

It seems that male aggression is genetically inherited from the evolution of what has been the aggressive male protecting family, tribe etc. Since women have become more empowered in more recent times, they have choices that once did not exist, and greater economic abilities. Leaving a partner is now an economic option for some/many. 'Man' now feels betrayed because he does not have control over his woman anymore, but he still has his aggression, genetic and environmentally/culturally reinforced. It is hard to change such ingrained behaviour. I think it is only a minority of males who are psychologically capable of adapting to social change of male/female re adaptations. This is the dilemma! Can males adapt quickly? No. In 10,000 years? Maybe. It may be difficult to change the consequences of evolutionary history, but it may be possible to modify it. But only if men are prepared to reassess themselves.

Steve attends a workers compensation hearing to support his friend Daryll, a Kamilaroi man originally from Tamworth. The hearing is conducted by video hook-up from a solicitor's office in Hunter Street, Newcastle, just across from the courthouse. After three hours of haggling, the two parties cannot reach an agreement – there is a difference of more than four hundred thousand dollars between what the insurer wants to pay and what Daryll's side will accept.

Acting on Daryll's behalf, Steve makes it clear to the solicitor that Daryll does not want the matter to land in court – they will need to reach an agreement. The solicitor is confident they will settle without going to court. As he explains, it is too risky for either side to pursue the matter in court. If the amount demanded in compensation is too high, they could be ordered to pay most of the court costs for both parties. If the party the claim is against offers too little, they could be ordered to pay the costs. The solicitor adds that the bias of the magistrate – whether they have an insurance or welfare background – can be paramount. It can make a difference of hundreds of thousands of dollars to the final payout, so it is financially risky for the parties not to agree.

The bias comment is not lost on Steve. Not just the police they have been dealing with, but the Family Law Registrars. All humans carry bias, unwittingly or not. Mansfield, the Registrar for the Interim Hearing, has a reputation for being fair, thorough, and astute. They are pinning their hopes on it – and that he is not replaced.

Narelle attempts to contact Sav's parents. They have met Narelle and Steve on social occasions in the past. Maybe they will at least discuss the situation – but they do not acknowledge the message. Perhaps it's a case of eyes wide shut; their son can do no wrong. Savington blood may be thicker than the truth.

Monica receives a call from the police. They want more information on the slashed tyre incident. Narelle goes into the station with Monica, and they are in there for about two hours. Monica again goes through the details – the location, the time, exactly where she saw Sav's red Ford.

DAY 84 – FISHING

Monica has a ReKonnect visit scheduled for Sunday. This time Daniel will accompany her. They plan to have lunch and a game or two of tenpin bowling.

Steve and Daniel meet Daryll at Pelican, on the lake near Swansea. He is with a friend, Amos, who is Papua New Guinean. They have an extra rod for Daniel. Steve will watch – he has no desire to fish. His father Jack had been a mad fisherman. They had lived at Malabar, in Sydney's eastern suburbs. Jack would get up at 4 am and head out to sea in his boat with a mate, usually Curly or Bluey. If the weather was right, they'd go forty kilometres east to fish off the continental shelf, where the deep ocean begins. They'd return early in the afternoon, often with a boatload of fish. Steve went with him a couple of times but got seasick. It turned him off fishing for good.

While Daniel and Daryll fish, Steve takes short walks, returning occasionally to check on them before heading off again. He is restless, unable to stay in one place. The scenario keeps running through his mind: Bauer will return in two weeks and ask for a statement. If the barrister's reasoning is correct, he will be arrested. He keeps his solicitor's number with him at all times. The barrister's words echo – they must have more than what's on the DVO, as it's barely enough to have one issued. He circles back to the same thought: what other lies has Sav coerced Benji into reporting? Poor kid… poor Pop.

He thinks of happier times, when he, Benji, and Daniel would go bike riding, swimming, or kicking a soccer ball in the park. Sav has stripped away Benji's innocence. With the police visits, the DVOs, and now these sexual abuse allegations, Steve is losing what little faith he has left – not only in the justice system, but in humanity.

Daniel does plenty of casting but catches nothing. Daryll lands two small bream, which he throws back. They enjoy each other's company, and Steve is glad Daniel is outside, breathing fresh air, rather than stuck inside playing computer games.

The next day there is a woman on the ABC morning program being interviewed about the escalating rates of domestic violence. A rally is planned for the weekend, with the issue now declared a national crisis. 'No More,' screams the headline. 'It's Time to Step Up.'

When Monica left Sav, one of Sav's sisters warned Monica about him. 'Take Benji and run,' was her advice. She knew what had happened to Sav's previous wife. Unless you have bucketloads of money and are adept at working the system, it is wise advice. If Monica's case is any indication, a woman fleeing an abusive relationship cannot rely on the police or the legal system for protection. The police signed off and served two DVOs framing her as the aggressor without speaking to her or anyone in her family. They had already denied her a DVO because Sav's children described the incident that led to her leaving as 'just another argument.' When is it one argument too many? Why did the police downplay the violence?

Unless systemic issues are addressed, nothing will change. Whether it is procedural flaws, a misogynistic culture, or police wanting to appear impartial, there is an assumption that males are just as likely to be victims of domestic violence as females. But the statistics show that deaths from domestic violence are not spread equally across genders – they are predominantly femicide (a male killing a female). Is a male ever killed by a female partner? Yes. Is a male ever killed by a male partner? Yes. But in Australia, the reality is that 77% of recorded murders related to family violence in 2024 involved a male killing a current or former female partner (ABS 2024).

'We are all trained in domestic violence,' the police officer told Monica when she asked to speak to someone from the Domestic Violence Unit. The training is meant to equip officers with the knowledge and skills necessary to respond effectively to domestic and family violence incidents, but it is flawed if police cannot detect those who manipulate the system. Sav's manipulation of the system to date has not been sophisticated – he has invented and changed dates and witnesses – but it has worked. The police served a court order to protect him from the woman he was harassing. They then granted Sav a second DVO (whatever the point of that was) when a two-minute phone call would have shown Monica was in hospital at the time of the alleged incident.

There has been a great deal of publicity from Government, heralding the new coercive control laws. 'From 1 July 2024, coercive control is a criminal offence in NSW where a person uses abusive behaviours towards a current or former intimate partner with the intention to coerce or control them.' But unless the flaws in the current systems are addressed, coercive control laws will not make a skerrick of difference. The new law may even assist the likes of Sav, becoming another weapon in the arsenal of the manipulator. In the opinion of those working in the domestic violence field, manipulating the system is widespread.

The latest death – 49-year-old Emma Bates – is the 11th woman to be killed in just 24 days, coming soon after the shocking death of Molly Ticehurst and the Bondi Junction attacks.

Monica, Narelle, Chantel, and Steve attend Benji's soccer game. Cameras are at the ready in case Sav tries another stunt. Daniel says he'd like to go and watch but doesn't want to be chased around the ground by Luca Savington. Steve offers to cook a curry for the troops, but they decide to get takeaway from Raja's Corner after the game.

Benji plays with enthusiasm and is aware his mother is watching and supporting him. Sav takes a photo of the four of them, then stays down the other end of the ground. Unlike a normal game of two halves, the younger teams play thirds. Sav collects Benji and leaves the ground before they start the final third. It's all about power and control with him. It must be embarrassing for Benji.

Steve is half expecting a visit from the police – that Sav will claim he was at the game and breached his DVO.

DAY 86 – FENCE SITTING

Monica, Daniel, and Steve take Roxie for a walk around the foreshore. Monica is nervous, anticipating how Sunday's visit will go. Narelle is working at the library – at least it gives her a break from hostilities, because it feels like they are at war. She has been knocked around by Sav's brutality and unrelenting nastiness as much as anyone.

Sienna to Georgia:

I think the accusations he made against your dad were obviously out of anger against me, because on Friday he was trying to coerce me into revoking my affidavit. Every time he called his behaviour would change. So, he'd be angry one call and hang up on me, or he'd be super calm and use reverse psychology on me. Then he'd be extremely changeable, especially when his threats of disowning me didn't faze me. I heard from Gabby and Marco about what's happened. If there's a character reference or anything you need me to provide, or anything you need me to say to help your dad's case, I will. Because Steve is not like that, and the accusations are harmful and damning. I understand if you are very angry because I am angry myself about it.

Georgia to Sienna:

Yeah, we're incredibly angry. But I am also very worried about what he is saying to Benji and exposing him to, to get him to say these things. I just hope Benji knows he can tell the truth to the right people and won't get into trouble.

Later that day, Georgia to Sienna:

Hey Sienna, how are you doing? Dad's barrister said he'd probably get arrested over this sexual abuse claim Sav has fabricated. The detectives mentioned your name. I'm wondering, do you know anything about it? Sorry to bother you, but we are really upset and worried about this.

Sienna to Georgia.

Why have they mentioned my name? I honestly have no idea what's going on. I understand you're really upset, and I really wish I could help, but I am no longer in contact with him. I'm in the dark just as much as you are about this.

Sienna is a victim, too. She fears her father – with good reason. She knows Sav set up her mother, his first wife, but what about the uncle who went to jail over Leonardo's allegations? Was that also a set-up? Does Sienna know? Would she speak to the authorities about it – and would they listen if she did?

The latest news is that Marco has moved out of the house. He had only been staying weekends. Maybe the text Narelle sent him, reminding him that Monica has always been there for them and that she was their mother, made him re-evaluate his position.

Marco has apparently borrowed money and bought an expensive European car. He had it transported from Queensland and plans to repair it and make a motza. According to Sienna, after moving the car to his uncle's place on the Central Coast, he cut communication with his father. She says he is conflicted – Sav is his father after all. But from the Kelty point of view, sitting on the fence is not an option after Sav's latest nefarious act.

DAY 87 – RALLIES ARE HELD

Violent deaths of women by partners in the first four months of 2024: NSW 10, Queensland 6, Western Australia 5, Victoria 5, South Australia 1, Tasmania 1, ACT 0, Northern Territory 0.
(ABC News – Georgia Roberts / Source: 'Counting Dead Women')

There are rallies across the country, with community advocates and politicians demanding an end to violence against women. In Canberra, thousands join a three-kilometre walk across Lake Burley Griffin to Parliament House. In Victoria, Premier Jacinta Allan addresses a rally at Federation Square: 'We need to stop talking about women's safety and get in and tackle men's violence.'

Monica sees her son for two hours. She isn't deterred by the $200 cost. They meet at Charlestown bowling alley. Benji is again standoffish with his mother but chats easily with Daniel. A short time later, the supervisor spots Sav lurking in the background. Once again, he is breaching regulations, trying to control the visit. 'I'll be watching you.' Benji would have been told. Why else would he hold back from the mother he loves, and who he knows loves him?

The supervisor tells Monica that after their first visit, Sav contacted her superior to lodge a complaint – because she hadn't allowed Benji to leave when he'd asked. More proof of Sav coaching the boy. He doesn't want Benji to connect with anyone, especially his mother.

The next day, Sav is back in court to answer for his DVO breaches. Chantel arrives around 8:30 am, carrying a cottage pie. It's the third time recently she's turned up with prepared food, and the residents at Hamilton appreciate the gesture. Half an hour later, Narelle and Chantel head for the courthouse. Steve decides it's wiser to avoid being near the miscreant, and Phillip can't make it. They arrive early, and when the courtroom opens, secure seats in the front row.

Sav has brought three statements of support – one from work, another from the men's group he has enrolled in, and the third a plea declaring his contrition. Narelle and Chantel exchange a pointed shake of the head when he tells the court how remorseful he is. His solicitor pleads for leniency, citing Sav's role as a carer for his child. Again, Narelle and Chantel signal their disapproval. The magistrate is unaware that the father snatched the child from a completely capable mother and has withheld him for three months.

Luca Savington must stand throughout proceedings, receiving a dressing-down from the female magistrate – something that would grate on him. His solicitor tries to have the breaches dealt with by way of a fine, but the magistrate rejects it, instead placing Sav on a twelve-month good behaviour bond. If he breaches the DVO again, or even commits a traffic offence, he will be hauled back before a magistrate. Aside from the soccer incident, where police dismissed Sav's account, this is the first real win Monica has had – the first time the court has held him to account.

On paper, the ruling should make Monica safer. At least Sav will only get one chance to breach. He has also been ordered to attend a men's behaviour program.

Later, Monica hears from a neighbour that Leonardo is back at the house. Sav's pattern continues. With Sienna and Marco on the outer, he has drawn Leonardo back into the fold. This is bad for Benji. Leonardo is charming and likeable, but he has no boundaries. Monica recalls something Sienna told her, soon after Benji was taken. She had chided Leonardo for dealing cocaine, only for Sav to tell her to leave him alone. According to Sienna, Sav had no problem with his son dealing drugs. It shocks Steve, but not Narelle. 'Surely you didn't believe Leonardo's nonsense about selling solar insulation systems, did you?

Leonardo's presence raises questions. If he was dealing cocaine, is he still doing it? Steve wonders if Leonardo is funding Sav's substantial legal bills. Unlikely – Leonardo is usually broke and borrowing money, leaning on parents or siblings to bail him out of tricky situations. Once, when he owed Narelle money, he pretended to transfer the funds and even showed her a fake confirmation on his phone. The money never arrived. Had he simply said he didn't have it; she would have accepted it. A month later, at a family gathering, he behaved as though the swindle had never happened. On another occasion, he rang Monica from a service station after filling his car with fuel, claiming he couldn't pay.

DAY 90 – ESCAPE

It is May Day, or International Workers' Day. It's also Save the Rhino Day, Couple Appreciation Day, International Victorious Women's Day – honouring resilience and strength – and Law Day, a reminder to support the freedoms and civility afforded under the rule of law.

Steve catches the 9:30 am train to Sydney from Broadmeadow Station. Everyone has urged him to take a break, to get out of Newcastle for a while. Often, when a person is deep in turmoil, they are the last to recognise how much it is taking its toll.

Georgia meets him at Central with baby Emma. Her smiling face is a lift – proof there is still beauty in the world. Steve spends the day with them, then drives Matt's car to Roselands to stay with friends Barry and Janet, and their daughter Olivia. Friends since childhood, their kids grew up together. Like Monica's family and other friends, they cannot believe how easily Sav has manipulated the police and the Family Court. They've seen Monica in action and know she has been an excellent mother to Daniel and Benji, and to Sav's three children as well.

While Janet is busy during the day, Barry and Steve head out for lunch and a walk around Botany Bay, talking about music and old times. After dinner, they watch the football. Their childhood team, the South Sydney Rabbitohs, lose yet another game – not like the old days when they seemed to win everything.

DAY 92 – GREY CLOUDS

It is World Press Freedom Day. It is also Garden Meditation Day.

Steve sits in the front garden of Barry and Janet's Roselands home, contemplating his dire situation, when a call comes through from Georgia. She has just spoken to Monica, who is upset after talking with her solicitor, Adele. Adele has advised Monica to move out of the Hamilton house with Daniel because of the allegations and DVO against Steve. She also warned her not to trust the woman from ReKonnect who has been supervising Monica's visits with Benji. Adele has dealt with her before and claims she can be duplicitous. There is, however, a silver lining. The Savington case has been placed on the Evatt List.

- **The Evatt List** involves a specialist team, including highly skilled and trained Judicial Registrars and court child experts. To be placed on the Evatt List, one or more of the parties must have completed the DOORS triage risk-screening process.

- **DOORS risk-screening process** identifies risk or exposure to harm (child abuse and neglect, family violence, mental health issues, drug, or alcohol misuse) experienced by a party or child in family law proceedings. The process involves completing an online risk questionnaire called the Family DOORS Triage Risk Screen.

Monica completed the questionnaire soon after Benji was taken. Whether the Evatt listing was triggered by that, or by Sav's accusations against Steve and Monica, is unknown. Either way, it means a more thorough investigation into Benji's case, which is welcome news. The Evatt team will begin their work soon.

That night, Steve stays in Camperdown with Georgia, Matt, and baby Emma. The next morning, the four of them drive to Newcastle, with Georgia and her family staying at Grandma's. Georgia later brings Emma to the Hamilton house – her presence, as always, a panacea for their troubles.

On Sunday, Sienna drops by late in the afternoon. She is distressed and not in a good mental space. Although she has kept her new address secret, she fears her father will find out. She has asked for a DVO to protect herself from him, visiting the police station three times to plead her case, but has been denied. She stays for dinner. The atmosphere is calm, the conversation congenial, and the allegations against Steve are not mentioned.

Monica receives a text from ReKonnect that includes a message from Sav: he wants Benji's iPad and clothes. Nothing has been mentioned about either for months. Sav can't help himself. According to Monica's solicitor, the message is another breach of the DVO, and Monica is advised to inform police.

Monica must brace herself to do it, but she again visits the local police station. This time she goes in alone. While she is waiting to being attended to, a female officer she has spoken to previously comes into the station with her partner. Monica proffers a friendly 'Hi,' to which the officer replies, 'I'm not your friend.'
Monica isn't thrown by the officer's bluntness. 'I'm not here to see you,' she replies.
The duty officer considers Sav's message a breach, but his superior disagrees. Still, it is logged, along with the solicitor's opinion.

Steve visits his doctor and discusses recent events. It is the second time this year he has cried – the first was when Monica vanished on her walk and ended up in the Mater Hospital. His doctor recommends he see a forensic psychologist. 'Male or female?' she asks.
Steve doesn't care, so she books the first available appointment nearby, explaining that a forensic psychologist's report can be subpoenaed if he is charged and the case reaches court. It will also create a record of the damage the accusations are causing to his mental health.

On his way home, the psychologist's secretary calls – there has been a cancellation, and Steve can come in the next day. He accepts.

It is the first time in his life Steve has seen a psychologist. If the aim was to feel better, the visit is a failure. The psychologist paints a bleak picture of his short-term prospects. Be in it for the long haul, he warns. Be ready for anything, and do not trust the detectives. He tells Steve of a client who was betrayed by detectives he had confided in. What the psychologist says next is in line with what James, the barrister, had already said – and is deeply unsettling. Men accused of sexual offences against children are assumed guilty. There is no 'typical' offender; they can present just like him. 'All men over fifty fit the sexual predator profile,' the psychologist explains.

Steve tries to calculate the age Leonardo would have been when his testimony resulted in Sav's previous wife's uncle being charged and convicted of sexual abuse. Probably around the age Benji is now. Again, Steve considers the possibility that Leonardo was also coached and coaxed into lying. Is Sav using what he learnt from a genuine case of sexual abuse, or did he manipulate Leonardo? Had a man been wrongly imprisoned?

What Steve doesn't want to admit is that he has begun to resent Benji for lying. He knows the boy is only eight and a victim of coercive control, but he can't help thinking an 8-year-old Daniel wouldn't have been as easily manipulated. Still, he reminds himself that the pressure on Benji would have been immense. Sav has even coerced Sienna into lying for him – and she is an adult.

The psychologist is familiar with men like Sav. 'The type who'll bash someone, then bang their own head against a wall and claim the victim did it.'

Steve recalls the scar on Sav's forearm – a wound Sav had once blamed on his 'crazy, drugged-out ex-wife,' saying she slashed him with a knife. At the time, no-one questioned it. But recently, Sienna revealed the truth; she'd seen Sav throw himself through a plate glass window, then claim his wife pushed him.

'Yes,' Steve says, 'that's exactly what he's like.'

'He's the criminal type,' the psychologist replies.

After the session, Steve is more anxious than before – afraid of being arrested and charged. Sav might know exactly how to pull it off. How do you defend yourself against something that never happened? The powerlessness is draining him.

That afternoon, Daryl drops by. Steve has known him since he was a teenager at risk, living in an Indigenous hostel where Steve worked as a teacher. Daryl knows the allegations are nonsense. They go for a drive and a walk along the Anzac Bridge. Daryl is deeply upset by what Sav has done.

'I hope you don't mind, but I said a prayer for you in church last night,' he says.

Steve isn't religious, but he knows Daryl's friends practise what they preach. They've helped him with accommodation and stood by him in hard times. Steve thanks him for the prayer. Maybe God will wake from His slumber.

DAY 98 – WAKE IN FRIGHT

Excerpt from Monica's diary:
When I went to sleep in the spare bed, he screamed (waking the children) that I wasn't acting like a married woman. I remember Sav waking up the children in the night to accuse them of things. Throwing the phone at my leg and leaving a bruise. Blocking me from leaving. If I locked the bedroom door to get away, he would bang it down. Yelling so loud at me and the children, the neighbours could hear. Calling the children "little shits' and swearing at them, then saying I do it too, which I never have.

Steve is watching the British crime series 'Wire in the Blood.' In both episodes, the villains are women – and both are violent. The night before, he switched off 'Baby Reindeer,' which Monica had recommended, because once again the perpetrator was a woman. Perhaps women make more compelling criminals and victims on screen, but in real life the picture is quite different; the overwhelming majority of violent crime is committed by men against men. In Australia, between 2022 and 2023, 87% of homicide offenders and 69% of victims were male (Australian Institute of Criminology).

Steve reflects on the police actions that led to Monica being denied a DVO. Sav had been granted two DVOs based on the police accepting his claim that he feared Monica – and that she had assaulted him. Yet four out of five domestic violence victims are female, and perpetrators are overwhelmingly male. Monicas don't usually beat up the Savs of this world. Sure, David beat Goliath, but he had a slingshot – and the rarity of his victory is exactly why the story endures. In reality, Goliath usually wins.

One of the falsified DVOs against Monica remains in place. It must be listed in the Evatt List paperwork and weighs heavily on her mind. The police officers who interviewed Sav, the senior officer who signed off on it, and those who served it have again bolstered Sav's case. Each has played a part in Benji's and Monica's ongoing abuse.

The suggestion that Monica and Daniel should leave the Hamilton house and rent elsewhere is neither sound nor realistic. Rentals are scarce and prohibitively expensive. Uprooting would also be unsettling for Daniel. There are other considerations: Narelle and Steve are known in the neighbourhood, which offers some measure of protection; security cameras are in place; and the wide street makes it difficult for Sav to approach unnoticed. If Monica moved, she would be a sitting duck for the scheming Sav and at risk of further police accusations.

Steve:
It is three weeks since the detectives came to the house with the DVO. Maybe tomorrow is the day I'll be charged. I don't want them to return but, if they do, at least I'll know what I am fighting. I still need to change my address to Grandma's place at New Lambton but have been delaying it because the last thing I want is for the detectives turning up and pestering Narelle's 93-year-old mother. Irene, like us, has lost faith in the authorities.

Monica receives two more no-ID calls. She answers, but no-one speaks. Wonder who? Her friend Beth then gets a disturbing call from Sav, asking her to tell Monica that he loves her. Can you believe this man? Oblivious to the damage he's caused, or simply indifferent? The truth is, Luca Savington is delusional and treacherous. He has no self-control and doesn't care. The words he claims Monica wrote on the death threat – 'I love you; I hate you' – sound far more like his own conflicted feelings.

There is something inherently wrong with a system that empowers the abuser, punishes the victim – a mother whose only 'crime' was leaving a toxic relationship to seek a decent life for herself and her children – and leaves a child at risk. The long-term effect of Benji's isolation and brainwashing is impossible to measure. Some psychologists say he will recover once he's back with his mother; others warn of lasting harm. With the amount of publicity and discussion about domestic violence, it's as if Monica is living in a parallel universe.

Narelle picks Daniel up from school and talks about the difficult four months they've had.
'I've had a good year,' Daniel says.
'Really? You like living with me and Poppy?'
'Yeah, I do.'

At least Monica has saved Daniel, herself, and Roxie – and now Sienna is out of Sav's control. Still, one more to go. Monica remains classified by domestic-violence experts as high-risk. Meanwhile her main protector, Steve, must leave the house. He will move down the coast to stay with his sister Chantel.

On the ABC, a woman was recently interviewed about her study on the importance of mothers in their sons' development. It came in the wake of a prestigious private school expelling boys for ranking female classmates on appearance, using degrading terms such as 'wifey' and 'rapeable.' The role of the internet in fueling toxic masculinity is a hot topic.

The following information is from Kellianne Costello and Brian Greenwald's 'Update on Domestic Violence and Traumatic Brain Injury: A Narrative Review' (US National Library of Medicine, 2022):
In the US, it is estimated that women suffering traumatic brain injury (TBI) due to domestic violence outnumber military and sports-related TBIs by a factor of 11 to 12. Victims often do not report abuse for fear of retribution or losing their children. Seventy-two percent are not identified when they present to emergency departments. Untreated TBI can lead to chronic traumatic encephalopathy, depression, suicidality, and Alzheimer-like symptoms.

In the US, intimate partner violence costs the economy an estimated $5–10 billion annually. The Department of Justice reports that 95% of assaults on spouses and ex-spouses are committed by men against women, and nearly 99% of rape and sexual-assault perpetrators are male ('Violence Against Women Report, 2002').

On May 1, 2018, Brain Injury Australia launched a report into the nation's first research on family violence and brain injury, 'The Prevalence of Acquired Brain Injury Among Victims and Perpetrators of Family Violence.' Among the findings: of the 16 000 Victorians who attended hospital due to family violence, two in every five sustained brain injury; and one in three victims were children. The violence was overwhelmingly male-on-female. Experts consider this only the tip of the iceberg as much goes unreported.

DAY 99 – LOW ACT

In the afternoon, Monica receives an email from Adele. Because of the allegations Sav has made against both Steve and Monica – and the fact they have each been served with DVOs – Adele suggests Monica save money, forgo the interim hearing, and move straight to a final hearing, where Sav will be cross-examined. The advice hits them all like a brick. Until now, every solicitor and expert has said that once the case came before an experienced senior registrar like Mansfield, Luca Savington's lies and manipulations would be exposed. Monica is distraught. So is everyone else. When the interim hearing date was set, it was already months away, but no-one had contemplated Benji's virtual imprisonment dragging on even longer. Yet Adele is an experienced solicitor, and if she thinks the odds are against Monica regaining Benji at an interim hearing, then that is the reality they must face. Which means Sav's tactics are working.

That night, when Chantel and Stephen arrive for Benji's soccer game, the mood is grim. Steve has cooked a chicken and vegetable curry. He has just added the final ingredients when he opens the cupboard above the stove and two cups tumble out, smashing on the granite benchtop and showering the curry with porcelain splinters. Chicken korma with chinaware is not very appetising.

It is a cold, wet night, and after soccer everyone is glad to return to the warmth. They had seats close to the action; Benji played well and clearly knew his support crew were there cheering him on. Sav kept to the far end of the grounds, well away from them.

They order takeaway pizza. Sienna arrives as the food does. Steve feels raw tonight and finds it hard to be pleasant to her. He is sympathetic to her predicament, but without her initial cooperation Sav may have found it far harder to manipulate the police. After dinner, Monica and Sienna take Daniel to his basketball game.

Monica returns from basketball in tears. How cruel and unrelenting can one man be? Sav has cancelled her Sunday visit with Benji. It is Mother's Day, and she has a present for him. The following week will be his ninth birthday.

Monica texts the supervisor, who says the reason given for the cancellation is that Monica breached a DVO. It is a fabrication – another example of Sav projecting his own actions onto her. By cancelling the visit, Sav has breached court orders. It should count against him in the long run, but that means little to Monica who desperately wants to see her son.

DAY 100 – UNDER ARREST

The wet weather continues. So much for the dry May that had been predicted. Monica visits the police station with her friend Beth. They have separate matters to file. When Monica reports the no-ID calls from Sav, Officer Reddington asks why she has waited so long to come in.

'Because I work all day and have a teenager to care for who plays sport,' Monica replies.

Reddington logs the report into the system but says the no-ID calls don't coincide with times Sav has used his phone to contact her. Monica can't believe what she's hearing. She keeps her composure as she points out that Sav uses multiple phones. The police's public rhetoric on domestic violence doesn't match the reality on the ground. Monica is an old hand by now and determined by nature. She insists the calls be formally logged.

Police stations can be intimidating places, and domestic violence victims are often fragile. Yet to get any action, the person must be assertive and articulate. If the experience is too confronting, victims don't return. Millions may be spent tackling domestic violence, but unless procedural inconsistency and ineptness are addressed at the first point of contact, progress will stall.

Beth, already nervous, finds the process stressful. Inside the station her phone won't work, sending her into a brief panic until she restarts it. The officer assigned to her is empathetic and treats her as a credible witness. She is taken into an interview room to make a statement. Sav's call to her is deemed another breach of the DVO.

When Monica returns home, she's buoyant. A text from ReKonnect has confirmed her visit with Benji is back on.

Later she realises she forgot to get an event number from Reddington – something her solicitor insists is important. She calls the station and asks to speak to Reddington, only to be told they don't allocate numbers that quickly. Monica knows this isn't true; she's been given event numbers immediately in the past. But what is she supposed to do – call the officer a liar? She shakes her head and ends the call. She's had enough for one day.

In the evening, around 8:30, Monica's former neighbour, Sarah, phones. Police have just left Sav's house. They were there for twenty minutes – and Sav, with Benji in tow, has been taken away in a police wagon. It is significant news – and deeply upsetting for Monica to know Benji has been carted off to the police station.

Monica discusses the situation briefly with Narelle and Steve, then calls the station where Benji has most likely been taken. She explains that she is Benji Savington's mother and wants to collect her son. The officer is unsure about the outcome of the arrest – whether Sav will be held overnight or not.

Monica and Narelle decide to drive up to the police station on the chance they can bring Benji back with them. With the interim DVO in place against Steve, if Benji comes home, Steve must leave. It is too late at night to turn up at his mother-in-law's, so he rings a friend of his and Narelle's in Maryville, just ten minutes away, who offers him a bed for the night.

When Monica and Narelle arrive at the police station, Benji won't even come out to say hello – a clear sign of the control his father exerts over him. When it becomes known that the police are keeping Sav locked up overnight, Monica insists she should be able to take her son. But Sav complains. He says he would rather Benji go with a welfare officer from DCJ than leave with his mother. It speaks volumes about the calibre of the man – but comes as no surprise. For a brief period, it seems they might get Benji, but the system shows Monica is only permitted supervised visits and that there is a DVO in place against her. The DVO against Steve is also a red flag and does nothing to help their cause.

The upshot is that Monica and Narelle leave without Benji. The police contact Sienna. While Monica and Narelle are driving back home, Sienna phones. She wants Monica to know she is on her way to collect Benji from the police station.

DAY 101 – SIENNA STANDS STRONG

Sienna rings Monica in the morning. She wants to bring Benji to the Mother's Day gathering at Beckie's place, where he would see familiar faces – people he has known all his life. But the catch is that if he goes, neither Monica nor Steve can be there. The court order states Monica is only allowed supervised visits with her son – and Steve has a DVO against him forbidding contact with his grandson.

They decide Benji should have the opportunity to see family he hasn't seen for well over three months. But a short time later, Sienna calls back. Benji is refusing to go. The reason he gives is that everyone will hate him because of the lies he's told. They do not force the issue. It is soul-destroying for Monica to hear that Benji is carrying such guilt.

Sienna contacts Monica again around 10 am. Sav has been released from custody. He wants Sienna to drive to the police station with Benji to pick him up, claiming he is stuck without enough money to get home. Sienna refuses, so Sav contacts Marco and gets him to phone Sienna to do his bidding. Monica reminds Sienna her father has other options – Leonardo is in the area and could drive over, or Sav could catch a bus or taxi. She tells Sienna not to believe his story about not having money.

Sienna holds firm. She has come too far to cave in now. She hasn't had contact with her father since she left, and Sav doesn't know where she lives – and she wants to keep it that way. Monica tells her to keep Benji and bring him to the scheduled 2 pm visit. Sienna equivocates, calling Monica back a couple of times. Sav has told her it is against the law for her to keep Benji.
'That's rubbish,' says Monica. It is difficult for Sienna, being pressured by her father, her brother and Monica. Sav is using the situation to try to gain sympathy from his daughter and to drag her back into his nefarious orbit. Sienna knows it is a trap – but resisting him is still difficult.

Sienna phones Georgia. She, Matt, and baby Emma speak with Benji, telling him how much they miss him and reminding him he is loved. Benji has always looked up to Matt and would gravitate towards him at family gatherings. Matt is of Portuguese descent and has similar brown skin to Benji, and they share a love of soccer and video games.

More went on the previous night at the police station than was first realised. The police told Sienna that before contacting her, they had phoned Leonardo – but he was deemed too drunk to collect Benji. Meanwhile, a perfectly capable mother who was present at the station was sent home, not permitted to take her son. There was no reason Benji could not have gone into the care of his nan, Narelle – his grandmother who has never had a DVO issued against her or so much as a parking fine. But Sav made such a fuss that the police did as he wanted and called Sienna. Once again, the police allowed Luca Savington to dictate.

Sienna defies her father, keeping Benji and bringing him to the scheduled visit in the afternoon. Benji is in a much better frame of mind than on any previous visit. He laughs and jokes with them. He hasn't been prepped by Sav and knows his father isn't lurking in the background. Monica gives Benji his presents and shares his birthday cake with him – he has two slices. Benji is sad when it comes time to say goodbye to Daniel and his mother. He will return to his life of seclusion with a mentally unhinged father.

As they are leaving, Daniel sees Sav on the escalator – dishevelled and angry. He is not supposed to arrive until after Monica has had time to leave, but he does as he wishes.

Narelle and Steve meet Monica and Daniel after the visit. Monica is in good spirits – it's the best interaction she has had with Benji so far. Steve says good-bye to the three of them and they part ways. He travels down to the Central Coast to stay with his sister.

SOMETHING IS SERIOUSLY WRONG 127

DAY 103 – EVATT FIRST RETURN

Today is the Evatt first return event. The judicial registrar will address procedural requirements such as subpoena requests and any further directions. With an interim hearing already set, no new date needs to be allocated. Benji has been assigned his own solicitor, and hopes are it is someone with insight, empathy, and experience – someone who will dig into the background and study the evidence.

Sav's neighbour contacts Monica: Leonardo has his car dashcam trained directly on her house. Sav must have worked out how Monica knew about his arrest and overnight stint in the cells. Leonardo's presence at Sav's home is becoming more regular, which is concerning. When Sienna lived there, Monica could at least be certain Benji was looked after. With Leonardo, there is no such reassurance.

Monica and Narelle get back from the First Return Event in high spirits. The barrister believes there is enough in the brief to argue Monica's case successfully and advises proceeding with the interim hearing. Adele, too, is more optimistic now. Something has clearly shifted since she initially advised against pursuing the hearing, though the reason is not disclosed.

Through his solicitor, Luca Savington claims he is running out of money and is pushing to avoid the interim hearing. He also wants the house sold quickly, asserting that because he has been paying the mortgage, he is entitled to a larger share of the assets. On top of that, he proposes each party keeps the household goods they currently hold – a suggestion skewed in his favour, as he possesses almost the entire contents of the house, apart from what he has already sold. Then there's the expensive car; 'All mine,' he says.

Adele confirms there are well over a hundred pages of DCJ reports on Benji's welfare, most detailing risks posed while in Sav's care. She has also floated the possibility that, due to Sav's lies and misinformation, he could be ordered to pay 70% of court costs. In family law, this is rare and would only be decided at the final hearing. Without substantial resources, a person in Monica's position could not realistically match Sav's litigation power unless they accessed Legal

Aid – and even that comes with limits.

- **Legal Aid in NSW** offers assistance with family law, but it is not entirely free. Applicants may have to contribute to costs, and the funding limit for a matter is $15,000 (excluding certain fees). If a legally aided person receives more than $30,000 from a property settlement, they must contribute towards costs. Legal aid is not available at all locations.

Monica's expenses have already exceeded $10,000 – and the plane is still on the runway.

Billy Holden returns Steve's earlier call for advice about whether to proceed with the interim hearing. The decision has now been made, but Billy's opinion mirrors that of the barrister; it is worth pursuing.

DAY 105 – BENJI IS UNSAFE

Monica:
Adele called me today and asked lots of questions about Leonardo and Saturday night. She's pushing for Benji to be with us much sooner. Should I drop cupcakes off for Benji's birthday to the class tomorrow morning?
Narelle:
Yes.
Monica:
Benji's been off school sick for most of the week. He didn't look sick on Sunday.

On Friday. Monica's solicitor Adele sent an email to Sav's solicitor, enquiring about Benji's care arrangements. Why had there been nobody to care for him the previous Saturday night? Was it true that the police had phoned Leonardo but deemed him too drunk to pick up Benji from the police station?

By putting forward Leonardo as a carer for Benji, Sav has inadvertently provided ammunition for Monica's legal team. In addition to his suspected drug dealings, Leonardo harassed and stalked his ex-girlfriend a couple of years previously, and a DVO was put in place to protect her.

According to Sav, Leonardo lives with him on a full-time basis, while his other son, Marco, comes home on weekends. On Saturday night, Sav claims, Leonardo had work commitments in Sydney. He maintains that Leonardo usually cares for Benji until he gets home from work.

There is also a DVO Leonardo obtained against his father in 2021. He had to persist, visiting several police stations before one was finally granted. Narelle and Steve remember the time well – Leonardo had come and stayed with them. Sav claimed then that it was his son who was the aggressor.

Monica, Narelle, Georgia, and Steve sometimes communicate through an online chat group, where they are privy to each other's posts.
Monica:
Benji turned nine today. I dropped off cupcakes and bouncing balls and Slinkys at Benji's school for the class to share with him.
Daniel got 7 points tonight. And got a few fouls because he played hard.
Georgia:
Woohoo Daniel! Well done! Did Daniel get his KFC?
Narelle:
Of course.

Chantel suggests they get the Life 360 app for Monica to share her location in case of an emergency.

DAY 107 – SAV ON THE BACKFOOT

Monica, 2:15 pm group chat:
Sienna confirmed with me that the police officer told her that on Saturday night Leonardo sounded too intoxicated on the phone to pick up Benji. She also said he had been staying at Merryland, occasionally going to Sav's. Sarah said Marco was there last night.

Georgia:
Marco Flip-Flop Savington.
Monica:
I think I'll send an email to Elle requesting a drug test.
Georgia:
Yes. Sav should do one too. If he's caring for Benji.

Monica 5:09 pm:
Policeman Blackwell called. Sav has a warrant out for his arrest for slashing tyres and private calls. That may have been what he was charged with last Saturday night.
Georgia:
Wow. How did they prove the tyres?
Monica:
Unsure.
Georgia:
No wonder he doesn't want the interim hearing. On the 28th of May he might be in a lot of trouble.

Blackwell is the police officer who visited the Hamilton house to question Monica about Sav's latest alleged death threat. He was also the officer Monica and Steve had first spoken to about the tyre slashing. Officer Blackwell also happened to be on front-desk duty when Steve and Narelle dropped by the station to collect Steve's DVO. Narelle told him about Sav's arrest, and he replied that he hadn't yet put in his report on the tyres.
'I wish he'd hurry up,' Steve said afterwards with annoyance.

But Officer Blackwell had been anything but slack. At the time of the tyre slashing, he asked Monica to return to the station to draw a map of exactly where she had seen Sav. It seems he was the one who pinged Sav's phone to establish he was in the area. He must have put in a lot of work to lay the accusation that Sav slashed the tyres – it's commendable.

Monica:
Earlier, I saw Benji play soccer. Went with Chantel and Daryl. His team lost. Didn't play his best. Sav went over and stood behind Benji, and the coach yelled, really loud, 'Sav, move.'
That was my highlight for the night.

Georgia:

He'll probably get an AVO out on the coach.

Monica to her solicitor, Adele:

I spoke with Sienna Savington over the weekend, and she confirmed the police told her on Saturday, when Sav was arrested, that Leonardo was too intoxicated to care for Benji. As Sav has advised, Leonardo is caring for Benji, I would like to request Leonardo is drug tested to see if he is still using. With Sav's recent arrest and Leonardo's drug history I am becoming increasingly concerned for Benji's safety in the care of Sav and Leonardo.

Kind regards,

Monica Savington.

Steve:

Benji was about six at the time. We were about to walk our bikes through the railway tunnel at Broadmeadow Station. Benji looked at the signage and began breaking the words into syllables and sounded them out: skate boards, per mitt ed, pen al ties, trans port, pass en ger. And he knew what they meant. It was impressive, having a grasp of phonetics at such an early age. Like with Daniel, Monica always read to him. So did Narelle when he stayed over at Hamilton. He'd select a book from the bookcase near the television. Benji and I would have these crazy conversations using made-up phrases. We'd banter back and forth, using tone and inflection to express the meaning. Narelle used to think our exchanges were hilarious. 'Fgrr nrr mss opps ti, Benji' The response. 'Arrr. Vineto dring. Impi cardo. Herr fundi.'

Benji loved playing hide and seek. Once the game started, he would want to play forever. There weren't that many places to hide inside the house, so I'd pretend I didn't know where he was, making silly comments until he'd crack up and reveal where he was hiding. When he got older, we'd play the same game at Gregson Park. He was impossible to see if he hid in the bush or climbed a tree, and I'd sometimes get worried when I couldn't find him. Benji loved playing cards and board games. He was hard to beat at Connect Four. He could plan three or four moves ahead. He loved to win, hated losing. Whenever Monica took the boys to New Lambton for a visit, he'd play cards with Great Grandma Irene.

DAY 110 – BAD BEHAVIOUR

Monica:

Sienna called. Marco went ballistic in her car. His girlfriend broke up with him, and he took it out on his sister. She called the police on him.

Georgia:

Oh… the poor girl.

Monica:

The police said, 'We know your father.' They took Marco into the station.

Georgia:

Like father like son.

Monica:

Sienna said she didn't want him charged, but they said they might need to put an DVO out on her behalf.

Georgia:

He needs to address his own problems. Remember the trouble he caused his last girlfriend? And he tried to sue for defamation. Is Sienna ok? Did he hurt her?

Monica:

She seemed ok. He didn't physically hurt her but lots of yelling and banging on her car.

Georgia:

Would've been scary. Was he doing it when the police came?

Monica:

Leonardo came and got him before the police arrived.

Georgia:

Did Marco call Leonardo?

Monica:

Yep.

Georgia:

Its good Sienna called you. Do the boys know where she lives?

Monica:

Marco does.

Georgia:

Eek. That's concerning. It would be very isolating. She tried really hard to hold onto the thought that Marco was different. She seems to be doing a good job at setting her boundaries. But it's lonely when it's all the family. I feel for her. I hope Benji is ok.

Monica:

I heard from one of the mums that Benji is playing up in class, saying inappropriate things to the kids. One of the kids asked him where his mother was. Benji said she was in gaol. I feel gutted. And helpless.

Georgia:

He'll come through this.

Monica:

Yes xxx.

DAY 112 – THE TIDE TURNS

ReKonnect 9:22 am:

Hey Monica, just confirming the visit for this weekend. We have it for Sunday 3:45 at the Swinburne Sports Complex. That is located at 28C Harris Avenue, Aberdeen Park. If you please park near the basketball courts and meet supervisor Anne at the tables.

ReKonnect 10:46 am:

Hi Monica, unfortunately Sav is unable to make that time. We are going to have to reschedule to next weekend. Apologies.

Monica:

Oh no. I was going to help Benji with his speech for school. Did he give a reason?

Fionna:

Just because it was so late in the day. I'm sorry Monica. I will try for next weekend.

Narelle:

Interesting, especially before your Child Impact Assessment. Won't look good for him, but so disappointing for you.

Georgia:

This sucks Monica. Keep hanging in there. His power is declining, and he knows it.

Steve:

Is it worth contacting the main office?

Monica:
We'll tell Adele tomorrow.

On Friday, Monica and Narelle have an extended meeting with Adele. They both prepare their affidavits for the upcoming hearing. Solicitors tend to play their cards close to the chest – they probably need to, as gossip can cost the element of surprise. But Adele does reveal that the Child Impact Report has labelled Sav as an abusive father who is using his child to get back at the mother. This might seem obvious, but such a declaration is rare and bodes well for the interim hearing. Furthermore, the Independent Children's Lawyer (ICL) is furious with Sav's solicitor for not disclosing that Sav was incarcerated – that Benji was taken to the police station with him and ended up spending the night with Sienna. Benji's solicitor now wants Sienna's address.

In what appears to be a tactical move to deter Monica from proceeding with the interim hearing, Sav's solicitor has offered weekly Sunday visits. It is the first sign that Sav is on the defensive. His stated reason for denying Monica access to Benji is that she is an unfit mother – yet suddenly Sunday visits, without ReKonnect's involvement, are on the table. Perhaps the tide is beginning to turn.

The ludicrous claims of alcohol abuse have already been discredited by follicle test results and Monica's professional work history. But the lines of attack Sav and his solicitor have used for the past three months are unlikely to change at the interim hearing. His main weapon will likely be Monica's mental health – a fear-driven tactic. Medicare records, doctor's statements, and reports from the Hunter Mental Health team all show Monica to be a perfectly capable parent. Still, Adele wants a backstop. That is where Narelle comes in – a retired deputy principal with no criminal record, who later worked at the university running community education programs, she will be hard to discredit.

Adele requires Monica's account of what transpired at Benji's last soccer game. According to Sav, Benji wet his pants because he was upset by his mother and family being present. But when Narelle, Beckie and Steve later spoke with the coach, he said he noticed no change in Benji's behaviour. Nobody saw Benji wet his pants.

Adele also wants a copy of the texts Monica received from the parents of Benji's classmates about Benj's inappropriate behaviour at school. 'I'm going home to lick a vagina,' was one example – a shocking phrase for a child to repeat. Another mother had texted Monica after her own child said Benji claimed his mother was in gaol.

Monica's solicitor has also obtained two DCJ reports from the past. One relates to Sav physically abusing Sienna at age 16. Monica remembers the incident well. The second relates to Daniel when he was eight. Details are vague, but whoever made the report knew the family well enough to name the children. Monica had not known about either report until now.

Meanwhile, Steve attends his appointment with the forensic psychologist. The discussion inevitably circles back to Sav's behaviour – and the criminal patterns that have emerged. The psychologist echoes what Monica has already been told by domestic violence workers: Sav will be more dangerous if he believes he is losing. The sessions do little to ease Steve's fears over the allegations made against him, but they offer insight. From his behaviour since the separation, Sav appears vengeful, incapable of empathy or guilt, and perfectly comfortable manipulating others for personal gain. Although the psychologist does not label him, he advises that arguing or appealing to decency with such a person seldom works.

Steve:
From my perspective, having an understanding into his behaviour is useful for everyone's safety. Much of what Sav has done so far, apart from harassing Monica at the soccer, has been underhand. His vengeful acts have been relentless and brazen and always preferring manipulation rather than direct confrontation. But will he act in a similar manner if Benji is placed in Monica's care? Will he cause damage to those who happen to be near him, and seek out those who have abandoned him?

Sienna meets Monica and Steve at Broadmeadow Stadium to watch Daniel's basketball game. She expresses concern about Marco, saying he is stuck in the middle and doesn't know who to trust. Steve thinks that's a cop-out, but he holds his tongue. Sienna then talks about her recent trip to Sydney. Her demeanour changes when Monica tells her the ICL wants to contact her. She becomes defensive, not wanting to get involved.

Later that night, Narelle and Steve are watching Television when a news item soon has their attention. In the affluent Perth suburb of Floreat, Jennifer Petelczyc and her youngest daughter are murdered after becoming the unsuspected victims following the marriage breakdown of a family friend. The pair were fatally shot by Mark Bombara who stormed their house. Bombara is the husband of one of Jennifer's closest friends. Bombara went to the address after finding out his partner had sought refuge there. Neighbours saw Bombara driving up and down the street multiple times before he entered the house. After shooting both women, he then turned the gun on himself.

Steve glances across at Narelle. Both are shaken by the story, at the senseless waste of lives. But there is something else. No words are needed. Each knows what the other is thinking, the fear – the elephant in the room. Just how far is Sav willing to go? He has already crossed lines that once seemed unimaginable, with total disregard for Benji, Monica and Steve. They know he has a bullet. Does he have access to a gun?

DAY 117 – THE WAITING GAME

Steve:

It's been over five weeks, and the detectives haven't come back. The DVO is still in place, and the dark shadow still hangs over me. It is unnerving, constantly wondering if they will turn up. Whenever a car pulls up outside, I check to see if it is the detectives coming to arrest me. It is difficult to concentrate on anything, impossible to relax. As the barrister postulated, it is likely the detectives have more information than they have so far revealed. And there is the real possibility that Sav has concocted more fabrications.

Steve and Narelle discuss his appointment with the forensic psychologist. Narelle says there is no point appearing calm and unperturbed, putting up a stoic front. They were both raised to be resilient – to grin and bear it, not to indulge in self-pity. In their working-class world, not coping was seen as weakness. The unfortunate reality is that people like Sav – skilled at playing the victim, lying, exaggerating, and free of any moral compass – often succeed within our systems.

What is beginning to undo Sav is his ego, impulsiveness, and the fact that he is not clever enough to keep up with his own fiction. Recent fabrications contradict past ones. Witnesses can dismiss his claims. But for now, it is still working for him.

Narelle, Chantel, and Steve attend court. Sav is charged with breaching his DVO by use of a carriage service – the two no-ID calls to Monica. He arrives after 10 am and pleads not guilty. He is granted bail until the hearing.

At 10:30 am, Monica attends her interview for the Evatt List Impact Study. Benji will be interviewed the following day. Sav had already completed his interview, which explains his late arrival at court.

During her interview, Monica is asked probing questions about her mental health. She has nothing to hide – the truth is clear in the medical records. She has control of her mental health and is high functioning and reliable. She explains how Benji was taken, isolated, kept from her without reason, lied to, and told to lie. She describes the recent calls from mothers at Benji's school, alarmed at his inappropriate behaviour. Asked whether she would keep Benji at the same school if she gained custody, she answers yes – her work is nearby, and Daniel attends a neighbouring school.

Monica is told that Sav has claimed she frequently bashed him and that he has witnesses. She denies it. Surely the interviewer is too canny to fall for such gaslighting. Sienna is free of Sav's control, so the only 'witnesses' could be Marco and Leonardo. This devastates Narelle, knowing how much Monica has done for Sav's older boys. That they would betray her with such lies is painful. But Steve points out the boys might not even know their names are being used.

Sav has also claimed that his parents once had to care for Monica because she fought with her own family. Who does he think she is living with now? The truth is simple – twelve years ago Monica stayed at his parents' property in Bulga for a few days to recuperate. Sav's story is just another projection. In fact, leading up to Christmas last year – only weeks before the separation – Monica and the boys had been at a family gathering at Narelle and Steve's. Afterwards, Sav was in a foul mood and drove dangerously on the way home, terrifying Monica and the children. His reason? Monica's family all got along, and he was jealous because his own family were always fighting.

Monica's interview runs for over an hour. At the end, the interviewer thanks her for her honesty – a positive sign.

On Friday, Donald Trump is found guilty in New York on numerous charges relating to the Stormy Daniels affair. His body language in court – slumped shoulders, head downcast – is strikingly similar to Luca Savington's mannerisms. Both play the victim. Woe is me; I've been so badly maligned by a woman. To many, it looks weak and unmanly – yet for them, it seems to work.

Steve:
These narcissists seem to fool a lot of people with their lies and bluster. Remind you of someone?
Georgia:
Definitely like Sav. Maybe the tide is turning on narcissists. It won't affect Trump's chances of becoming president though.

It's International Children's Day. Monica receives an email from her solicitor. Sav is again pressing her to sell the house. His solicitor demands details of all assets within 28 days to avoid court proceedings. Monica's solicitor intends to play along – she will accept Sav's material but not respond in kind.

Sienna phones Monica. Her car has broken down, and she needs two thousand dollars for repairs. In the past she would have called her father. Monica drives over to collect her so she can attend Daniel's basketball game. Steve meets them at the stadium. The team loses, but Daniel plays well and scores a few goals.

It's Sunday, the first day of winter, and one of the quietest periods since Benji was taken over four months ago. Monica has her scheduled visit with Benji. Returning from the visit, Daniel enters the house first. Narelle asks him how it went. His response is brief, in the way of teenage boys: 'Good.' Monica, however, is upbeat. Benji was reserved at first but relaxed as the visit went on. He gave his mother a hug before she left. With the interim hearing due Friday week, they hope it will be the last of the supervised visits.

DAY 123 – DETECTIVE BAUER

Steve is at Gosford Courthouse with his sister Chantel, waiting for their nephew to appear. Until this year, Steve had rarely been to court or dealt with police and lawyers – apart from job-related matters when he worked with youth at risk. This year, it has been nothing but. They have come hoping their nephew, who is facing drug-related charges, might be eligible for a rehabilitation program as an alternative to jail.

As they wait for the 11 o'clock deadline, Chantel receives a phone call from Narelle, wanting to speak to Steve who has left his phone in the car. Leaving the courtroom, Steve has an innate feeling – the same one he had when detectives first visited – that the call relates to the sexual interference allegations. He paces the foyer, jumpy as a joey at a gym, waiting for Narelle to answer.

His hunch was correct. Detective Lizbeth Bauer has just left the Hamilton house. She was in the company of a police officer. When they asked for Steve, Narelle told them he was staying down the coast with his sister Chantel and wouldn't be back until later in the week. Narelle's conversation with Bauer was interesting. Bauer told Narelle she didn't get the impression Steve was the intimidating type. Apparently, Sav had told Bauer he was terrified of Steve. For that reason, the detective accompanying her when she first came to speak with Steve was carrying a gun. Once again, Sav overcooked it. Steve is over seventy and Luca Savington is a large, strong man in his forties. When Narelle tells Steve that Bauer is aware Benji has been schooled by Sav, he feels enormous relief. They hadn't come to arrest him. Bauer is sympathetic to Steve's predicament but still wants to talk to him. She will phone him in a couple of hours.

When they spoke about the case, Bauer asked Narelle if they had thought of snatching Benji back? Narelle explained that they didn't get the opportunity. After Benji was taken, Sav kept him from school and didn't even allow him to venture outside the house, not even into the backyard. Then Monica's mental health began to deteriorate, which lead to her hospitalisation. She was still recovering when Bancroft served her with two DVOs.

If Monica had gone near Sav or her son with the DVOs in place, not only would

Benji have been returned to the father, but Monica would have been charged with breaching the DVOs. They'd also been under the impression that once the case came before a court, the registrar would see through Sav's lies and mischief, and order that Benji be returned to his mother. But the junior registrar did nothing. Which resulted in the bizarre situation of Monica having to pay for supervised visits.

Steve goes back into the court knowing the worst is over. His nephew Luke is yet to arrive. Two cases came before the magistrate, and both involve threats that breach DVOs. The magistrate dresses down the offenders and warns them not to threaten their ex-partners. Both men are given bail.

On the drive home, Bauer calls. She makes it clear she does not believe the allegations, and that Sav has a history of this sort of behaviour – whether she means lying to police or coercing children to make false claims, he is unsure – though she must follow process. She asks Steve if he will make a statement. He replies, 'There is nothing to say.'

Bauer says she will speak with her boss. While Steve is mulling over just what that means, Bauer speaks. What she says gives him reason to be jubilant. The investigation is complete. He will not be charged. Bauer, almost apologetic, explains it is not within her scope to withdraw the DVO – she apparently wants to, but her boss won't allow it – yet the most damaging clause, restricting Steve from being within 200 metres of Benji, will be removed. Only the generic conditions will remain: no stalking, harassment, threats, intimidation, or destruction of property. The new order will take effect in two weeks when it is due to be heard in court. She will call back tomorrow after speaking further with her boss, but she repeats – the investigation is finished.

Although a DVO is still in place, a weight lifts from Steve's shoulders. It has been a harrowing time, and the relief is palpable. Chantel feels it too. False accusations are still allegations, and if the matter had gone to court, the cost – both financial and reputational – would have been severe. As the forensic psychologist said, mud sticks. Steve contacts the friends and family who stood by him, people who felt his pain vicariously.

Text from Detective Lizbeth Bauer to Monica:
Hi Monica,
I was wondering if you could give me a call when you have a spare minute. I

am the officer in charge of the complaint made by Benji against your father.
It's not urgent.
Thanks,
Lizbeth Bauer
Newcastle Child Abuse Squad.
Georgia:
Oooo good. It's urgent to us, officer.

Monica, Narelle, and Steve receive notification in the mail. They have been subpoenaed by the ICL representing Benji to supply details of criminal charges and DVO orders by the end of the month. Sav, Leonardo, Marco, and Sienna have been ordered to do likewise, according to the letter.

DAY 124 – DRAMATIC TURNAROUND

Monica 8:17 am:
Detective Lizbeth Bauer is coming to house tomorrow at 4 pm. She said it's nothing to worry about. She needs to ask me about something Benji said in his statement. To tick off she has investigated it.
Georgia:
Yeah… ok.
Narelle:
We'll see. I'll be there.
Georgia:
Be careful with detectives. They're not your friends. I think they pretend. So they don't have to do formal interviews. And that way it's easier for them to get information. No lawyers, and the person willingly did the interview. That's my experience from TV shows anyway.
Monica:
Yeah. I'll be careful.
Narelle:
Lisbeth is working to get rid of Steve's DVO. The two I spoke to yesterday were very real. They said they knew what was going on.
Georgia:
Ok, that's good.

Narelle:
They didn't ask any tricky questions.
Steve:
Monica will know what to say. She's an old hand at this. The truth is all we need.

Steve has been visiting a friend at Empire Bay and is driving back through Budgewoi when Monica calls. She has just heard from her solicitor, Adele – the Child Impact Study report has been released.

Sav, as always, tried to play the victim. He repeated the lies that had worked with police and earned him two DVOs: that Monica drank excessively, had untreated mental health issues, was violent, and had sent him death threats. This time, the tactics backfired. The interviewer was not as gullible and saw through the manipulation. She is critical of Sav for withholding Benji from his mother and family and rejects his excuses for keeping the boy from school, sport, and social activities.

Benji claimed his mother hit him 'all the time,' echoing Sav's police report – yet Sav never mentioned it during the interview, which struck the assessor as odd. When asked, 'How long did your mother smack you? Was it all the time or just for a week?' Benji replied, 'Just for a week.' The lack of detail – the clipped phrases, the absence of context – mirrored the sexual interference allegations. It was obvious to the interviewer that Benji had been coached.

The recommendation is unequivocal; Monica should have full custody of Benji, with Sav limited to supervised visits. A dramatic turnaround.

After months of distress and heartache, the outcome feels almost surreal. Monica and her supporters breathe a collective sigh of relief. With the interim hearing ten days away, the prospect of Benji's return has grown stronger.

DAY 125 – DASHCAM

Detective Bauer contacts Monica but postpones their meeting until the following Wednesday. Monica had braced herself for the appointment, so the delay is frustrating. The house had been scrubbed in preparation – no small task with Roxie's shedding fur and the added clutter of Monica and Daniel living there. Bauer insists the meeting is procedural, so she cannot be accused of cutting corners. Even so, the accusations against Steve were grave, and the visit must be taken seriously.

Sav will be ropeable when he finds out about the Impact Study outcome. Will he be capable of waiting calmly for nine days, knowing Benji might be taken from him? News from Monica's former neighbours suggests Sav hasn't been to work in over a week. With his absences piling up between court dates and interviews, perhaps he has already lost his job. A friend offers to install a dashcam system in Monica's car. Both Narelle and Steve urge her to accept. She arranges to have it done the following week.

Meanwhile, Sienna's car remains off the road, making her commute to university difficult. Monica helps where she can, ferrying her to and from classes.

Chantel and Phillip drive up from Budgewoi to celebrate Steve's birthday. The family goes to Verde Luna, the Italian restaurant just down the road. They order Sicilian seafood pasta, chicken parmi, and pizza. The food is excellent. Dessert is enjoyed back at the house – a simple, warm celebration.

DAY 132 – PREDICTABLE TACTIC

Chantel and Steve go for an ocean swim at Norah Head. The water is cold but exhilarating. A few others are also braving a dip, while onlookers stare as though they are unhinged. Steve notices the chill barely registers. His mental anguish is so intense that physical discomfort scarcely touches him.

Detective Bauer visits the house and speaks with Monica. She reiterates what Narelle and Steve were already told – the DVO against Steve will remain, but the restriction on his proximity to Benji will be removed, and there will be no charges or further investigation. Once the DVO is formalised in court next week, Steve can legally stay in the same house as Benji. Bauer again makes it clear she is aware of Sav's manipulations. When Monica asks if Sav will face any consequences, Bauer does not answer.

The neighbours watch as Sav's Ford is towed away. It must have broken down. Perhaps parts are hard to come by, or he cannot afford repairs. If Sav has another vehicle, it is problematic for Monica, though the neighbours may yet manage to get a photo.

Later, Monica and Narelle meet with Adele and their barrister to prepare for Friday's interim hearing. Adele remains confident about Monica's chances but also stresses the need to be ready if the decision does not go her way. Then Adele reveals something remarkable, one more window into Luca Savington's ego – he has sent an email directly to the senior registrar. Adele does not know the content, but surely Sav must realise that attempting to interfere with the judiciary is something the court will not take lightly.

Sav's tactics for the interim hearing are predictable. In his affidavit he rehashes the lies he has already fed to police and solicitors: that Monica suffers serious mental health issues, has been admitted to the Mater hospital on multiple occasions, and is incapable of caring for her child. Sav's solicitor has access to her medical records, so they know the ambos took her to hospital. He claims her alcoholism makes the problem worse – that she drinks two bottles of wine each night (sometimes four) and becomes violent, assaulting both him and Benji. That he has been called names in front of Benji – arsehole, shithead, wanker, wog – and casts himself as the saviour who has kept the boy safe. He asserts Monica could not manage daily tasks and that he was always stepping in to help. And a new development is his claim: that Monica punched Sienna.

Sav's team also seeks to undermine the maternal grandfather by pointing to the DVO and accusations against him. That line of attack has lost bite now that Steve no longer lives at the Hamilton house. Instead, Sav twists the sexual abuse allegations, claiming Benji told Monica, but she ignored it, and that Narelle screamed at the boy when he confided in her.

Sav's ploy of shifting dates and inventing witnesses is again apparent. At the soccer game where he chased Monica and Narelle, Sav now claims Leonardo was present – though Leonardo was never mentioned in his original account to police. Five witnesses can swear he was not there. The police have already dealt with that incident and found Sav in breach of his DVO.

Sav revives another story: that Benji urinated himself at soccer. The reason now changes – not because of Monica, but from fear of Steve. Sav even claims a Child Abuse Squad detective told him Benji disclosed 'a significant amount of concerning detail' and that Steve would have to be interviewed.

Sav asserts he is stressed from Monica's supposed death threats and now needs psychological support. He downplays the DVO served on him by Leonardo, saying it was merely over a scratch on Narelle's car.

He relies on the two DVOs police granted him: one to argue Monica is violent, the other to claim she placed death threats in his mailbox. He laments his estrangement from Sienna, professes his love for her, and adds further malicious accounts of Poppy smacking Benji and pushing him down a stairwell. He denies bringing flowers to Monica's workplace, though witnesses saw him. He denies making hundreds of phone calls, though the police have the records.

Leonardo has also sworn an affidavit. He states that he lived in Melbourne for three months before moving in with Sav. He falsely claims he runs a solar installation business, and that he played premier league soccer. He says he attended the April 7 soccer match where he heard Monica and Steve abuse his father, and that he comforted Benji, saying 'Do not worry, I will help you.' Five witnesses contradict him, and the police have already ruled on the incident. Leonardo perjures himself further, claiming he was the one who rang Monica from his father's phone, that he saw her drinking to excess, and that in December 2023 she threw eight or nine punches at Sav – punches that, conveniently, had no effect.

Steve:
No bruises this time. Get the story straight, Leonardo. That Leonardo is prepared to lie for his father and defame his stepmother, despite all that Monica has done for him, is despicable, and immoral. The statements again show the power Sav exerts over his family. That Leonardo

has put himself in the firing line, shows his naivety.

Sav is seeking sole responsibility for Benji. His proposal allows Monica only limited, supervised contact, each alternate Saturday and Sunday from 9 am to 5 pm, with the supervision to be carried out by the maternal grandmother. He offers only restricted access on special occasions and at Christmas. Communication, he says, should occur solely through the Talking Parent app. He further insists that Benji have no contact with his paternal grandfather, Steve Kelty.

Benji is absent from school. It raises immediate concern. There is a persistent, nagging fear that Sav might run off with the boy. It seems unlikely he would do so before securing his share of the property settlement – but the possibility lingers.

DAY 134 – INTERIM HEARING

- **The Family Court** was established by Gough Whitlam in 1975. It began in a time of political turmoil, and when it opened its doors the following year, it lacked resources and expertise. It also had to contend with strong moral and social objections, those who saw twelve-month no-fault divorce as contrary to the social and moral standards of the day. (John Fogarty, Judge designate 1975)

The interim hearing has been a slow train coming. Yet, being on the Evatt List, this case has moved faster than most. Many parents, including Monica, could never afford both a barrister and a solicitor without financial assistance. Technically, it is possible to represent oneself, but few could master the legal requirements while enduring the emotional toll of having their child's future on the line.

Monica has played by the rules – honest, consistent, and straightforward. Will it pay off? The barrister is confident. But those with little faith, who have watched the justice and welfare systems fail at every turn, are not so sure. Adele, experienced and pragmatic, warns Monica to be ready for the worst. That advice alone is sobering and does little to inspire confidence in the process.

Georgia travels up from Sydney on Thursday night with baby Emma so she can support Monica in court. Narelle joins the pre-court meeting with the solicitor and barrister.

For legal reasons, the actual Family Court proceedings have been omitted.

PRE-COURT MEETING

Adele has received the ReKonnect supervisor's report. It is favourable to Monica – meticulous, detailed, and leaving nothing unnoticed:
On the first visit, Benji doesn't engage with Monica. Adele makes a note, that it had been ten weeks since the child has seen his mother. Monica is patient and engages in an activity that brings Benji out of his shell.
Next visit with Daniel – his brother that is closest in age. Benji goes off playing with his brother. Mother is persistent and Benji opens up.
Third visit, Sienna took Benji to the supervised visit. Unlike the earlier visits, Benji engages freely with his mother. It is reported that he immediately hugged Daniel and Monica and enjoyed his birthday cake. Benji knows that this time his father is not in the vicinity. He plays games at Time Zone with Daniel and keeps checking that his mum is watching him play.

What wasn't known, but comes as no surprise, is that the ReKonnect states the father attempted to cancel every single visit between Benji and his mother:
Visit 1 – father requests an extension, saying Benji is sick. When the supervisor informs him, he will have to pay for the canceled visit as it's within 24 hours, the father calls back, saying Benji is OK after some Panadol and will attend.
Visit 2 – father texts again to say Benji is sick. Again, he is notified he will have to pay. Again, Benji makes a recovery and attends the visit.
Visit 3 – father cancels. Goes to jail. Sienna can take Benji, so the visit is on.
Visit 4 – father postpones visit as 3.45 pm, saying it is too late in the day.

THE BARRISTER'S STRATEGY

Monica's barrister will use Sienna's affidavit if it strengthens Monica's case at the right moment. Sienna has told Narelle, Steve, and Georgia that Sav was physically abusive towards her and coerced her into making false statements to police. She describes the disturbing repetition of his behaviour; what he is doing to Monica, he also did to Sienna's mother. Sienna recalls Sav fabricating death threats and making sure she and Benji were present when he opened the letters. Her fear now is that he is instilling the same fear in Benji – and she worries he may even abscond with the child, having mentioned plans to 'visit the country' for six weeks.

DEPARTMENT OF COMMUNITIES AND JUSTICE (DCJ) REPORTS

Monica's solicitor holds notes from the DCJ case worker confirming that Benji is enduring significant psychological harm. The full DCJ reports – over one hundred pages – have been obtained. While some material was supplied by Sav, the overwhelming majority favour Monica.

ESTABLISHING THE HISTORY

The barrister intends to start from when Monica first left Sav. For six weeks, Monica had both boys in her care, while Sav saw Benji only on weekends. This was the accepted status quo; the child's home was with his mother and maternal grandparents.

That changed when Sav unilaterally removed Benji from school, drove him five hours to his parents' home and kept him out of school for over six weeks. This shows both his capacity for control and the harm he has caused. Afterwards, he withheld Benji from Monica without justification.

The mother didn't want supervised visits, but it was all the father would agree to. According to the barrister, the junior registrar who heard the initial application didn't have the power to make changes. If that was the case, Monica wasted thousands of dollars on solicitor and court fees for nothing.

MENTAL HEALTH AND ALCOHOL CLAIMS

The barrister will show Monica's mental health only became fragile after Benji was taken. This is supported by the hospital social worker's report, Monica's medical records, and her doctor's statement.

The allegations of alcohol abuse are disproven by the follicle test and her treating doctor. The barrister will emphasise that the DVO against Monica is disputed and inconsistent – it does not establish any risk to Benji. Sav's claim of receiving death threats has already been disproven; if others sent threats, it is irrelevant to Monica's parenting.

Monica's hospital admission will be directly addressed. This approach could result in the court allowing the social worker's damning letter about Sav to be admitted as evidence. The emergency triage notes show Monica was briefly confused and disoriented but stabilised within hours and voluntarily admitted herself for a medication review.

This demonstrates a mother who recognises her health needs and acts responsibly. She has managed her mental health for years with low-dose medication, while working full time and completing an Associate Diploma in Aged Care. In stark contrast, Sav shows no responsibility for his behaviour.

EVIDENCE OF COERCIVE CONTROL

The barrister will highlight Sav's coercive control: bringing Benji to a mental health ward, impersonating a police officer on the phone, and even posing as Monica's cousin – all to pressure her into contact. His aggressive behaviour towards staff is further evidence of his controlling tendencies.

The Child Impact Study, together with the hospital social worker's letter, demonstrate that Sav has consistently used Benji as a tool against Monica. The pattern of coercive control is not speculative – it is established.

INCONSISTENCIES AND FALSEHOODS

The barrister will expose the contradictions between Sav's affidavits, police statements, and the accounts of his sons. His fabrications shift with each telling, undermining his credibility.

In the Child Impact Statement, Sav even trivialised his breach of the DVO: 'Silly me, I didn't realise I couldn't call her.' Such flippancy in relation to court orders speaks volumes about his contempt for the law.

THE INDEPENDENT CHILDREN'S LAWYER (ICL)

The Independent Children's Lawyer (ICL) holds powerful evidence that supports Monica and undermines Sav. As the child's advocate, she speaks directly on Benji's behalf and is in a position of influence. The ICL has compiled two full pages of police records documenting attendances at Sav's house while Benji was present. She has never seen so many incidents. The relevance is clear; repeated police call-outs are causing ongoing psychological harm to the child.

The ICL and Monica's barrister will press for Sav's long history of domestic violence orders (DVOs) to be admitted. Monica herself had been unaware of earlier incidents that predate their relationship, but the record is telling:

2021 (Feb) – DVO
2021 (Feb) – Assault
2019 (Mar) – DVO
2019 (Feb) – DVO
2010 – Police called, child at risk
2009 – Police called, child at risk
2008 – DV incident
2007 (Oct) – DVO
2007 (Sept) – Assault
2007 (Aug) – Assault
2001 – DVO

DEATH THREAT ALLEGATIONS

Sav has accused Monica of sending death threats. These were investigated and no charges resulted. He claims the notes were delivered with banging on the door. Evidence shows Monica was in hospital then, proving she was not responsible. The obvious conclusion: Sav himself is engineering fear in Benji. This is psychological abuse, deliberately damaging Benji's relationship with his mother.

WITHDRAWAL OF COMPLAINTS

The ICL notes a disturbing pattern; complaints against Sav are routinely withdrawn by victims, a hallmark of coercive control. In 2021, Leonardo himself obtained a DVO against Sav. Sav later claimed it was withdrawn, that he did not need to attend court, and that Leonardo was the aggressor. Yet hospital records show Leonardo presented with a dislocated shoulder. He stayed with Narelle and Steve afterwards, and only later did they realise how serious the injury was.

The ICL's argument is damning; if Sav can cause such an injury to a fit 20-year-old male, what risk does a nine-year-old boy face? And if Sav's version is true – that Leonardo injured himself by throwing items – then he is plainly unfit to provide safe care for any child.

SOCCER INCIDENT

The soccer incident further exposes Sav's lies. He claims Monica harassed Benji at the soccer game, and Leonardo now asserts he was present. Evidence from five witnesses proves Leonardo was not there, and the police have already dealt with Sav's own breach of DVO on that occasion. The real issue is the psychological abuse of Benji, being manipulated into fear and used as a pawn in Sav's conflict with Monica.

OPTIMSTIC

Narelle came back from the meeting with Adele in an optimistic mood. Both the ICL and Monica's legal team are on the same page. The Child Impact Report concludes that the child's views are being influenced by Father. The child is now 'scared' of his mother after an extended period with no visits. This is detrimental to the child. There has been no contact with the mother for over sixteen weeks. How could Benji fear his mother unless the father is feeding him these ideas?

It was also revealed by the ICL that phrases Benji used in his interview with the Child Abuse Squad (watched me in the shower, touched me all over) were the same ones that Leonardo used to accuse his uncle all those years ago.

According to DCJ, the child is at serious risk of harm and is being psychologically abused. The ICL will be arguing for a six-week moratorium on the father's time with the child. The child needs a break – time solely in his mother's care – to re-establish the safe and secure attachment he had before his father snatched him away. In this matter, there is a complexity of risk with the father.

The ICL is recommending to the court that Benji have no contact with Steve while the DVO remains in place. Adele wants to contest this, but with limited court time the barrister advises letting it stand for now. To press the issue would complicate the case.

Narelle and Steve realise that Adele's request for a psychologist's report was a clever tactic. They have no idea whether the father has complied but, either way, he loses. If he has failed to provide a report, he is in breach of a court order. If he complies and, as is likely for a narcissist, insists he has no anger-management issues and does not display anti-social behaviour, the police and DCJ records will expose him. They will show he has little insight into domestic violence and refuses to see himself as the perpetrator.

TIME CONSTRAINTS

The clouds break, and sunlight pierces through the grey sky. The outlook is the brightest it has been since this torturous ordeal began. Monica and Georgia enter the safe room on level one. Chantel and Phillip take the lift to the fourth floor, where the case will be heard.

When the doors slide open, Sav is there – sitting alone in the small foyer. They walk past him without a word, refusing to acknowledge his presence. At around 10 am, the senior registrar sets the priority and running order. Benji's case is listed second.

Georgia's notes:
We go in at 10 and the Registrar asks if we have all agreed on an outcome. No. Father's barrister says he hasn't had a chance to review all the documentation. That police documents came in at 9 pm the previous night. Monica's solicitor Adele was awake at 4 am to read everything and it would appear from the knowledge she had of the police reports, a similar

effort was put in by the child's lawyer. Registrar says we will come back at 12 to give the father's barrister a chance to read the information, and he hopes the three parties can agree on an outcome (his sense of humor is showing). Lots of talk about the time the Registrar has available today. He has been told this matter must be heard but he also has another urgent matter to attend to at 2 pm. This is nerve-wracking, because if they can't get through everything today, it will get postponed, and the new hearing date could be weeks/months away. Earlier, before proceedings began, I overheard Sav's solicitor giving him advice; 'Just take deep breaths,' he told him.

We come back in, and father's barrister said father has withdrawn the offer for Monica to have Benji alternate weekends, 9-5 Saturday and Sunday, and he is going back to the two hours of supervised visits. Basically, father has thrown his toys out of the cart because he's just found out that the child's lawyer thinks Monica should have full custody. And court hasn't even started yet...

Text from Georgia to Narelle and Steve:
Sav has disagreed with his solicitor. Of course. So, it will be going before the Registrar. Hopefully, as soon as possible.

Georgia's notes:
We go back in at 12 and the Registrar asks if all parties are open to working through lunch, which would mean we have from 12-2 pm to get through this. Father's barrister insists that he cannot miss lunch and must have a sandwich at 1.30 pm, even though we've just had an hour out of the court room. Father's barrister takes as much time as possible and tries to get the matter postponed. This brings us to around 1:30/2pm and we need to leave the court room. Both Monica's barrister and the ICL agreed to use just 30 minutes, so the case can be heard today.

13:51, Georgia to Narelle and Steve:
We are coming home. We need to be back at 2:50. Papers won't get issued today. But, hopefully, a resolution. If the decision comes today, the paperwork won't. So Benji won't come to Monica today. Barrister said he is still waiting on paperwork from last Friday. But this case is more urgent.

Georgia:
We return at 3 pm. The lawyers have made up a document. While we wait for a decision to be made on the case (as this can take time) Monica will have Benji on alternate weekends, from 9-5, both Sat and Sun. Narelle James will do the handovers and be the supervisor. Monica disagrees, saying she wants full custody. She agrees after her lawyer explains that this

arrangement is just temporary, while the judgement is being made, and will commence tomorrow.

For some reason, the barristers keep referencing to each other as friends. It almost sounds comical, as though they are being condescending towards each other. 'My friend' stated, blah, blah, blah.

Ok we are back on! Father's lawyer takes some more time to say God knows what, and we are all just trying to stay awake at this point. The earliest the Registrar can deliver orders is 3 pm the following Thursday.

The temporary court order requires that Narelle be with Benji and Monica as supervisor. Steve is not allowed contact with Benji, and Monica is not permitted to be alone with him. Monica is a perfectly fit mother – but because of Sav's lies, and his refusal to give an inch, Monica's solicitor agreed to these terms. For Sav's barrister, it's all about creating the impression that Monica is incapable. Narelle believes there is systemic bias against Monica because of her history of mental illness, even though it hasn't been an issue for fourteen years, apart from the short relapse after Benji was taken.

Steve:
This decision means Narelle must give up her job at the library on Saturday mornings. That Narelle must supervise Benji's visits while Sav has no conditions placed on his parenting is clearly absurd. Once again, it highlights the flaws in the system. The abuser, the child snatcher, the coercive controller, the manipulator, the liar, calls the shots.

Monica's solicitor ushers the group past the father, who is outside the courtroom in conversation with his solicitor. A few minutes later Phillip is alone downstairs waiting for Monica, Georgia, and Chantel to return from the toilets. The elevator door opens. Sav and his solicitor come out. Sav won't move while Phillip is standing nearby, so at Sav's solicitor's insistence, Philip moves away. When Phillip tells Steve about it later, he scoffs. 'Poor Sav, still trying to play the victim. If police and DCJ records could speak, they might say the game's up, Luca Savington. Aka Constable Larry, Battered Sav, Batterer Sav, or just plain BS.'

A few weeks back, Daniel ordered cologne from an online site as a birthday present for Steve. It arrives late in the day. Steve is down the coast at Chantel's so Daniel sends him a text.

Daniel:
Your birthday present arrived. I can't lie, I smelt it once and it smells sooo good. Like better than mine.
Steve:
Wow. I can hardly wait.
Daniel:
It smells sort of like a fireplace in a nice way.
Steve:
Hope I'm not tooo hot.
Daniel:
😂😂😂😂😂

DAY 135 – MOTHER AND CHILD

At around 8.30 am, Monica and Narelle leave the house and drive to McDonald's Hexham to pick up Benji. Narelle's sister Beckie and her husband Martin meet them there for back-up, ensuring Sav behaves and stays for the required ten minutes after the changeover. Cameras inside and outside record the event, which goes ahead without incident. Narelle drives Monica and Benji to soccer. Benji plays games on the iPad along the way – Four in a Row, Memory, Match, Roblox, Wordle.

After soccer they stop at the shops. Monica's neighbour Sarah is holding a birthday party on Sunday at Stockton for her son, Ross. Benji chooses a present for Ross, and Monica lets him pick something for himself as well.

From there they return to Hamilton – Benji's first visit to his mother's home since Sav took him more than four months earlier. Monica has kept his birthday presents, show bags and even Easter eggs. It is a heartfelt moment when Benji realises he hasn't been forgotten, and that his mother has loved him all along and isn't the fiend his father portrayed her to be. Benji is thrilled to see a bed and room set up for him. He plays upstairs, stacking toilet rolls to build a barrier between his and Monica's space.

'I'm making it into my castle,' he says.

Benji tells Monica she'll have to move the music stand. 'It isn't my thing,' he says. But music could yet be his thing – he has a melodic singing voice and keeps rhythm with ease. A mini drum kit still sits beside the piano downstairs. Like Daniel, Benji used to play the drums while Pop played piano. Sometimes Benji would improvise at the keys, making up words to his own music and singing them out loud.

Late in the morning, Georgia arrives with baby Emma. Benji's eyes light up, and he relishes playing with the cousin he hasn't seen in more than five months. Georgia and Emma head back to Sydney after lunch.

It is a cold and rainy afternoon. Benji wants to go for a swim at Auntie Beckie's. When he's told it's too cold, he throws a tantrum. Tantrums aren't uncommon for 8-year-olds and at least it shows he isn't afraid of his mother, as Sav claims. Monica wants to take him to a heated pool to placate him, but Narelle needs a rest and isn't keen on the idea. Monica hugs him and assures him they'll swim another day.

Benji is cheerful on the drive back to McDonald's, playing Wordle on the iPad. At the handover, Monica keeps the soccer jersey, shorts, and socks she bought, while Benji takes the shin pads and boots Sav provided. Sav sends him back to ask for the rest. Narelle explains they'll wash the clothes and return them tomorrow. Monica has no intention of returning them but relents when Narelle urges her to pick her battles.

That evening, Monica receives a call from Gosford Police Station. They want Leonardo's phone number – none of the three numbers he gave them are connecting. When Monica asks why, she is told it involves his ex, Simone.

On Sunday, Benji is friendlier towards Narelle than he was the previous day. In the afternoon, Monica and Narelle take him to the birthday party at Stockton, where he reunites with friends he hasn't been allowed to see for the past four and a half months. It feels peculiar to him at first, but soon he is in the thick of it, the months of isolation behind him.

Later, Monica and the boys take Roxie for a walk to Gregson Park. Daniel turns to Benji and says, 'I bet you want to live back here now.'

Monica:

Met Benji at McDonald's. Went to Ross's party from 11 am to 1 pm. Benji played with Stu and interacted with the other children. Benji showed his caring nature, asking me to cheer Ross up when he was sad. Benji enjoyed interacting with me. Very chatty and laughing lots. We all took Roxie for a walk. Benji played and talked with Nana but when she was walking Benji back to McDonald's, Benji saw that Sav was there and he went quiet, shrugging when she asked if he had had a nice day.

DAY 137 – WHERE'S SAV

Georgia, 5:24 pm:

Emma has started trying to stand up from sitting. She sits there and flaps her arms down like she's trying to launch herself up.

Narelle:

She's a bird.

Georgia:

Ha, ha, ha. She thinks that's how you stand up.

Monica:

I just checked Benji's school attendance. He had an early departure at 1:17 pm. The records say he went with his older brother, Leonardo. I wonder why Benji left early.

Georgia:

Probably to go to Time Zone.

Narelle:

No-one was home. No cars were there.

Georgia:

How do you know that?

Monica:

Mum drove past this afternoon. I asked Sarah if anything suss is happening.

Georgia:

Humm, a bit odd. I asked the solicitor when we were at court what to do if we know he's taken off with Benji, and she said to call the cops. I can call the sister if we need to. I wonder if he's taken off with Benji, so he isn't there for Thursday. Let's see if he goes to school tomorrow.

Sarah to Monica, 8:53 pm:

Oooo! How worrying for you. There's nothing I could see and there were no cars there when I was coming and going. Wonder what they are up to?

Steve:

Don't worry. He'll turn up. Doesn't get it yet. Still house to sell as well.
Georgia:
That's right.

After dinner, Chantel is reading the upcoming court listings. Steve's DVO is listed for Tuesday. Chantel also discovered that Monica's DVO is to be mentioned in two weeks.

Steve:

Just when we thought that chapter might be finished, Monica's DVO, where she purportedly bashed Sav, pops up again. When we hadn't seen it listed, and Monica hadn't received any notification in the mail, we'd wrongly assumed that it had been withdrawn, as the police are now aware they were hoodwinked by Sav. This was naive of us. But really? Why is it still doing the rounds? Maybe the Police Crime Manager figures the police prosecutor doesn't have enough work to do. What a farcical system! What a waste of resources, money, and everyone's time. One of Monica's support workers told her that some police precincts were notoriously bad with domestic violence issues. How can the escalating rates of domestic violence be addressed when the police stand by DVOs they know were issued on false grounds.

The headline reads: 'Woman hid in paddock after brutal domestic violence attack in regional NSW.' The article is by Stephanie Gardiner, AAP – June 17, 2024:

When the couple began arguing in the early hours of Sunday morning, the woman got in a car to escape, according to police. The man grabbed her, dragged her onto the ground, and pushed her through a window in the garage, causing the glass to shatter.

As she lay on the ground crying, he told her he loved her.

The man then dragged her through the house, before kicking her while she was on the floor. He then dragged the woman by the hair, repeatedly smashed her face into the bathroom tiles, and continually jumped on her. He took her phone.

She found his phone and fled to the paddock, from where she called the police, who found her with cuts, bruises, and swelling. During the man's bail application, the court was told he has no prior history of violence. The police prosecutor opposed bail, citing concerns for the safety of the victim.

NSW Police say domestic violence was more prevalent across the region compared with rates of assault in the city. Quakers Hill, Western Sydney, and Wyong, on the Central Coast, were urban suburbs with similar domestic violence spikes, according to authorities.

DAY 138 – STEVE'S DVO

Steve is anxious about his impending DVO hearing. Although Detective Bauer has said his DVO will be adjusted, until it happens, he cannot relax. Lisa was supposed to contact him on Monday night to discuss it, but he has heard nothing. He doesn't know whether he is supposed to turn up in court or simply wait to be informed of the outcome. Whatever the solicitor and barrister plan to do, it hasn't been shared with him. Being kept in the dark is frustrating. Even capable solicitors with integrity, like Lisa, seem oblivious to what their clients are going through. Perhaps they become desensitised over time.

Steve is annoyed not only with his solicitor but also with Detective Bauer. It seems Bauer knew Benji's claims were fabricated from the start, yet she imposed a DVO and put him through weeks of hell because she was going on holidays. While the DVO is still in place, Sav's solicitor has been able to use it to his advantage – with the ICL now recommending Steve doesn't have contact with Benji.

After 9 am, Steve finally gets through to Lisa. He is not required to attend court. The case will be mentioned, and the barrister is making representations to have the DVO withdrawn. Lisa says she is 'all over it' – and Steve doesn't doubt she is – but he would have slept better had he been told this earlier. Lisa has contacted Bauer, who has confirmed in writing that the investigation is complete, and that Steve will not be charged.

Narelle, 9:58 am:
Is Benji at school?

Monica:

No. I'll call the school when I get the chance at 11:30 and see why he is absent.

Georgia:

Yeah. Has Sarah seen cars?

Monica:

Sarah said the lights were on last night. We could get a welfare check.

Narelle:

Were the cars there last night?

Monica:

The Ute was.

Georgia:

The red car is probably in the garage. Or sold.

Monica:

It was on the trailer. Maybe sold. Maybe being repaired.

Georgia:

Oooooh! Interesting.

Monica:

Should I ask Adele?

Georgia:

I would.

Monica:

Adele has called Sav's solicitor. If we don't hear back by 12:30 we call police for a welfare check. Adele said, 'I understand why you are worried.'

Georgia:

Good.

Half an hour later.

Monica:

So, Sav has been arrested, and it is looking like he'll be out on bail this afternoon. Benji is with Gabby on the Central Coast. We can't get Benji until court order is in place.

Georgia:

Ok. Bloody hell! So sorry for you, Monica. This would just be so awful for you. Hopefully, Thursday is a big turnaround.

Monica:

Do you want to message Gabby and check Benji is alright?

Georgia posts her conversation with Gabby on Messenger.

Georgia:

Hi Gabby, I hope you're well. Can you please let us know that Benji is ok? This must be very tough and confusing for him without his mother. Thank you.

Gabby:

Hi Georgia, he is fine. Watching a movie, waiting for his cousin to finish school to play. How did you know he was here if you don't mind me asking?

Georgia doesn't reply.

Gabby:

All this is confusing for any kid. No kid should go through this.

Georgia to Monica:

I feel like writing, 'He should be at school.'

Monica:

Exactly. Write that. Obviously, she is feeling sorry for her brother.

Georgia:

Yeah.

Monica:

So odd they don't blame their brother's behaviour.

Georgia replies to Gabby:

No, that is right. What your brother has done is absolutely disgusting and is psychological abuse as Benji's lawyer stated in court last week. Benji should be in his mother's care in a loving and stable environment and attending school.

Gabby:

I don't know what is going on because I don't want to be involved too much. I have my own family to look after. I am sorry. How did you know Benji was here?

Georgia wants to tell Gabby that her response is pathetic because Benji is a nine-year-old who is being abused by his father. She wants to berate Gabby for supporting her brother. But she decides the best course of action is to simply not reply.

Gabby:

Like I said to everyone, I love my brother. He is family but keep me out of it.

I'm happy to help and love to see cousins together and I do hope that if Monica gets full custody, they still see each other, because Giana is attached to Benji.

Georgia to Monica:
I want to reply to Gabby, 'Keep dreaming. You don't deserve to see Benji again because you think it's ok not to get involved.'
Monica:
All Gabby is worried about is how we found out.
Narelle:
Don't tell her.
Georgia:
Absolutely not.

A short time later.

Georgia:
Lorna found Sav selling stuff on FB.
(Georgia posts images).
Monica:
I paid for that coffee table. Good researching, Lorna.
Georgia:
It's not his to sell.
Narelle:
Keep that. Are there more? They are assets.
Georgia:
She couldn't find the dates.
(Georgia posts more images).
Monica:
That's the scan tool, I think.
Georgia:
Send to solicitor.
Narelle:
Just keep it until the assets are divided.
Georgia continues to post more:
Mahogany table $500
Snapon scan tool $1800
Cement mix $400
Office desk chair $50

Georgia receives a text from Gabby:
Do you want to speak with Benji?
Georgia ignores the text, as she does two phone calls. She tells Monica.

Later, Georgia to Monica:
They're all cut from the same cloth.
In the afternoon, Steve is walking Roxie. He left his phone back at the house, and when it rings, Narelle answers. It is an Officer Rollo, asking to speak with Steve. The name means nothing to him. He tries twice to call the station, but the phone just rings out. Later, on his way to collect Daniel from school, he misses a call from Bauer. He returns it once he gets home.

Bauer organises a time and comes to the Hamilton house. The amended DVO has the distance restrictions removed. The original grounds – inappropriate touching and watching the child in the shower – are gone. Bauer is now firmly on Steve's side. She even offers to find out how long Sav will be held in custody. An hour later she texts him: *He won't be kept overnight.*

That evening, Monica receives a message from Adele. Senior Registrar Mansfield has put forward his decision on the interim hearing to 12 am Thursday. Steve stays for dinner at Hamilton before driving back to the Central Coast.

At the table, Monica cracks them up. Adele had told her Sav was incarcerated, which she misheard as 'incinerated.' Monica adds that when she walked into court on Tuesday, Lisa was already there. She saw Monica, pointed to the seat beside her, and said: 'Sit here with me. I'll be your bodyguard. I'll protect you from that Pen creep.'

They laugh again when recalling Sav's barrister, who kept referring to Monica as 'The Wife' – an attempt to diminish her that only made him sound like a relic from the past. The ICL certainly wasn't impressed. When Sav's barrister asked her to repeat a point, she shot back,
'Let me slow it down for you, friend.'

DAY 139 – PREVENTABLE HOMICIDE

With escalating rates of domestic violence, and new legislation on coercive control coming into effect in NSW from July, the topic is receiving substantial media attention.

Sydney Morning Herald, June 18, 2024:
More than 70% of men who killed their current or past female partners had at least two interactions with the police, the legal system or child protection before the killings, an analysis of a decade's worth of sentencing comments has revealed.

The findings are from the Monash University Report, 'Securing Woman's Lives.' The report examined sentencing remarks from 235 cases of men who had been convicted in Australia for killing their current or former intimate partner over a decade. According to Professor Kate Fitzgibbon, family violence academic and lead author of the report:
The number of different points of intervention that the perpetrators of these killings have with the system show us these killings are inherently preventable. We can see these are not men for whom violence comes out of the blue. These are often men with significant histories.

What many experts argue is that, rather than a whole population approach, the focus should be on those living with trauma, alcohol and drug abuse, and mental health issues. Sixty-eight percent of the perpetrators had alcohol and drug issues. Nearly half had mental health issues.

Victorian Victims of Crime Commissioner, Fiona McCormack: *The women in these 235 cases were reaching out for help, they were seeking it. So many are seeking protection, and they were failed. Parole and bail emerged as a key point of risk for the occurrence of intimate partner femicide, but there is no obligation to consult the victim. This report makes it clear, and research recognises that intimate partner violence is the most preventable type of homicide.*

Monica, 2:58 pm:
My Woman's Advisory Case Manager rang. She had some news about Sav's arrest. The police did a body search and prepared him to go to gaol. Hopefully, this has scared him not to do anything further. He has come to the attention

of the Chief Police Prosecutor who was alarmed at the offences on his file.
Georgia:
Omg that's scary.

DAY 140 – INTERIM HEARING RESTARTS

Monica:
Benji's athletics carnival is on Friday. If I get custody I can stay all day. Lots of parents and teachers around to keep us safe.
Steve:
Chantel and Phillip said they'd go. I don't think it's wise to go alone.
Georgia:
I got a text from a friend who works in the courts. She wanted to know how we got on. I asked her what weight the children's lawyer's report had. She said all the weight.
Monica:
That's positive. Hopefully, I'll get Benji today. I hope they brought the time forward, so I have time to get him from school.
Georgia:
Yeah. You'd think so. Who knows? Is Benji at school?
Monica:
Late, but there.

Narelle and Steve drive to Monica's workplace to help Monica and be there in case the decision doesn't go her way. While Monica sets up for the video hook-up, Steve sits at the piano and plays a few songs. Narelle chats with some of the clients, while Monica heads into a meeting room with her solicitor online.

Ten minutes later, the door opens. Monica emerges in a distressed state, headphones still on, her voice breaking as she speaks with her solicitor.

Monica, 12:18 pm
Benji's solicitor, the ICL, has new evidence about Leonardo, and she wants

the case to be reopened. He spelt his name differently when he was arrested. The ICL is also peeved that the court wasn't informed Sav had been arrested and charged with breaching his DVO, and Benji was withdrawn from school and dropped at Sav's sister's place.

Georgia:
Oh. When?
Monica:
2 pm tomorrow.
Georgia:
Omg.
Narelle:
Oh no.
Monica:
Decision may not be made until 3 o'clock next Monday.
Georgia:
Oh, you're kidding.
Monica:
It's to ensure I get full custody.
Georgia:
Surely in the meantime they need to remove Benji.

Monica remains upset for hours afterwards. She had believed she was finally getting Benji back. The disappointment is crushing, but what is also unsettling is knowing that Leonardo has been nominated as Benji's carer.

Later in the day, Monica signs the new affidavit. While she is speaking with Lisa, she remarks on how strongly Benji's solicitor is now advocating for her.
'She wasn't always on board,' Lisa replies.
It hits Monica that the solicitor, who now seems powerful and astute in her advocacy, must once have believed Sav's lies. That may have been the reason Adele suggested bypassing the interim hearing. At some point, though, the solicitor came to see she had been duped – possibly after the release of the Child Impact Statement.

Because the postponement of the decision and the ICL's move to reopen the interim hearing stem directly from Sav's side withholding information, Lisa will file for the extra costs to be borne by Sav and his team.

DAY 141 – ANSWERS PLEASE

They hear through their solicitor that the ICL was livid and tore shreds off the father's solicitor for failing to disclose that the father had been arrested, or that Benji spent the night with the father's sister. She immediately sought to have the hearing reopened. The ICL also wants the registrar to know that Leonardo has a DVO against him for harassing a woman. Sav made a serious error of judgement naming Leonardo as Benji's carer.

Like Monica, the ICL wants answers about Benji not attending school. He wasn't sick the day before – yet suddenly he was when placed with his aunt. When the father was arrested for breaching his DVO, why was Benji placed with the aunt and Leonardo? The father had a clear alternative – the mother. Once again, there are glaring discrepancies between police records and the father's version of events. The same pattern as January – remove the child from his mother at all costs.

1:50 pm:
Monica goes upstairs with Steve for the video hook up. Discussion centres on whether the hearing should be reopened to include the new material. Predictably, the father's legal team has filed to have it disallowed. A twenty-minute adjournment follows while solicitors search for a compromise. They don't find one.

Fifteen minutes into the resumed hearing, the Ring app sounds. Steve looks at his phone and freezes – a police officer is at the front door. Oh no, not again, he thinks, hurrying down the stairwell, dreading what Monica will be accused of this time. But when he opens the door, the officer is alone – and smiling. He explains, 'Monica was stopped at a roadside breath test earlier in the day. She left her licence behind. I'm just returning it.' Relief floods through the house.

The senior registrar allows the new material on the ICL's argument that it relates to the child's exposure to family violence. Mansfield grants leave to reopen the interim hearing at 3 pm the following Monday, via Microsoft Teams. Though the decision favours Monica, the delay is agonising.

Georgia:

Sav's barrister mentioned the strain the proceedings have placed on Sav (boo hoo) and his difficult financial situation (bring out the violins). Furthermore, because of his financial position, he might no longer be able to avail himself of high-level (insert comical cough here) legal representation. Sav has the added stress of caring for a child. Nothing to do with Benji. All to do with him.

With the convoluted web of lies Sav has been spinning, it's not surprising that he is coming unstuck. Or more accurately, stuck in the web of deceit he's woven.

Monica's solicitor is exultant about how the case is now unfolding, but for Monica it is just another weekend without her son. The ICL's insistence that these recent events be included is entirely understandable. They are a stark snapshot of the father's conduct over the past five – going on six – months. Nothing has changed. The lies, the withholding of information, the disregard for Benji's welfare, the animosity towards the mother – all of it laid bare before the Chief Registrar.

Sav's attempt to cast himself as the victim is unlikely to fool an experienced registrar like Mansfield. As Monica's barrister has said of him – it's not his first rodeo.

Then comes word from Sarah, Sav's neighbour; he has a new set of wheels. A blue Hyundai with garish gold rims. 'Hideous,' is Sarah's verdict. Monica barely cares what it looks like – what matters is knowing it. If Benji is returned on Monday, bells of joy will ring across the land. But alarm bells will sound as well. How will a wounded, isolated, and cornered Sav react? It is crucial Monica recognises the cars he might be driving.

Perhaps he will do nothing drastic. He could attempt an appeal, as his barrister hinted. But an appeal cannot be lodged merely because a party dislikes the outcome. The decision must be shown to be errant, biased, or unjust – that there was an error of law or a denial of natural justice.

Is to be violent simply a choice some men make? Psychologists and domestic violence workers are divided over its causes. Is it rooted in psychological dysfunction, childhood trauma, mental illness, or the patriarchy – the belief that men are inherently superior? Is the 'alpha male' a social construct, or the outcome of evolutionary roles of man as protector and provider?

There is no doubt some men take pleasure in watching their partners and children squirm. For them, power and control are intoxicating. Self-described misogynist, Andrew Tate – a figure teachers say is heavily influencing young male students – has become the face of anti-equality resentment. But he is far from alone. Entire online movements, and indeed entire countries, continue to denigrate women and promote rigid masculine ideals. These ideas seep easily into the minds of teenage boys. Even political leaders reinforce them; US president Donald Trump has boasted about 'grabbing women by the pussy' without their consent. He has been accused of sexual misconduct by at least twenty-six women. Yet it does nothing to diminish his popularity.

There are varying opinions on the role of men's behavioural change programs. While some argue the limited funding should be spent on the abused, others say that without attempts at changing male behaviour, nothing can change. The woman might escape an abusive relationship, while the perpetrator moves on, finding another woman to abuse. This is the case with Sav, who is repeating the abusive and demeaning behaviours that he perpetrated on his first wife. Some experts have noted that the children of abusers will likely grow up to be victims of or abusers themselves. Both Leonardo and Marco, still in their early twenties, have had DVO's taken out against them by females.

Intimate perpetrators often escalate their violence during separation. Separation-instigated violence involves men who might display 'low level' violence in a relationship, but in the context of separation, become emotionally or physically violent.

Chuck Derry is from the Gender Violence Institute of Minnesota in the USA. He asked a group of offenders ('Created to Thrive,' CBE International, 2021) about their behaviour and their answers were blunt: to get their way and feel superior. *These men clearly understood the benefits of violence, and how much they gained from it. That's why they didn't want to stop.* After they spoke about the benefits of violence and control, Derry posed the question: Why would they give it up?

While some males attend men's behavioural change programs because of a court order, others are genuine. 'The biggest motivator we see for men is children,' says Megan Boshell, who runs programs for Mission Australia. Relationships Australia has 220 men on its waiting list and receives four referrals a day. The waiting period is over six months. If a program is not readily available, the opportunity to seize the moment is lost.

That Sav, who is driven by revenge, would attend such a program with an open mind is doubtful. It is likely his behavioural patterns are too ingrained.

DAY 144 – WE HAVE PROBLEMS

At 3 pm, the interim hearing reopens. While Monica waits for proceedings to begin, Sav's solicitor can be heard speaking – presumably to Sav. 'I'll do the best I can, but we've got problems.' He doesn't seem to realise everyone can hear his conversation. Or perhaps he does, already laying the groundwork for excuses. A few seconds later, Lisa's voice cuts in, telling him to hit mute. The line goes quiet. That Sav's own barrister is pessimistic gives Monica reason to be optimistic.

The senior registrar has barely begun when the father's barrister announces he has just received 126 pages of new material from the DCJ. The registrar is reluctant to delay, but a brief pause is agreed on to give the solicitors time to scan the documents.

3:15 pm:
When the hearing recommences, the father's barrister immediately seeks an adjournment. He claims he could be sued for negligence if forced to proceed without studying the new material. The ICL pushes back. She has more than enough evidence to recommend Benji be returned to his mother. If the case is reopened, she will also add further material.

Sav's barrister will not budge. He insists that without time to review the documents, his client will be denied procedural fairness. He must receive instructions from Sav based on this new evidence and presses hard for an adjournment.

The registrar relents and adjourns until 10 am the next day.

For Monica, it is yet another bitter setback. More time off work, more mounting legal costs, more days without her son. And the so-called 126 pages of new material? A fiction. All but the final eight pages had been available when the hearing opened nearly two weeks earlier. Still, the tactic worked. Delay achieved.

DAY 145 – ANOTHER WAIT

It is 10 am. Hopes are high as Mansfield reopens the hearing. After a brief technical exchange with the parties – where it is clarified that Sav is deemed to be the applicant – proceedings begin.

Lisa immediately points out she has only just received the barrister's bundle from Sav's side. The registrar allows a short adjournment while she runs the documents through her printer. As the machine clatters away, Lisa shares a lighthearted exchange with Mansfield – the two seem to know each other – about the rebuild in her office and the need to comply with building codes. With a smile, Mansfield accuses her of 'destroying a tree' as the printer spits out page after page.

The substance of Sav's case is hollow. His team presents no genuine evidence, only a rehash of the same fabrications about Monica and Steve that have already been dealt with. Even the ICL's so-called 'additional material' is not entirely new – Marco's DVO is already known to Monica's side. What has changed is that Marco, like Leonardo before him, has come under the microscope because Sav has named him as Benji's carer. This adds weight to the case that the father consistently minimises violence – whether his own or that of his sons.

Monica:
The registrar will publish his decision from chambers at 3 pm next Monday.
Georgia:
What! The decision won't come until a week's time? Another wait.

Georgia later chats with her friend who works in the system.
Georgia's friend:
You know why. It's the magistrates conference break. They all broke for the

conference today and won't be back until Monday.
Georgia:
Oh what! He said he was off to Brisbane.
Georgia's friend:
I'm not back until Tuesday next week. They only keep an emergency registrar on for fresh custodies. All the local, district, supreme and family magistrates break and go to this conference. It's massive. We have our DVCAS conference. And the police have theirs as well.

DAY 146 – DCJ

At 3:30 pm there is a visit from two DCJ representatives. It was supposed to have happened the previous week. Julia Presgraves, the case manager, had told Monica the visit was just to 'cross the Ts,' but they have since decided to do a more thorough investigation, the likely reason being Luca Savington's end-of-week allegations to the DCJ.

Monica is anxious. She's had a full day and is tiring of dealing with the authorities.

Presgraves speaks with Monica, Narelle, and then Daniel. She asks Daniel about his favourite food and the video games he plays. He tells her he is worried about Benji and glad to be away from the fighting. Presgraves is reaching into areas that should have been examined when Benji was first taken five months earlier. Presgraves says she knows Sav's type. In her experience, men like him often 'clear out' once they realise they have lost control, and their power game is up. Time will tell.

Although it is right that Sav's claims be investigated, one and a half hours of interviewing at this late stage is like turning up to a football match as the final whistle blows. Still, this DCJ report will, hopefully, shine a light on Luca Savington's fabrications and his weaponising of Benji. It could be useful at the final hearing.

Steve:
Whatever the result on Monday, the final hearing will be intriguing. BS will be cross-examined by Monica's barrister and must account for the monumental lies he's put in the affidavits. A date has not been set, but book early for a seat to that one. It will be standing room only.

The following statistics are from the Australian Institute of Family Studies (October 2019) Parenting Arrangements after separation:
Evidence Summary: Only 3% of parents use the court system as their primary method of determining custody. There are claims that fathers are hard done by at custody hearings, that courts favour mothers. According to the Australian Institute of Family studies, more than 90% of the time, the mother is the prime custodial parent in cases where the court approved joint custody arrangements. Approximately 80% of custodial parents are mothers. So, fathers are not disadvantaged; it's simply a reflection of the fact that mothers are, in most cases, the prime caregiver:
27%: where the mother has sole parental responsibility
46%: where the mother is granted the majority of time
21%: where there is a shared care/time arrangement
3%: where the father is granted the majority of time
2%: where the father has sole parental responsibility.

Steve receives a call from his barrister's secretary. They need to meet and discuss progress on his DVO. The matter will be back in court at the end of July. Monica's DVO, where she allegedly bashed Sav, is listed for mention this Tuesday.

Sav's lies serve no purpose other than to waste money, clog police and court resources, and damage the reputations of innocent people. How many nonsense DVOs like this are in the system? How many cases mirror Monica's and Sienna's – where genuine applicants have had their DVO requests rejected?

DAY 148 – PLAYTIME

On Friday, a letter arrives in the post from Monica's barrister. Enclosed is his bill – $6,600 – with the solicitor's fees running at nearly double that for the interim hearing. He also provides an overview of the case, noting the more-than-obvious efforts of the father's legal team to delay proceedings:

'I formed the view it was a deliberate attempt by Father to cement a status quo of Benji living with Father, which would be wielded with advantage at any subsequent hearing.'

The barrister adds that the tactic irritated the senior registrar, who kept the parties in court until nearly 6 pm.

As per the temporary court orders, Monica has Benji for Saturday and Sunday, though he must return to Sav's care each night. On Saturday morning, Benji doesn't want to attend soccer – another indictment of Sav. Just six months earlier, he loved the game. Monica insists he go, but while he plays his heart isn't in it. After the match they visit Grandma's, just around the corner from the field. Before he was taken, Benji was a regular visitor there. Grandma makes a fuss over him, but Benji stays guarded, slipping out to eat his pancakes in the car.

In the afternoon, Monica takes him tenpin bowling with a school friend he hasn't seen since he was taken. Daniel joins them, and for a while Benji reconnects with normal childhood fun.

That night, more items appear for sale on Sav's Facebook page. Among them is the basketball hoop Narelle and Steve had bought the boys the previous Christmas. Once again, Sav shows his selfishness and disregard for Benji and Daniel – selling what isn't his for a couple of hundred dollars.

On Sunday, Chantel drives to Hamilton with her daughter-in-law, Indira, so Benji can spend time with his three-year-old cousin, Nadia. Chantel brings a tray of sausage rolls that are an instant hit. Benji is happy, relaxed, and bonds quickly with Nadia. The two play upstairs together. Sienna drops by. She spends most of the time upstairs playing with Benji and Nadia. Steve must stay away as per temporary court orders.

DAY 151 – JUDGEMENT POSTPONED

8:54 am:

Delivery of the judgement has been postponed until next Thursday. The reason given: unavoidable competing and emergent court commitments. With most of the legal fraternity away last week at the Brisbane conference, one would have thought the backlog might have been anticipated. The senior registrar's message ends with an apology to the parties for any inconvenience. Inconvenience! That's not the appropriate word. Being inconvenienced is when your train arrives late, or the supermarket runs out of milk. Try frustration, immense disappointment, and disbelief.

Steve receives another call from his barrister's secretary the next day. The police prosecutor is considering removing his DVO, so the scheduled meeting with the barrister on Friday will no longer be necessary. Although the court order still prevents Steve from seeing Benji, and the practical effect on his day-to-day life is minimal, at least he will be spared thousands of dollars in legal costs.

On Wednesday, Daniel has his school athletics carnival at Maitland Regional Athletics Centre. He is a natural at the high jump and has impressed in PE lessons, despite never having trained formally. Monica has just received his school report. Given the chaos of recent months and Daniel's habit of playing video games late into the night, she had been bracing herself for poor results. But to her surprise, his grades are solid. He's excelled in both Mathematics and English.

Narelle and Steve pick up Daniel after the carnival. He has bandages on his arm and leg. He won his two-hundred-metre heat but fell over on the finish line. He spewed up afterwards in the toilet. The high jump was postponed due to insufficient time, which was fortunate. The remaining field events will be held at school during sports period.

Monica is advised that tomorrow, at three o'clock, Registrar Mansfield's orders are scheduled to be handed down. Nearly three weeks have passed since the interim hearing commenced, and the decision is long overdue. Steve and Monica remain confident, but Narelle and Grandma are more cautious.

Grandma has lost all trust in the system after witnessing months of injustice. Steve, however, clings to what Billy Holden told him four months earlier: 'Mansfield is thorough, and nothing gets past him.' Narelle remains wary of what she perceives as systemic mental health bias.

Narelle:

The claims in Sav's affidavits keep being referred to in all the hearings, even though the alcohol claim has been addressed (hair follicle test), as has the mental health claim (report from Mater Hospital, Medicare records, and the Newcastle Mental Health Team). It is brought up in every interview. With DCJ workers, alcohol intake was discussed. These claims are constantly weaponised. Although Monica had not been in hospital for the fourteen years previous and has remained stable, her mental health has continually been referred to in all hearings. But the reasons for the relapse seem to be skipped over and carry no weight.

The real issues:
1. The child was snatched from school by Sav.
2. The child has been withheld from his mother.
3. The mother was unable to get a DVO from gatekeepers, the police.
4 At the time of the child's abduction, the mother had been weaned off medication and was on a very small dose.

The legal system seems to see a mental health issue as a barrier to parenting. They seem to think that at any minute Monica will run amok and injure someone, even though she has never been violent and has maintained continuous employment for more than 10 years while studying and achieving higher level qualifications. They have no understanding of the deterioration and don't realise it is not a sudden decline; that her recent deterioration was directly linked to Sav's behaviour.

DAY 154 – RIP VAN WINKLE

3 pm:

The time for the senior registrar's decision arrives. Nothing happens. No call from the solicitor, no judgement handed down. Monica contacts Lisa, who tells her that Benji's solicitor is following it up. Five o'clock comes and goes. Still nothing. Messages stream in from friends and family, all using the same word to describe the silence: CRUEL. If Mansfield is postponing the decision for a genuine reason – even something as serious as a health emergency – why doesn't his secretary simply say so?

The next day they are all on edge. Nine o'clock, ten o'clock, eleven, twelve… still nothing. It's not just cruel – it is unprofessional. One text, that is all it would take to ease the torment. There have been diversions and delays. It might be a complex case, but if the registrar sticks to the evidence, the path is clear. The Child Impact Study and DCJ reports are unequivocal. The ICL left no stone unturned. The conclusion was inescapable: the child is at risk and should be returned to his mother.

By three o'clock, still nothing. Everyone waits with bated breath for an email. Four-thirty – still silence. Both the ICL and the Child Impact Statement stressed the urgency. For Monica, it is torture. The longer it drags on, the stronger Sav feels, and the longer Benji's psychological recovery will take.

That evening, Monica downloads Benji's school report. Academically, he is doing well, concentrating on his lessons. But he isn't mixing with his peers and is struggling in the playground. Alarm bells.

DAY 157 – STILL NOTHING

In early July emergency services rushed to a home in Lalor Park, Sydney, where a man, a woman, and seven children lived. The house was engulfed in flames. NSW police allege the father attempted to prevent rescue workers from saving his family. Two boys, aged three and six, were taken to Westmead Hospital in a critical condition but died a short time later. Four other children, three boys aged four, seven and eleven, as well as a nine-year-old girl, were treated by paramedics at the scene and taken to hospital in a stable condition. The body of a ten-month-old girl was found after firefighters extinguished the blaze. The father, 28, was burnt and had inhaled smoke. He was arrested at the scene and put into an induced coma, under police guard. The mother 29, suffered smoke inhalation, and was kept in hospital under sedation.

'It's completely devastating for people who know the family, that go to school with the other children. It's a close-knit community and will have a lasting impact,' said NSW acting Police Superintendent Jason Pietruszka.

The tragedy is being treated by detectives as a domestic-related multiple homicide.

An article, posted on July 8, 2024, by ABC journalist Hayley Gleeson. is based on findings from a group of Australian pathologists. The study, published in *Acta Neurotological,* discovered that the degenerative brain disease found mostly in deceased footballers and boxers was also prevalent amongst abused women with histories of repetitive head injury. The pathologists, after reviewing clinical records, found they had at least seventy assault related presentations and thirty-five documented head injuries relating to partner violence between them. Two women who endured decades of intimate partner violence, including brutal assaults and head injuries before they died, have been diagnosed with chronic traumatic encephalopathy, the mildest form of the disease.

Although CTE is only likely in the most extreme cases of domestic violence, experts say it highlights the importance of screening victims at autopsy, and the urgent need to support women to leave violent relationships. CTE was first linked to domestic violence in Britain in 1990.

Michael Buckland, head of Neurology at Sydney's Royal Price Alfred Hospital, and one of the paper's authors, has found CTE in several footballers and a small number of autopsy brains in the general population.
'I was a bit shocked that in this first-world country with supposedly world-class public health care, these sorts of cases were popping up through women's exposure to violence,' said Buckland. 'And really, I think for any person who has a history of domestic violence and goes to a coroner, consideration should be given to screening the brain for CTE. That's the only way we're going to understand how common this problem is in the general population.'

At 1:30pm the next day, there is still not a word from Senior Registrar Mansfield or his office.
Monica contacts Lisa Jones, but she too is in the dark.

Steve:
In the Hollywood movie 'The Never-Ending Story,' the boy fights The Nothing. Benji, Monica, Narelle, Steve, indeed everyone concerned for Benji's welfare, are in their own never-

ending story, fighting The Nothing. The decision that is not made.

Georgia:

What the hell!

Narelle:

It's terrible.

Steve:

Hopeless.

Monica:

I feel too scared to complain.

Steve:

Mansfield has nothing listed. The solicitors don't even know. Alien abduction maybe!

Monica:

Benji's solicitor wanted Benji in my care before Sav's court date. which is tomorrow. I think she would be chasing it up.

Georgia:

He is listed for 9:30. Is anyone going?

Monica:

Chantel and Phillip, I think.

DAY 159 – SAV IN COURT

Monica must go to work. Her clients rely on her, and she doesn't yet have a reliable substitute. It is hard, but she pulls herself together. Still, the waiting game is wearing thin. A decision originally scheduled a week ago – from a case meant to be resolved three weeks ago – has still not been handed down. If nothing comes by Friday, Monica is due to have Benji for the weekend, though Narelle, who must supervise, is scheduled to work.

For Benji, more than five months have slipped away. If Sav were gaoled, Leonardo would be his nominated carer – a man already deemed unreliable and unsuitable. But Sav is unlikely to face prison, according to court workers who know the system. His solicitor will argue that Sav is a sole parent – a situation of his own making – and Mansfield's non-decision will be weaponised, just as the DVOs against Monica and Steve have been.

'Dad tried to kill us,' the surviving children told the neighbours who ran to save them from the flames of their Lalor Park house fire. The neighbours who saved the children had to force their way into the house, past a father who didn't want anybody left alive.

Details are emerging about the increasing erratic and aggressive background of the father who allegedly committed filicide, the second most common type of domestic crime in Australia. The father had no criminal history. Police, who had done a welfare check a week earlier, were told all was fine. But neighbours said the man had been driving erratically down the street and was angry with the children, behaving aggressively when he dropped them off at school. 'He struggled with the workload,' said one neighbour.

Monica has seen Sav's car at his workplace, a sign he is still employed. That offers some short-term stability, but his behaviour remains alarming and is escalating. Which leads again to the question: How he will react if Mansfield rules in Monica's favour?

Chantel and Phillip attend court. Sav sits at the back, staring straight ahead. He pleads guilty to wishing Monica happy birthday. On the face of it, this seems trivial. But in the context of undermining Monica and abusing a child, it becomes another form of harassment and control. His solicitor pushes to adjourn the hearing until November, when two other breaches will be heard.

Sav is pleading not guilty to the no-ID phone calls. Police must have traced them to his phone, but he now claims it was Leonardo who made the calls back in April. The reason: his own phone had run out of credit. Leonardo, he says, rang Monica to ask for his passport and was devastated when his father was arrested for something he himself had done. Two weeks later, using the same phone, Leonardo supposedly rang Monica again – this time to demand the return of belongings. The passport was forgotten. The story strains belief. If Sav presses ahead, Leonardo risks cross-examination in November. And perjury is no small offence.

Sav also admits to contacting Monica's friend – previously denied – claiming he was chasing payment for plumbing work. The problem is, he never did the work.

Sav must have done a creative writing course. He told the court he called

Monica because he needed financial help.

The magistrate takes his time perusing documents. Then he looks at Sav's solicitor.
'Have you told him to wake up to himself? He's running the risk of being locked up before the sentencing hearing.'
'Yes, we've had that discussion,' replies the solicitor.
Sav is ordered back to court in mid-October.

DAY 161 – LOLLY BAGS

Still nothing from Senior Registrar Mansfield. He had listings yesterday and today, both at 4 o'clock. Perhaps he is catching up on his backlog in between. It is now almost a month since he first heard the case. Being on the Evatt List, it is supposed to be given priority.

Steve:
To say the case is moving at a snail's pace is an exaggeration. It seems the 88-armed octopus has fallen into a deep sleep, comatose even.

Monica contacts her solicitor. As the days tick by it's getting beyond a joke.

Lisa Jones:
I've never experienced anything like this before. I've checked the portal and nothing. I'm hoping for 3 pm today. If nothing is posted by 3:00pm today, I'll check with the ICL and see what she suggests,
Yours faithfully,
Lisa.

Monica:
It answers one question. This is not normal.
Narelle:
Weird.
Steve:
But why?

On Saturday Monica drives with Narelle to Hexham McDonald's to pick up Benji for the day. They enjoy themselves, and Benji is more relaxed with each visit. When Monica drops him back at the carpark, Sav waves as if they are friends – as though the months of harassment have never happened.

On Sunday, when they collect Benji again, he is carrying two brown paper bags filled with packets of lollies. Faces are drawn on them. One reads 'To Mum,' the other 'To Daniel' (each with, Love Papa). What goes through his head to think that after all the damage he's caused, this is acceptable?

Later, Monica, Narelle, Benji, and Sienna drive to Sydney to celebrate Emma's birthday. It is a warm family gathering, albeit incomplete. Steve cannot be there with Benji because of the Family Court orders. His absence hangs heavy over the day.

DAY 165 – CHILD SINKS

Monica is told by her solicitor to take the paper bags to the police station and make a report. She is reluctant, but she knows she must. It's Monday night. The station is buzzing with arrests and parole reporting. The officer tells Monica it will be a two-hour wait but offers an alternative – someone can come to her house before 8 o'clock that evening.

A letter arrives from Monica's barrister. A date has been set for her DVO to return to court in five weeks. He now has the DVEC recording of Sav's statement. Sav should be held to account for his lies, but instead it is Monica who must defend herself. Madness. More solicitor and barrister fees.

On Tuesday morning, the police finally call in at Hamilton to take Monica's statement about the 'paper bag incident.' But she is at work. It goes back on the job list.

That evening, around 8:30, the police ring Monica. They want to come and record the breach. But Monica is exhausted and ready for bed. The officer reassures her about the importance of documenting breaches – an encouraging sign. Monica promises to attend the station on her way to work. With coercive control laws now in place in NSW, even a bag of sweets can be seen in its true light: an act of control coming from a man with Sav's history.

Later, Monica is shopping when she bumps into a neighbour from her old address. What she hears is disturbing. The neighbour suspects Benji is being left alone all day while Sav works long hours. Monica alerts Lisa and the DCJ. Again, the DCJ do not consider Benji's case serious enough to act.

Sienna drops by the Hamilton house for a visit. The Savington family is shunning her, but she's spoken to Marco. Marco is concerned his name was mentioned in court. He is blaming Sienna, but he should be blaming his father for having listed him as one of Benji's carers.

Narelle remarks that when Benji is with them he is guarded in conversation, constantly saying he 'can't remember' when asked simple questions. No degree in psychology is needed to see the damage. Months of manipulation and coercive control have silenced him.

Steve:
The octopus sleeps. And while it slumbers, the child sinks deeper into the abyss.

That night the final State of Origin match will be held in Brisbane. For twelve hours from 6 pm, Australian women and children are at more risk of harm than any other Wednesday night throughout the year. Rates of domestic violence soar by over 40% on Origin game nights, according to a 2018 study by NSW Bureau of Statistics and the Foundation for Alcohol Research and Education.

Domestic violence advocates want the NRL to do more to prevent violence against woman and children around this this time. The sport is intrinsically linked to the alcohol and gaming industries through sponsorships. Victims of violence around sporting events tell a similar tale. Towards the end of a big game, where there has been partying with lots of drinking, the violence escalates and they've had to escape.

Emma Haskin (ABC, July 17, 2024) reports that the Northern Territory sees higher rates of domestic violence than anywhere else in the country. Doctor Gourley, the director of the Alice Springs Hospital emergency department, said there has been a steady increase in domestic violence over time. He said alcohol was a significant contributing factor and called on both major political parties to address the underlying causes of why people drink to excess and lash out at each other.

'We need to address housing, we need to address unemployment, we need to address that basic hope for the future,' he said.

Steve dreams he is at a football match. Two minutes before full time, the referee stops play, promising to return in a month to finish the game. Players file off into the sheds; spectators drift out of the stadium. No protest, no outrage.

DAY 167 – POLICE STATION

They are still waiting for the senior registrar to hand down his decision. Custody of children and separation is emotional for all parties. But when there is no trust or clarity – when the court is fraught with delays – people become increasingly frustrated and more likely to react badly when a decision is finally made.

Steve accompanies Monica to the police station. It is a long wait. While they sit in the reception area, they overhear a conversation between the duty officer and a middle-aged woman trying to apply for a DVO against a bellicose neighbour. Steve can tell by her compliant manner and politeness that she has no chance. She is far too reasonable. He recognises himself in her – back when all this started, naive and too reasonable. She is turned away. The officer tells her to go to the courthouse. Steve jokes with Monica that they should give the woman Sav's number – he will set her straight.

By the time Monica's turn comes, there is a different officer at the desk. He is personable and takes the matter seriously. While Monica is in the interview room, a police officer steps out from her workspace and offers Steve the *Newcastle Herald* to read. The kindness catches him by surprise. She had been stern and uncompromising with the men reporting for bail and bond requirements. Police deal daily with difficult customers and fraught situations, and showing softness can leave them vulnerable.

The Herald carries a story critiquing the new coercive control laws. It notes that

NSW police receive one domestic violence call every four minutes, and that a dozen coercive control investigations have already begun since the law came into effect at the end of June in NSW. Police Commissioner Karen Webb reveals that senior executives are considering a dedicated command, like those in Queensland and Victoria.

Queensland established its Domestic Violence and Vulnerable Persons Command in 2021. Its purpose: to deliver effective and efficient policing strategies, to drive prevention, and to ensure investigation of domestic and family violence incidents. Commissioner Webb also raises the possibility of involving detectives early in domestic violence cases.

If detectives had been involved in Monica's case, it would have made a significant difference. They would have seen through Sav's trickery from the start.

Monica is in the interview room for nearly forty-five minutes. The officer is thorough, taking detailed information that can be relied upon in court. Waving to Monica is deemed a breach – as is sending Benji home with paper bags of sweets. According to the officer, Sav will likely be arrested. If that happens, it is just as likely he will retaliate – as he has in the past.

DAY 168 – DISTRAUGHT

Imagine being a loving, law-abiding parent, and knowing your now nine-year-old child is being left in isolation for nine to ten hours a day and that you are forbidden from going near them.

Monica is at her wits' end. She wants to contact the police and ask them to intervene, to save Benji from his dismal situation. Narelle advises her to contact the DCJ first. She contacts the DCJ again, and they tell her the request will carry more weight if it comes from a neighbour. Monica reaches out to Sarah, who does as the DCJ suggests. But when Sarah contacts the police, they ask why the mother hasn't called herself – or simply collected the child. They tell her there is nothing they can do.

The system is failing the child, supporting the abductor, and punishing the victim. It is easy to see why people lose their cool – why they sometimes take matters into their own hands.

Friday comes and still nothing. Monica contacts her solicitor. The entire office is distraught at Benji's plight. Narelle joins the court chatline and makes an enquiry. Late in the day she receives a reply claiming the decision has been posted. They get excited – only to realise the case number Narelle has been given differs from Monica's.

For Monica to check, she needs an ID number. It raises the possibility that the court orders have been posted under the wrong number. There is nothing they can do until Monday, as the department's online service is closed over the weekend.

It is confusing. It is nerve-racking. And it means Benji will spend another weekend in captivity.

DAY 172 – SCHOOL'S BACK

Good morning, everyone. Still nothing on the portal.
Yours faithfully.
Lisa Jones

Monica:
Lisa sent her email to the barrister and Adele, as well as me. Hopefully, the barrister can do something further. Funny how that's all she needs to write, and they all know it's about our case.
Steve:
Like the time when we asked for someone who knew about the case. The cop shook his head and said, 'Everyone knows about this case.'

Bad news. Narelle had the case number wrong. The case is becalmed, in the doldrums.

Steve:

Can someone wake up the octopus. It may need mouth to mouth. There is barely a pulse. If Mansfield misses nothing, as Billy Holden said, what in heaven's sake is this. The urgency of the situation was spelt out by the Child Impact Statement and Benji's solicitor. Three weeks have passed since Mansfield set a date for the decision.

Daniel returns to school today, Benji is due back tomorrow. With all the attention on Benji, it is worth remembering that Daniel has had a turbulent twelve months. He was in the house when the police kept turning up on the doorstep, interrogating, and accusing his mother. He was home alone when Detective Bauer and her partner knocked and even asked him to relay a message to his grandfather. He was there when they returned to serve the DVO. It has been impossible to protect him from the fallout of Luca Savington's malice. He knows his younger brother is in danger – kept captive by an unstable father – a father who rejected him, thereby trashing their relationship.

In addition to that, Daniel has lost contact with his two older brothers, who he had known since he was three and to whom he was strongly bonded. He has had his grandfather effectively removed from his life by police and the Family Court. Every significant male figure gone. To Monica's solicitor and the ICL, Daniel was a bargaining chip – the brother it was in Benji's best interest to be reunited with. When DCJ spoke with him, it was only to confirm Benji would be returning to a safe house. Considering what he has endured, Daniel is faring remarkably well. He is more introverted, but resilient, grounded by his mother's and her family's love. Through most of the drama he has been the invisible one.

Narelle is off to Sydney to care for baby Emma while Georgia is in Melbourne for work. Steve is tinkering on the Nord piano he inherited from his brother, Warren. He plans to gift it to Daniel and Benji.

As each day passes without a decision, Benji's confusion must grow. At least Monica can see her son every second weekend. The solicitors are powerless to do more. Monica receives an email address after contacting the court chat line, raising hope. Briefly. She asks if a date has been set and receives an automated response, promising her enquiry will be addressed in 3–5 days. That is far too long. To make matters worse, there is a notice for electronic requests: The Newcastle Registry of the Family Law and the Federal Circuit Court are currently experiencing delays processing electronic access requests.

'It's clearly another arm of the 88-armed octopus,' says Steve.

DAY 175 – ACTION TAKEN

Something must be done. Monica is a party to the case and cannot jeopardise the outcome. Steve has no credibility because of the Family Court ruling. Narelle takes the bull by the horns. They have been weighing this course of action for days. She emails the senior registrar's office, asking when a decision is likely. At this stage there is nothing to lose. After all, Sav contacted Mansfield's office before the interim hearing had even begun.

Meanwhile, Julia Presgraves, the DCJ officer handling Benji's case, wants to speak with Steve about the sexual abuse allegations. Monica and Narelle trust her, but Steve is not so sure. Presgraves was the one who interviewed Benji alongside Detective Bauer – the interview that resulted in a DVO filled with sexual abuse claims.

When Presgraves phones Steve and asks to hear his side of the story, he bristles. 'There is no story to hear about,' he tells her.
 Presgraves doesn't respond. They agree to meet the next day at the Hamilton house. She will bring someone to record the conversation. Steve ensures Narelle will be home, so he has a witness.

DAY 176 – PRONOUNCEMENT PENDING

'Can you please, *please* help Benji?' Steve implores Presgraves. 'We all fear for him. Just six months ago, he was a carefree, innocent boy. Now, he is in the grip of a heartless ogre, who is causing immense psychological harm in his twisted quest for power and revenge.'

When Benji was taken by his father over five months ago, he was crying and fretting for his mother. Since then, the 8-year-old has been kept in seclusion – a virtual prisoner – except for the one night he stayed with his half-sister Sienna when his father was in gaol. On that occasion, Sienna wanted to take Benji to a family barbeque, but he refused to go. When she asked him why, he told her that everyone would all hate him because of the lies he'd told... lies his father forced him to tell. Meanwhile, a capable mother is left without her son, watching helplessly as he slowly suffocates.

Steve continues, his eyes practically jumping from their sockets, as he makes sure Presgraves is aware of the urgency of the situation. 'Benji is experiencing ongoing trauma. There's been numerous reports to DCJ (the Department of Communities and Justice) about this.' He sneaks a glance at his wife Narelle and contains his fury – fury she too feels. 'These are the cornerstones of your charter. Surely you can do something?'

Presgraves can't. She does not have the authority.

Presgraves is part of The Joint Child Protection Response Program, a partnership between the DCJ, NSW police (NSWPF), and NSW Health.

Narelle and Steve speak with Presgraves and her associate about the danger their family is in – not only their daughter Monica and grandson Benji, but themselves as well. They describe Luca Savington's (Sav's) escalating behaviour: stalking, vandalism, threats and relentless harassment. The hundreds of text messages, emails and phone calls at all hours of the day and night, meant to intimidate Monica. Many of them from no-ID numbers and multiple disposable phones.

What makes the situation even more volatile, they tell Presgraves, is that Sav has succeeded in deceiving police. He has portrayed Monica as a mentally unstable alcoholic – violent towards him and their son and threatening to kill him. He claims to be terrified of her. The lies have been accepted without scrutiny and as a result Sav has been emboldened. The danger has only intensified.

Although Narelle and Steve know there is little Presgraves can do, they relish the opportunity to voice their fears and frustrations to someone in authority. To be fair to Presgraves, she is not there to resolve their difficulties. Her purpose is to formally conclude her investigation into one of Luca Savington's spiteful and malicious lies.

Presgraves knows Benji was coached by his father and is almost apologetic as she explains that she is obliged to ask Steve for his response to Luca Savington's claim that he sexually abused Benji.

'How can I respond to something that didn't happen?' he says.

Nothing more is required, and the investigation is complete.

After Presgraves and her associate leave the Percy Street house, Narelle and Steve make a cup of tea and sit in the courtyard. They are relieved that this part of the saga – which has greatly affected their lives – is finally over, but they remain fearful for their daughter and grandson. And it is so frustrating.

'Surely somebody can save Benji!' Steve roars.

'Shush,' says Narelle, in a scolding tone. 'The whole neighborhood can hear you.'

Steve lowers his voice. 'For months now DCJ have known Benji is in serious danger, yet nobody does anything. Like Presgraves, they listen but do nothing.'

'You can't blame her. She's just doing her job.'

'That's the problem? Everyone is just doing their job. Presgraves's unit, DCJ, the police, the Family Court. They operate in a vacuum. Each is like an arm of a 88-armed octopus, reaching in a different direction – oblivious to what the other is doing. Nobody connects the dots. That's why psychos like Sav get away with it.'

Then it happened. It's likely the senior registrar reacted to the text Narelle sent to his office. That afternoon, a court date for Mansfield's decision appeared on the portal – 3 pm the following Wednesday, to be delivered by video.

The inability to tell the truth is a pathological condition Luca Savington suffers from – as do others like him. They are incapable of telling the truth, even when there is nothing to gain. Sav's solicitor instructed Monica's solicitor that Benji didn't have soccer this weekend. But Monica has access to the coach's portal and knows the team's draw for the season.

Narelle:

It's not true. Soccer's on tonight.

Monica:

I'll contact Lisa.

Georgia:

Good. Liar!

Monica:

Good morning, Lisa. This is the info confirming Benji's game was tonight.

It's a shame Benji has been missing them.
Kind regards,
Monica.

Missing yet another soccer game must put Benji in danger of being dropped from the squad. Sav has probably decided soccer is no longer worth the bother – the court has heard all the evidence, and Mansfield's decision is already made. Once again, Sav proves how little he cares about Benji's ambitions and aspirations. He made such a big deal of soccer in the past, but the reality is he's not prepared to do the hard yards the way Monica did, driving to trials and practice sessions to support her son.

Daniel plays basketball at Broadmeadow Stadium. His team wins, and he plays with passion and purpose, scoring a few goals. They defeat the top-rated side in their group, but there's a catch. They are short of players, and his coach allows a 'ring-in' from A grade to step in – a poor decision since the player is well known to officials. For the next competition, Daniel must decide whether to move up to the under-17 age bracket with most of his present team, or to stay in the under-15s and find a new side.

DAY 178 – FRUSTRATION AND ANGER

In the *Sunday Telegraph* (July 28, 2024) Danielle Miller wrote about a new campaign launched by the paper to address domestic violence. Her article highlighted the media's long-standing tendency to frame perpetrators as 'good blokes who were pushed too far.' She pointed out that 60% of reporting excluded any information about the perpetrator. Miller argued that the way the media reports on violence against women matters because it shapes how audiences understand abuse and influences how they respond to both victims and perpetrators.

The *Telegraph* has since launched the 'Coward Campaign,' aiming to name and shame the perpetrators and call out 'these hideous assailants and end their reign of terror.' The campaign features respected sports stars urging men to take ownership of their behaviour, and it attempts to amplify the stories of those who live with the violence.

Whether the campaign will keep its momentum once the media spotlight moves to another issue remains to be seen. Miller's article is posted on Facebook and of the twenty-five comments beneath it, twenty-four are by women. Monica has received help and support from males. Phillip, with Chantel, attended nearly every court hearing. But most of the ongoing assistance is from women. The truth is that domestic violence is regarded as 'a women's problem.'

On the way back to Hexham, Benji becomes upset. After a good day with friends, he unravels when told he cannot take his iPad. In the car he lashes out – punching, pinching, and spitting at his mother. Seven months earlier such behaviour would have been unthinkable. Across the iPad screen he scrawls *I wish you'd never had me.*

DAY 179 – THE IPAD

On Monday afternoon, Monica receives disturbing news: Sav's solicitor has filed an urgent application 'to re-open the application in a proceeding for the purpose of adducing new evidence.' They want the matter relisted. Sav is claiming that Monica hit Benji. His request is for a return to supervised visits.

Luca Savington:
When Benji was returning from visiting his mother, his Nana snatched his iPad from him and his mother, and his grandmother yelled at him. After the visit, Benji ran towards me. I cuddled him tightly, and he said, 'I do not want to see Mum because she hurt me.'
I turned towards Narelle and said, 'What happened?'
'It's about the iPad,' she replied.
Walking towards the car, Benji was almost hyperventilating. When we got to the car, I asked Benji what had happened?
'Mummy kept screaming at me. She did not let me take the iPad. She hit me.'
'Where did she hit you?' I asked.
'On my chest.'
Benji cried intensely throughout the drive back home. Benji told me Mummy had spat on his sleeve. 'And she hit me on the chest while we were at McDonalds car park. It hurt... I do

not want to go back there.'

I felt shocked and concerned by Benji's disclosures. I contacted the police, and an officer attended the house. The officer had a brief conversation and said he would obtain CCTV footage from McDonalds and would be in contact once support was available to formally interview Benji. That night Benji repeated, 'I do not want to go back and see my mummy.'
I told Benji everything would be ok. He told me he was worried and scared of his mother.

I have extreme fears Benji is not coping with spending time with his mother. I do not believe that Monica has the capacity to care for Benji.

In the afternoon, Monica speaks with her ex-neighbour, Sarah. She was getting out of the car with her family just as Benji arrived home from school. Sarah saw Benji's eyes light up, only to withdraw into himself. He walked past his good friend Stu – the boy he had played with for years, and whose brother's party Monica had taken him to only a day earlier – and went straight into his house. He would have had three hours to wait until his father arrived home from work.

Benji must be extremely lonely, and it breaks Monica's heart. It breaks Steve's and Narelle's hearts when she tells them. Before Monica walked out on Sav, Benji would spend hours next door, but now he acts as though they don't even exist. The DCJ knows the situation but does not intervene. Psychological abuse doesn't register – they will react to physical abuse only. Yet, as mentioned earlier, it is widely known that psychological abuse can be just as damaging.

Narelle and Monica are asked by Monica's solicitor to respond to Sav's accusations. There is grave concern that Sav will succeed in delaying the case yet again. Benji was upset, and based on everything they have experienced so far, they have little reason to feel confident in the police force's capacity to deal with these bogus allegations.

Monica says, 'Sav is now saying he was born in Italy. He also has Marco's and my birthdates wrong.'
'I don't think he's capable of telling the truth,' Steve replies.

Monica responds to Sav's claims by stating that supervised visits were only a negotiated position while waiting for the outcome of the interim hearing – and that Benji should be returned to her care immediately.

Monica:

The time I have been spending with Benji has been going very well. We have lots of laughs. We have spent time at the library, had lunch with family members, and gone to soccer, gotten sushi and milkshakes and chatted. Last visit we were trying to win a football on the Claw Machine. I could see he was determined to beat the machine. Benji has been very chatty, and we cuddle each other a lot.

Monica explains that Narelle drove to Hexham while she sat in the backseat with Benji so they could keep chatting. She kept the iPad so that Benji would have something to look forward to when he was with her. She didn't want him to take it back to the house because Sav had been selling off the children's belongings on Facebook Marketplace – items such as the trampoline, the basketball hoop, and others. Besides, Benji already had PlayStation at the house to play on. The solicitor chose to exclude the issue of asset sales to keep the response uncomplicated.

Monica:

I had a conversation with Benji that the iPad would be staying with me. During the first visit, he started to negotiate. Sienna, Narelle, Benji and I went to Benji's cousin's party in Sydney. We had a good day. Afterwards we drove to Hexham. Benji was upset at the changeover because he couldn't take the iPad with him.

When Benji visited two weeks later, we attended a friend's birthday party at Revolution Sports Park. Benji told me he had been invited to two parties. I said I'd take him as it fell on the dates I had him. I was able to get the details of one of the parties. Sav did not provide me with the invites or any information. Benji told me Sav doesn't let him attend parties.

We got a present at K-Mart and Benji enjoyed himself at the party. He came to me for things like food, drink, his jumper, but mainly played with his friends. Benji played with his iPad in the afternoon and chatted with his friend Zoe online. We left for Hexham to drop him off. He played on his iPad and chatted. After a while Benji stopped chatting and stared out the window. His body was stiff, and he said words to the effect, 'Dad's house is boring, and he never plays with me. Can I take the iPad back with me?'

'You have Playstation.at your house,' I replied.

We travelled in silence for the rest of the way. When we pulled up at McDonalds, Benji grabbed the iPad and wouldn't let go.

'You need to give me the iPad, and you'll have it when I see you next,' I said.

'Two weeks is too far away.'

'You need to give me the iPad. I'll count to three. 1 2 3...'

Benji still didn't give it back, so I proceeded to take it off him. As I reached for the iPad, Benji pulled it to his chest and began hitting me with an open hand to the shoulder. I told him he couldn't do that to his mum. He then spat at me, kicking his feet in my direction. I quickly took the iPad, got out of the car, and passed it to Mum. I told Benji to get out of the car, as his dad would be arriving soon. I never screamed at Benji, I never spat at Benji, I remained calm. Benji was angry and said, 'I hate you and never want to come back.' I replied, 'Well I love you Benji, and can't wait to see you again.' Benji and Narelle went into McDonalds, while I locked myself in the car.

Narelle's account is consistent with Monica's, with a few additions. She includes the details of handing Benji over to Sav inside McDonald's after each of the two visits.

Narelle:
I heard Benji ask if he could take his iPad back with him. Monica replied something to the effect that he knew he had to leave it with her so he could play with it next time. Sienna also said, 'You need to leave it Benji.' Benji would not hand over the iPad and became increasingly angry. When we got back, Sienna took the iPad and handed it to Monica. Benji was agitated and got out of the car, ran into the restaurant, and started crying when he saw Sav and ran to him. I followed him and said to Sav, 'He wasn't allowed to keep the iPad.' Sav embraced Benji, stood for a while then left. He said nothing to me, and as they left, I said, 'See you next time.' I did not yell or scream at Benji.

As we were driving Benji back to the rendezvous after the next visit, Benji started to argue he should be able to keep his iPad because it belonged to him. Monica explained he had his PlayStation, so his iPad stayed at Hamilton. Benji argued that we were trying to upset him. Monica, and I replied that was not true and we wanted him to be happy. Benji replied that it was not working and to make him happy he should be able to keep his iPad.

By the time we arrived at McDonalds, Benji just kept repeating, 'I'm keeping it.' Monica took the iPad and put it into the door's side pocket. I had parked by this time, and I saw Benji lunge across Monica trying to get the iPad and shouting at her, 'I hate you and I never want to see you again.' He spat at Monica, pinched and slapped her. I left the car and went around to Monica's door, opened it, and Monica passed me the iPad. I took it and put it under my coat. Benji kept yelling and refused to leave the car to go inside. Monica got out of the car and said (she did not yell), 'You have to get out, your father is waiting.' Benji left and ran into the restaurant. I followed behind and Benji ran to his father, crying and saying, 'I hate mummy.' Sav looked at me and mouthed, 'What happened?'

I replied, 'It's about the iPad.' Sav pulled a face and kept patting Benji and saying it will be alright.

He then asked, 'Is there any chance of getting the iPad?'

I replied, 'No, he has the X-box.' Sav said, 'He hasn't got an X box. It's a PlayStation and he doesn't play it. We both paid for the iPad.'

I replied, 'He has the PlayStation at your place and the iPad at Hamilton.'

Sav said to me, 'You leave,' so I did.

Benji had continued crying through this exchange and would not look at me.

Narelle is at her wits' end. It feels wrong that she must be near Sav just to facilitate the handovers. She also worries the police will come knocking again over Sav's latest fabrications. It is wearing her down, and she is fed up.

They all fear for Benji. Just six months ago, he was a carefree, innocent boy. Now, he is in the grip of a heartless ogre, suffering immense psychological harm in his twisted quest for power and revenge. Meanwhile, a capable mother is left without her son, watching helplessly as he is slowly suffocating.

Sienna has offered to make a statement in support, confirming she was in the car with them during the first visit in mid-July. But Monica's solicitor says they have enough evidence, and her account is not required.

DAY 180 – ON THE DEFENSIVE

Before Monica leaves for work, she asks Steve if the police will come to her workplace.

'Call me if they do,' he replies.

Sav's tactics are a repeat of the rubbish he claimed happened at the soccer game. No death threats this time – just coercing Benji into lying in an attempt to influence the Family Court.

Myra, a real estate agent, visits the Hamilton house. Narelle and Steve have been considering a move for some time and now feels like the right time. They need more space. Ideally, two houses on one property – and by chance, the perfect place is for sale near Daniel's school. In conversation, Myra mentions she recently did a valuation near Monica and Sav's house. By coincidence, the property turned out to be theirs. Sav presented himself as the sole owner and never once mentioned Monica. That night, Narelle and Steve agree on terms to sell. Steve warns Myra that if Sav learns she is handling the Hamilton sale, he will never allow her to sell the house. Monica must approve the sale, despite Sav pretending it is his call. With Myra managing the process, they will have visibility over what is happening.

Around 2 pm Monica rings Steve. She has been contacted by the police. The police prosecutor has confirmed that no action will be taken against Steve, and his DVO will 'dissolve' over the next few months.

'Dissolve' is the legal term for bringing an order to an end. Under a new scheme being trailed in Newcastle, selected DVOs that are not breached within three months are dissolved – unlike the past, when they remained on record for two years.

Steve shares a joke with Narelle where he wants the DVO to be dissolved immediately due to no solid evidence.

The police officer who contacted Monica seemed as though he wanted to deliver some positive news to the family. When Monica tells him that her father would never harm Benji, he agrees, and it becomes clear he knows the truth. Steve is not overly excited when he hears the update; Bauer had already tried to have the DVO removed weeks earlier. But Monica insists they should celebrate every win, and Steve does not disagree.

While Narelle is driving Daniel home from school, he asks about his brother, and she tells him about Benji hitting at and spitting on Monica when he wasn't allowed to take his iPad back home.
'That's wrong,' says Daniel. 'What will we do about his spitting?'
'Sav is saying it was Monica who did the spitting.'
'What! How can he get away with that? I should make stuff up about him.'
Daniel pauses for a moment, 'Actually, I don't have to make anything up. I only have to say what he's really done to me. Maybe I should make a list.'

Only one more day remains until the court orders are due. Sav's latest claims are already listed on the website. Narelle is shaken when she opens the

Savington v Savington file – it is full of vile accusations. Reading the sexual and child abuse claims makes her sick. She sees that the solicitors have already conferred, presumably about Sav's recent allegations. The ICL will not be fooled, and neither should the senior registrar be. Both know that Sav has coerced Benji into lying before.

DAY 181 – FORGOTTEN CHILD

Chantel and Phillip drive up from the Central Coast to help Narelle, Monica and Steve declutter the house. Using Phillip's Ute and the Ford, they make several trips to Grandma's place at New Lambton, storing three bookcases and ten large cardboard boxes full of household items in her garage.

Benji's case worker contacts Monica. She has completed her report and, as they had been told verbally, she and her father are cleared of Sav's accusations. The report states there is no evidence to support his claims. There are no repercussions for the person behind the malicious allegations. Like the police, the DCJ simply concludes there is no evidence to proceed.

The 3 pm deadline approaches. Outside it is overcast with intermittent showers. The weather reflects the atmosphere inside the house. They have had their hopes crushed before, and the tension is palpable as they await Mansfield's decision. Monica recalls the first time Benji managed to put on his shoes by himself. He was at preschool and said to the teacher, 'Don't tell Mum.'

Narelle leaves to collect Daniel from school. Ten minutes later, Chantel and Phillip are about to head to the airport to meet Chantel's son and his family, who are arriving from Brisbane, when Monica receives a text message from Lisa: *See you tomorrow.*

Confused, she calls immediately. More disappointment. Mansfield has postponed his decision. On Friday at 3 pm the court will hear an application from Sav's solicitor to have the case reopened. The delay tactic has worked, and once again they are forced onto the defensive.

Six weeks earlier the ICL told the court she had all the information needed to determine what was best for the child. Yet the child is forgotten again.

Police review the CCTV footage from McDonald's Hexham and will not be taking the matter further. The images show a boy running from a car, followed by his grandparent. Monica and Narelle are required to sign fresh affidavits. To attend the hearing on Friday into whether the case will be reopened – to respond to what everyone knows is another fake allegation, as well as blatant child abuse – will cost Monica another $5,000. That is the price she must pay to stay in the game, to have even a chance of saving her son from this unrelenting ogre. It is like a high-stakes poker game – winner takes all, with Benji's future on the line.

No wonder so many women stay in abusive relationships, trapped until their children grow up. No wonder so many women die.

DAY 182 – COACH

In South Australia today, the police carried out a domestic violence crackdown that resulted in 80 arrests. Police targeted 265 offenders. The announcement of the results comes after a week of national rallies demanding an end to domestic, family, and sexual violence.
'In 22/23 the rate of domestic violence matters reported to SAPOL was over 22,000,' said Deputy Commissioner Williams. 'It sends a strong message to people who, for example, are on bail or have an intervention order, that it will be policed, and we will be following up, and they will be held to account.'

Tomorrow, Narelle and Monica's affidavits will be presented to the court. Sav can't be cross-examined, which means he can assert whatever he likes. What purpose the reopening serves is anyone's guess. Monica is due to have Benji on Saturday and Sunday. There is a soccer game scheduled for Saturday morning and Monica wants Benji to play. She decides to text the coach.

Monica:
Hi Chris, has Benji attended any training or games recently?

Coach:
Not in the last 5 weeks.
Monica:
Thanks for the reply. It's really concerning to hear this. The custody decision has taken longer than anticipated. I know the team was important to Benji and I also don't like letting the team down.

Monica then sees that on the club's football app that Benji has not been selected for the Saturday game.

Monica:
Hi Chris. I have Benji this Saturday. I can bring him to play if he's OK to attend.
Coach:
Hello Monica, there is an issue that Benji's registration fees are still outstanding. Along with not having trained it will be difficult for Benji. Happy for him to attend and play but the registration would need to be rectified.

Monica contacts Georgia, Narelle, and Steve on Facebook Messenger:
Should I pay $500?
Georgia:
How much is rego?
Monica:
$1350.
Georgia:
Tell the soccer coach Sav told the courts he has paid, and you are confused.
Narelle:
Ask Lisa to say Sav must pay the outstanding amount. It's not the club's fault that Benji didn't go. He took a spot.

Coach:
Hi Monica, URGENT PAYMENT REQUIRED
Please see attached invoice:
The amount outstanding of AUD 1,350 due on Feb 28, 2024.

Monica pays the full amount then sends a copy of the receipt to Lisa. She may be able to bring it up if the hearing gets reopened. Sav has made a monumental deal about the soccer.

Monica to Lisa:

Hi Lisa, as you can see in correspondence with the coach, Sav hasn't paid the rego. Sav said in an earlier text that he paid the fees, clearly another lie. Benji will be lucky to have a spot on the team. I would like to take Benji to the game on Saturday, but we'll need to meet earlier than 9 am to make it in time. Kind regards,
Monica.

Monica:

The coach thanked me for paying the fees and said see you Saturday.

DAY 183 – NEVER-ENDING HEARING

Just before two o'clock, Chantel and Phillip arrive at the Hamilton house to accompany Monica and Narelle to the courthouse. Again, their support is invaluable. Steve doesn't attend. Monica and Narelle have discussed tactics with Lisa. The iPad incident can be turned against Sav. It shows Monica sets boundaries for her child, something Sav is incapable of doing. A decent father would have backed the mother.

There is also a strong point about Sav potentially getting the iPad and using it for stalking. Monica will also be able to bring to the court's attention the fact that Sav hasn't taken Benji to soccer training, or to a single game, for five weeks. He lied about this and lied about having paid the registration fees.

Monica waits in the safe room while Lisa sets herself up in a small space visible from the foyer. When Sav arrives with his solicitor and barrister, they plonk themselves directly outside where Lisa is working – an obvious attempt to intimidate. Lisa has a reputation for being a tough cookie, and the tactic is bound to fail. She has moved between criminal and family law throughout her career. She has stood up to motorcycle gangs and is not easily bullied.

The hearing begins an hour and a half after the scheduled time. Lisa takes Monica with her to the front of the courtroom. Sav and his team can only see her back. They will not see her reaction, although by now she has perfected the blank poker face that gives nothing away.

Sav's barrister claims the case should be reopened and quotes some vaguely related commercial law case from Victoria, as he can't find an equivalent in family law. Lisa writes a note to Monica: *There is a saying in law. When you lack evidence, you quote cases.*

The Independent Children's Lawyer is adamant the case should not be reopened. She refutes the claim that Benji was hit. She predicts Sav will make ongoing allegations in the future and says there is nothing in these new claims that differs from what has previously been disclosed to the court. But if there is a delay, she has more to add.

Lisa is originally against reopening the hearing but changes her mind. The texts from Benji's soccer coach show Sav doesn't care about Benji's soccer, despite the fuss he made over it. Lisa has another concern, and it may explain why the senior registrar is cautious. If Sav's new allegations are not defended, and Monica is given care of Benji, Sav's team will likely apply for a 'stay' in the orders. If successful, delivery of the court's orders could be delayed indefinitely.

Mansfield agrees to reopen the hearing on Thursday at 10 am, via Microsoft Teams. He notes that it is unusual to overturn a living arrangement at an interim hearing. He will hand down a decision from chambers the following Monday.

Steve:
The never-ending hearing continues. We are now in a movie called 'Groundhog Day.' In the background someone is singing, 'Where oh where is little Benji?'

While this legal discussion is going on, Benji is alone in the house. School finishes at three. By the time Sav gets back – after lingering at court and chatting heartily with his legal team about motor vehicles – it will be dark outside.

It is known the child has been coerced into lying to police and other authorities. It has been normalised. By now, Benji believes there is no alternative – that his father, despite setbacks and endless police visits, runs the show. He lies to please Sav, displaying the behaviours of Stockholm Syndrome, bound by a powerful attachment to his captor.

On Benji's school file, Monica notices the word 'meeting' written next to his name on a couple of occasions. She makes an enquiry. The business manager replies that Benji was not attending meetings. Instead, the school was meeting to discuss whether he needed support. But if Benji has been struggling – and it is unlikely to be academic – why has his mother not been told? Why have her enquiries about her son been ignored? The school principal does not seem to grasp that Monica is still a joint parent.

Under the previous principal, Monica was held in high regard. Daniel thrived both academically and as a student leader. To dismiss a mother's concern about her son's welfare is a serious blunder. Perhaps the principal has believed misinformation or yielded to Sav's pressure. Either way, the school has failed both mother and child.

Sav, meanwhile, must be feeling cocky. He is now trying to be friendly with the very neighbours he reported to police earlier in the year. He no longer pretends to fear Sarah. The hot-and-cold behaviour mirrors the tactic he uses with his own family – push, pull, alienate, charm.

Sarah:
Sav tried talking to me and the kids today. That's three times in three weeks. I'm going to the police. Stu told him, 'My mum thinks you are mean and rude.' I've warned him not to talk to Sav. He was speaking with him when I wasn't there. I'm so angry.

DAY 189 – PLAY DATE

Narelle accompanies Monica to the hearing at Lisa's office. Around 12:30 Monica rings Steve. She is upbeat, which is a relief. No, she doesn't have Benji – but Sav's tactics have backfired again. His accusations were discredited by the ICL: further proof of his deceitful, controlling nature. The senior registrar's decision will be handed down next Tuesday morning, five days from now. There is some discussion about how it should be done. It is agreed that the ICL will go to Benji's school and explain the situation to him. Monica and her team take this as a positive sign. Why would an explanation be needed if it were business as usual? Still, they've been disappointed before, and they resist the temptation to feel overconfident.

On Friday morning a photographer arrives at the Hamilton house to take footage for the upcoming sale. Everyone has been frantically tidying and are worn out by the time he shows up.

Benji is scheduled to visit on Saturday and Sunday. Monica is excited. She hasn't seen him for two weeks. She buys burger buns and hotdogs, his favourites, and arranges a play date with one of his best mates – a boy Sav has kept him from since the isolation began.

Lisa, 4pm:
Hi Monica, I've just finished the appointment run. There is an email from Sav's solicitor so there will be no contact this weekend. This is devastating now but will play into our hands come Tuesday. Please email the coach to ensure Benji is at soccer tomorrow, but no-one from your family, including yourself is to attend the game. This will become extremely important for the final hearing, in that his behaviour just reinforces his attitude towards orders. It demonstrates they don't apply to him. No matter how much everyone wants to see Benji tomorrow, DO NOT GO.
Tuesday at 11am for judgement.

Monica is upset. It makes her sick.

Georgia:
Course he has. Get Sarah to see if he leaves the house at all. I bet he takes Benji to his parents for the day on Tuesday.
Narelle:
Tuesday will be interesting.
Georgia:
The father knows any power he has is running out.
Narelle:
Yes. Definitely his last stand.
Monica:
Sarah is on the lookout. The police were at the house last night. A neighbour told Darren. They missed it, as it was late at night.
Georgia:
Oh… I wonder what for. Of the many things.

Monica:
Neighbour across the road told Darren they're very worried about Benji. Benji forgot his key and was out the front for hours alone.
Narelle:
Interesting. Send to Lisa.
Georgia:
OMG. Can they put it in writing?

Monica contacts Benji's soccer coach and explains Sav is refusing the scheduled visit. The coach says he will confirm if Benji attends. The soccer issue is making Sav appear stupid – and even more stupid if Monica had taken Benji to soccer on Saturday. It is unlikely Sav will take him. But who can predict how the narcissistic mind of Luca Savington works. His disregard of court orders makes him dangerous – and maybe even more so if Monica is given full care on Tuesday.

Around 4 pm Steve is coming back to the house after picking up Daniel from school. They are driving along Sandon Street, just about to turn into Percy, when Daniel says, 'That's Leonardo who just drove past.'
'Are you sure?' asks Steve.
'Yeah. I know his car.'
It's a busy street, but it's unusual for Leonardo to be in the area.
When they park the car Daniel says, 'You know Leonardo takes steroids.'
Steve's heard this before, but is surprised Daniel knows.
'Who told you?'
'He did. You can tell from the stretch marks on his skin.'

Monica takes Daniel to his basketball game at Gateshead around 6 pm. She picks up Sienna along the way. Still on the outer with the Savington family, she can hold her head high. Steve speaks to Daniel about being accepting of Benji if he comes back to live with them on Tuesday. Steve doesn't know if he will be allowed to stay if it happens – that might be another battle they must fight.

Narelle is checking the Savington court files after dinner. In the court diary she sees there is a chambers hearing listed for the following Monday. It is to be attended by the three solicitors and the senior registrar. The judgement delivery is still scheduled for 11 am Tuesday.

Due to the actions of a jealous, self-centred narcissist, a child has been torn from the life he knew and kept from his mother. The aggressor has been empowered and allowed to inflict psychological damage on both the child and the outcast parent. There is an alternative. If the parents cannot agree, equal access should automatically be granted as the starting point – or, as mothers are the prime carers in more than 90% of cases, fathers should be allowed time with their children every second weekend. It is far from perfect, but it is a vast improvement on the present system, where taking and withholding a child is legal.

With the present system, when the case finally reaches court, the abducting parent can not only argue it is 'the norm,' but they have a distinct advantage if the court wants to observe the child's behaviour with each parent. Without the interim hearing, Monica would barely have seen Benji until the final hearing, which might have been twelve months or more from when he was taken. By then, Benji would barely have known her. Monica's solicitor Adele warned Monica of this when she advised her to agree to the supervised visits. The status quo would have been established, which was why the interim hearing was crucial in Monica's case.

DAY 194 – D-DAY

D-Day has finally arrived. Everyone is desperate for a decision (except maybe Sav and his team) and will be shattered if there are more delays. Monica sets up her computer at the kitchen table, with Narelle and Steve sitting on either side.

As she logs on, a notification flashes across Steve's phone: *On this day in 1521, Spanish Conquistador Hernán Cortés captured Mexico City after a 93-day siege, ending the Aztec Empire.* Sav has kept Benji under siege for more than twice as long. It would be fitting if he were freed today.

They talk about Sav cancelling the weekend visit and Benji missing his soccer match.
'Lisa really spelt it out. DON'T GO TO SOCCER,' says Narelle.
'Sav was never going to take him anyway,' says Steve. 'He'd look like a complete fool after keeping him away for five weeks.'

'Who knows? Maybe he wanted one last shot at being father of the year,' says Monica.

The screen springs to life. The senior registrar's assistant checks that all parties are logged in. Curiously, Sav has logged on alone instead of appearing from his solicitor's office as usual. It is unclear where the ICL is, but the orders will be sent to Benji's school once finalised. The ICL intends to be there at 2 pm to explain the decision to him directly.

The senior registrar opens the hearing. He says he will send the orders to the solicitors by email unless someone objects and insists they be read aloud. Nobody objects. He notes his reasons will be published within twenty-four to forty-eight hours. He states there is an order concerning the paternal grandfather, Steve Kelty, then announces there are twenty-three orders and five notations. After just ten minutes, the hearing closes.

Monica waits anxiously for Lisa's call. Five minutes later, the phone rings. Lisa has only read the opening paragraph, but her entire office is jubilant, their celebration audible in the background.

CHILD TO LIVE WITH MOTHER

The mother has sole decision-making responsibility in relation to all major long-term issues for child.

Monica will collect Benji from school once the ICL has spoken to him about his new living arrangements. At last, she can fulfil her son's wish from what feels like a lifetime ago, just before he was taken, when he said: 'You won't ever leave me, will you, Mum?'

The relief is overwhelming. Supporters who have followed the case for six months are jubilant.

But as the saying goes, the devil is in the detail. Steve is banished – not allowed near Benji.

Another condition: Narelle must always be within hearing range of Monica and Benji. The only exception is if Benji is in the care of someone else.

The father will have no contact for four weeks. After that, he is entitled to supervised visits through ReKonnect, at his own expense – poetic justice. The ICL had pressed for this, to give mother and son time to rebuild their bond.

When Monica and Narelle collect Benji from school, he is cheerful and chatty. They had feared he might be unsettled, but instead he sings and talks happily all the way home. Over and over, he chants one line, 'I'm going home. I'm going home.'

Back at the house, Benji is thrilled to be reunited with his brother. After dinner, he plays with the infamous iPad and chats easily with his mother.

Monica:
Benji said to me, 'You made me miss sport today.'
Georgia:
Oh, ha, ha.
Monica:
That's been the biggest concern.
Georgia:
Did he say what the Independent Children's Lawyer said to him?
Monica:
No.

Sarah 10:40 pm:
Hi Monica, just letting you know Sav left in the Ute. He's not at Coles, because I'm down there. Just keep an eye on the cameras.

Georgia to Monica:
If you see anything call the police. Don't even hesitate.

DAY 1 – NEW ORDER

Georgia:
How was last night?
Narelle:
Good, all ok.
Georgia:
What was that about the iPad in the court orders. It seems crazy that an iPad is in a court order.
Narelle:
I think it was to rub it into Sav. The iPad was to stay with the mother. It was a big thing. Sav went to the police. The case had to be reopened.
Georgia:
Yeah, ok. Ha, ha. Crazy.
Narelle:
I think it was the last straw. Everyone knew Sav was lying and the registrar let him hang himself.
Georgia:
I'm curious to know how he keeps track of those lies in the final hearing. When he's cross-examined. How's Benji tonight?
Monica:
Happy. Just chat, chat, chat.
Georgia:
So good.
Monica:
Sarah doesn't think Sav has been back to the house since last night. Hopefully, he's taken off.
Georgia:
Oh, wow. I wonder. Hopefully.
Narelle:
He's probably gone to his parents. Maybe he won't come back.
Georgia:
That would be best for everyone. Unlikely. His first reaction is always, boohoo, poor me, but he'll plan something. He did it in the beginning. Moped around. Made the kids feel sorry for sad papa, then began terrorising them. He has no ability to give up because he doesn't think he is doing anything

wrong.
Monica:
That's true. Benji hasn't said, 'I miss my dad.' Which is good.
Georgia:
Or. 'I want to go back there.' Yeah. I'm sure he's happy to be with you and Daniel.
Monica:
Safe.
Georgia:
Relieved too. I told Matt about him missing sport and he said sport was the best subject at school.
Monica:
Sav keeps updating his soccer profile. Father and son and all that.
Georgia:
Maybe that's him trying to send messages to you. Report it.
Monica:
Yes.
Narelle:
Two more weeks.
Georgia:
Two more weeks for what?
Narelle:
Soccer. I don't think you should escalate at the moment. Ignore him. He can't do anything.
Steve:
Just leave it. You have Benji and that's all he has left.
Georgia:
Yeah, true.

The second night, Benji became upset as he lay in bed.
'You and Dad shouldn't have separated over a silly fight,' he told Monica, his voice breaking into tears. He cried harder as he explained that he felt sorry for his father. 'It's only fair I lived with Dad because you have Daniel, and he has nobody.'

As the time for the interim orders drew closer, Sav, fearing he might lose his son, would have been moping around the house, projecting his own anxieties onto Benji. Now the child feels responsible for his father's predicament. Too young to grasp the seriousness of his father's actions, he takes on a burden that isn't his to carry. One day, though, he will understand. Just as Sienna remembered how appallingly her mother had been treated, Benji too will see the truth.

DAY 3 – UNTRUTHS UNVEILED

Monica:
Benji was talking to me about falling downstairs.
Georgia:
What did he say?
Monica:
He said something like, 'No-one has pushed me.' That's a start.
Narelle:
It's on his mind. Especially now he's at the house with the stairs.
Georgia:
Poor thing. Did he bring it up?
Monica:
Yes. He said, 'Do you remember when I fell down the stairs?' I said, maybe at Nelsons Bay when you were little.
Georgia:
Its good he's talking and figuring it out.

Since returning to his mother, Benji hasn't let her out of his sight. If she steps into the yard, he follows. If she goes to the mailbox, he goes too. He shadows her every move, as though afraid she might vanish again. He keeps his distance from Narelle, wary and unsure. Sav has likely poisoned him with lies, telling him Monica's side of the family despise him because of the things he was forced to say. Sav worked to isolate the boy, to sever his ties and warp his trust. But Benji knows the truth. He knows he wasn't pushed down the stairs. He knows his mother never smacked him, despite what Sav made him claim. He knows, too, that the statements about sexual abuse were fabrications he was coerced into repeating. The knowledge sits inside him, confusing and heavy.

He must also be wondering about his Pop. Monica will wait until Benji raises it himself. Just as Sav once told him his mother was in gaol, it is likely he has been told the same about his grandfather. Another cruel invention to keep him cut off from those who love him.

On Sunday, another of the lies Benji was fed is unveiled. Sav had led Benji to believe the reason Benji wasn't allowed to see his mother was because the police wouldn't allow it. Monica sets him straight.

DAY 7 – DVO

Georgia:
Do you think it's funny if I send Emma to daycare as Sleeping Beauty? Because they keep telling me she won't sleep.
Narelle:
Yes. I think that's very funny. Not peculiar.
Georgia:
It's a rare blue supermoon tonight. It means change, transformation and new beginnings.
Narelle:
Nice. We can hope.

Monica received a message from the Hunter Valley Domestic Violence Court Advocacy Group:
Hi Monica, your DVO was mentioned in court today. The matter has been adjourned for further mention March 13, 2025. Interim order to continue.

Monica tells Georgia:
What! Why?
Monica:
No idea. Still an interim order. With everything else going on, I forgot it was still in the system.
Georgia:
What is taking so long? Honestly! $$$$
Steve:
It might be time for a serious complaint.

Georgia:
I agree. It's costing so much money, having to keep hiring a barrister.

The DVO still in the system was used to Sav's advantage in the initial Family Court hearing, enabling him to retain custody of Benji while they awaited the interim hearing. Sav used the documents to convince doctors, psychologists, soccer officials, and Benji's school that Monica was an unfit mother.

DVOs are a money spinner for solicitors and barristers, yet a time waster for police and the courts. Many women, through bitter experience, believe DVOs favour the abuser. How can that be changed? For a start, the officers who issue the DVO – and the higher-ranked officer who signs off on it – should be required to speak with both parties in person. A reasonable person with common sense would recognise the improbability of a man of Sav's size and strength living in fear of a woman like Monica. They might check their own records; which party has a history of violence? Sav dislocated his own son's shoulder and was reported to the DCJ on multiple occasions for child abuse. He has an extensive police record.

In Monica's case, the police officers (several) involved in issuing and authorising the two DVOs on Sav's behalf ignored or missed the fact that just a month earlier, Monica was on police video in a highly distressed state asking for protection. She was the one in need of the DVO – not the man stalking and harassing her, the one with a history of violence and harassment. Is there a history? Is there a credible witness? Is there evidence? These are some of the questions that need to be asked.

That two DVOs were issued against Monica based on what the abuser told police should be of serious concern to the NSW Police Commissioner. That one of those DVOs is still in the system more than six months later is indefensible.

Steve:
It is ridiculous that without a witness, nor one skerrick of evidence to back up the incredulous claims, it is still being prosecuted by the police. It makes a mockery of the claim, 'All police are trained in domestic violence.'

DAY 8 – SAV CAN'T STOP

Monica and Narelle attend a directions hearing. Nothing of substance is achieved. The only adjustment is a tinkering of the orders, allowing Benji to attend special events if they clash with soccer training or games. Soccer has taken on an outsized importance, especially as Benji hasn't played in five weeks and there are only two weeks left in the season.

The ICL suggests that sharing responsibility for soccer might encourage a cooperative parenting approach. To Monica and Narelle, the idea is laughable given Sav's history. It isn't even clear how such an arrangement could work when his contact is limited to two-hourly supervised visits.

By the end, both women are drained. The exercise has added to their legal costs without achieving anything tangible, apart from listing future court dates. What stings most is hearing the ICL thank Sav for signing the orders handed down by the senior registrar – a gesture that feels like misplaced gratitude to the man who caused all this.

Monica:
Sav has indicated on the soccer app that he's attending the JDL club dinner on Friday night. Should I send it to the solicitor or ignore it?
Georgia:
Send it.
Steve:
Sav is trying to get to you. Make a note of it and wait. He wants a response. Oh... I just noticed you are already down to go.
Georgia:
Or just go and call the police if he attends.

Monica contacts her solicitor. Lisa sends an email to Sav's solicitor asking him to explain the court orders to his client in a manner he can understand, noting that Sav added his name to the list of parents attending the dinner after today's court hearing.

Monica:
Daniel came fourth out of twelve participants in the regional high jump.

Georgia:
Wow! Imagine if he had training.
Monica:
He made lots of new friends.

Steve has become collateral damage. Restrictions remain despite DCJ, the Child Abuse Squad, and the ICL all knowing the accusations were fabricated – without a conviction, a charge, or even a formal interview. The reason (though none has been given) is that his DVO has not yet 'dissolved.' But this order is not in the best interests of the child. Benji knows his Pop can't live with them because of him, and Daniel feels some resentment towards his brother for making Pop live somewhere else.

The court ruling requires Narelle to always remain within hearing distance of Monica and Benji – an impossible burden. The order provides a release valve by allowing Benji to be cared for by relatives or friends without Narelle's presence, providing Monica is not there. In practical terms, it is meaningless. After months of isolation, Benji will not let Monica out of his sight. Which in effect means Monica never gets a break. It also means Narelle and her husband Steve cannot be together.

How can Narelle, a seventy-year-old woman, fulfill the court requirement? What happens if either Narelle or Benji falls ill? Both lives must be put on hold. The order prevents Monica from doing the simplest things with her son – taking him shopping, visiting friends, or walking to the park – without Narelle in tow. Unless Narelle is available, the order effectively restricts Benji from joining a soccer team or attending Little Athletics. Furthermore, it prevents Narelle from being able to work.

DAY 10 – DYING STAR

Monica took Benji to soccer training and later to the end-of-season presentation. The club was crowded, so they didn't stay long, but at least he was able to finish the season with his team. Sav didn't attend.

He is still posting inappropriate photos on the club's soccer app, which is viewed by the parents of the under-9 and under-10 teams. The profile image was first of himself with Benji but has since been changed to a wedding photo of himself and Monica.

Sav continues to misuse the soccer club app, posting a photo of himself with Daniel. The next day, the profile picture changes again – this time to an old photo of himself, Daniel, and Benji taken five or six years earlier. Neither boy is aware of what Sav is doing, and Daniel is far too astute to be taken in by such nonsense anyway. Soon after, Sav posts a photo of himself and Monica. The coach must find it peculiar.

It is the only power Luca Savington has left to wield – like a dying star whose light is fading. Whether he goes out with a whimper or explodes remains to be seen.

On Monday, Sarah texts Monica:
Hey honey, saw the weirdest thing today. Sav walking to the shops in the rain with a shopping bag. No Ute there the last few days. Very often just Marco's car. Wonder has he lost his license or something! I thoroughly enjoyed watching him drag his fat lazy arse up the road in the rain.
Monica:
I think Marco is waiting on parts for his car.
Sarah:
I slowed right down, and he looked everywhere but me.

Georgia:
It's sad but it's his fault. I have to remind myself what he's done. It's not in our nature to enjoy someone being down. But he would have no issues if we all went to gaol.

Steve:
I have no sympathy for him whatsoever. Not after what he's done.

On Tuesday, Monica texts Georgia:
Benji went to the tryouts for next year's JDL soccer. He did his best. There were a few trying out.
Georgia:
Oh, good on him. That's very brave to do after the year he's had.
Monica:
Yes, he was nervous.
Georgia:
Good on him. Getting himself there. We're proud of him.

Sav continues to post on Benji's soccer app, switching from photos to messages.
Sav:
It's ok to start over and love each other the right way.

Monica:
That's clearly a direct message.
Narelle:
Let's just ignore it. Don't give anything back.
Steve:
Keep a record but don't react. That's what he wants.

Sav puts up a new photo of himself with Daniel.
Georgia:
Oh, good to know he remembers him.
Sav posts a photo from their wedding.
Georgia:
He's testing. To see what he can get away with. Trying to provoke a reaction.
Narelle:
Did he send that directly to you? He turned off team notifications.
Monica:
The photos will still come up.
Georgia:
Funny for someone who is so scared of you.

The profile picture is gone. Sav posts a message:
How do I say I miss you that will make your heart ache as much as mine?

Narelle:
I think you should talk to the police about that one. What do you think?
Monica:
I feel sad for Benji because it looks stupid in his soccer team app.
Steve:
The club should close his access.
Monica:
I feel Sav doing this will disadvantage Benji getting on the team again.
Georgia:
He's already done that.

DAY 16 – SAV RUINS IT FOR BENJI

Monica:
Sav's no longer on the soccer app. I emailed Lisa yesterday afternoon. Not sure if she said something to the club or the coach had had enough.

Sav is too self-absorbed to consider the effect of his actions on his son. Whether he organises visits through ReKonnect remains to be seen – and whether paying to see his child will feel too much like a slight to his ego. He seems oblivious to the harm he has already caused. Monica forwards Sav's posts to her solicitor. She hasn't the energy for more of Sav's trickery, but still takes them to the police, knowing full well he is likely to retaliate.

On Friday, Monica receives Benji's NAPLAN (National Assessment in Literacy and Numeracy) results. He performed strongly across all areas. Surprisingly, his English ranked higher than his math. Considering he missed a significant amount of school earlier in the year while Sav kept him home – and endured considerable stress – his results are a source of pride for Monica.

In the meantime, Steve meets with solicitors Clark and Salisbury to discuss his situation. Narelle accompanies him to their Hunter Street offices, near the courts. The solicitor they consult is familiar with the ICL attached to Benji's case, as well as Sav's solicitor and barrister. Together, they consider whether Steve can apply to have his restrictive order removed.

The first option would involve Steve applying as a co-respondent and party to proceedings. That would require a hearing to have the restriction lifted, after which he could apply to leave the proceedings. The process could cost more than ten thousand dollars, with no guarantee of success. The solicitor warns that the application would likely fail while Steve's DVO remains in place (it does not dissolve until the end of October).

The alternative is for Monica's solicitor, together with the ICL, to apply for the condition to be removed. Even then, waiting until the DVO expires would be the safer strategy. At least now, they have some clarity about where they stand.

DAY 20 – GO TO POLICE

Lisa:
Hi Monica, you must go to the police. In my opinion, these messages are meant to intimidate you, and he is to have no contact with Benji until the Rekonnect visit.
Monica:
I've done that. The police have made a copy of the photos. The guy said it's unlikely to be a breach because he wasn't directly messaging me. He's going to talk to Sav about it and call me tomorrow to let me know what he says. At least it's on record.
Steve:
Talk to Sav about it! The officer must think he is dealing with a rational human being. Perhaps he should read the case history.

Rekonnect contacts Monica. Sav wants a visit next weekend.

On Tuesday, Benji's mood fluctuated during the day. He wasn't keen to go to soccer training, but once he was there, he did well. He'll need to regain his fitness to perform at his best.

DAY 22 – RETALIATION

At 7:58 in the morning, the Hamilton doorbell rings. It's busy inside – Daniel and Benji are getting ready for school, Monica is upstairs. Out the back, Narelle is pegging clothes on the line when she sees two police officers at the foot of the steps. She slips inside and opens the door.

'Hello. Just wondering… is Monique here?'

'Do you mean Monica?'

The officer quickly corrects herself. Narelle calls out, and Monica comes downstairs.

'Hi, Monica, how are you? My name's Constable Jameson. I think we've met. I have a body cam recording. I'm just here about an incident that happened a month ago… that ok?' Narelle edges away.

'Is that your mum?'

'Yeah.'

'Ok, alright. I'll need to talk to her about this matter as well. You're not under arrest or anything like that. Is it alright if I talk to you out here, then to your mum… if that's ok?'

'Yeah.'

The officers have come to investigate Sav's claim that Monica hit Benji on the chest. Monica tells the officer she has full custody. Constable Jameson replies, 'Yes, and he goes to Sav's house on weekends.'

'No,' Monica corrects her. 'Sav has supervised visits, and he hasn't seen Benji for three weeks.'

The exchange lasts about five minutes. Monica denies hitting Benji on the chest. Then it's Narelle's turn.

Steve:

I am lying on my bed at Chantel's place when the Ring app sounds. When I see it is the police, I turn the volume up. I hear Narelle say, 'What happened a month ago?' and know that the police are there about the supposed iPad incident at McDonalds. I watch the live view, and after the police leave, ring Narelle. She's in a hurry and doesn't want the boys to be late for school. She'll ring me later.

Do the police have any idea what they are putting the family through? If they wanted to investigate further, why didn't they do it five weeks ago when it happened? The police have already viewed the footage from the carpark after Sav's complaint and concluded there was nothing to answer for. Yet, five weeks later, an arm of the 88-armed-octopus decides to investigate? They could phone and organise an appropriate time, but they don't. They turn up at the door and insist on interrogating Monica and Narelle when the family is in the midst of an early morning rush.

Monica:
Hi Lisa,
Arrangements have been made for Sav to see Benji with ReKonnect on Saturday. Please ask Sav to bring Benji's soccer uniform as Benji needs it for Sunday's soccer presentation. The police were here this morning investigating the iPad incident. This is after I attended the station on Monday about the soccer app DVO breach.

It is the same pattern once again. Monica puts in a legitimate complaint to the police about Sav, and the police turn up at her door. Knowingly or not, it amounts to police intimidation. Does this happen because Sav puts pressure on the police? For whatever reason, the message to vulnerable women is clear – remain silent. Do not go to the police.

On Friday, Monica hears through ReKonnect that Sav has cancelled his Saturday afternoon visit. She had already told Benji about it, so Sav has let his son down. No reason is given for the cancellation.

An article in The Guardian, Friday April 26, 2024, quotes Jess Hill, the acclaimed Australian author and researcher on domestic violence, 'We won't stop violence against women with conversations about respect. This is not working. We need to get real.'

Jess Hill states, 'In one breath we are facing a national crisis, and in the next our solution is to call out disrespect and challenge harmful gender norms. But these aren't just stock answers or platitudes. They articulate our national prevention strategy, which focuses on changing the underlying social drivers of gendered violence by addressing harmful attitudes. The problem with this strategy is that it outsources its results to future generations.'

The Guardian article reports that Jess Hill has toured the country for the past five years, speaking about coercive control at hundreds of events. She has been working with Professor Michael Salter on a white paper, called 'Rethinking

Primary Prevention.' The paper argues against whole of population strategies. It identifies four missing pieces to the puzzle:

- *Accountability and consequences — for perpetrators and systems that enable them — is prevention: There are so many opportunities to introduce accountability across a system weaponised by perpetrators.* Sav's ability to weaponise the system would have failed if the police had examined his history. His past DVOs, DCJ and police records, efforts to manipulate the system, and his behaviour towards his previous wife, were all on file.
- *Recovery is prevention; there is the need to properly resource the frontline so they can work with child survivors so they can properly heal.*
- *Regulating damaging industries (including porn, gambling, alcohol, and social media) is prevention.*
- *Structural improvements to gender equality, such as the single parenting payment, is prevention.* Most women would find it impossible to escape an abusive relationship without financial assistance. This problem is accentuated in many parts of Australia because of the exorbitant cost and scarcity of housing.

The paper's argument against whole population strategies is supported by a recent report (September 17, 2024) by the Australian Institute of Criminology, which found that in NSW, 1.2 % of people born in the state were responsible for more than 50% of recorded family and domestic violence offences. More than half of reported incidents (54%) involved intimate partner violence. The other cases involved siblings, parents, children, relatives, housemates, or carers.

Steve and Daniel travel to Sydney on Saturday for Manuel's (Matt's dad's) eightieth birthday party. It is held at the Ashfield Leagues Club, in a room with glass walls and a glass ceiling, overlooking the main road and the railway line. Steve points out to Daniel and Georgia that across the road is the house Narelle lived in when Steve and her first met. A few kilometres away in Stanmore is the house they lived in when Monica was born. Closer still, in Lewisham, is the house they bought when Georgia was a baby.

Daniel has an extensive chat with Manual, who grew up on a small island off Portugal. Most of his family emigrated to Brazil, but he took the opportunity to come to Australia. A builder by trade, he lives nearby. Daniel is intrigued by Manual's story.

Narelle:

Daniel enjoyed it. He was so pleased to be asked.

Georgia:

He's such a nice boy. He went around at the end, saying goodbye and shaking everyone's hand.

Narelle:

He told us Matt's dad said he was part of the family. Daniel said, 'I used to be part Italian and now I'm part Portuguese.'

Georgia:

Matt's mum gave Emma a Portuguese tart, and Emma shoved it in her mouth. Matt's mum said, 'There's the Portuguese.' She thinks Emma looks like a carbon copy of me.

The *Sydney Morning Herald* front page the following Tuesday reads:
Violence against women. LET'S STOP IT AT THE START.
And the back page read: *STOP IT AT THE START is a primary intervention campaign that looks at how we, as adults, can help break the cycle of violence against women.*

The narrative speaks of powerful influences online and young people's exposure to online disrespect as one of the many ways violence-supporting attitudes can start to develop. The way social media algorithms tailor the content they show based on what consumers interact with the most. 'Not all disrespect towards women results in violence, but all violence against women starts with disrespect.'

DAY 31 – MANIPULATIONS

Monica:

Benji doesn't have a spot on the JBL team. Coach said he missed too much of the season and there were some really strong kids trying out. He said, 'I know it's not your fault and I know it's not Benji's.' He'll play for a local team now.

Georgia:

Probably better for him at the moment.

On Monday, Monica receives a message from Rekonnect:

Hi Monica, Sav has confirmed he wants to do the visit next weekend. We have it for Saturday at Speers Point Park.

Supervisor Gail.

Monica posts the Rekonnect message for Narelle, Georgia, and Steve to see.

Georgia:

Let's see.

Monica:

He's asking if Daniel can attend too.

Georgia:

Yeah, Daniel can choose, right?

Narelle:

Well, he can, but I bet he won't want to go.

Georgia:

Sav will try and use this to say you're not supporting the kids to see him. Like the ICL said, 'If Benji doesn't want to see his mum it's a reflection on the dad.' But it's different with Daniel because Sav never wanted to see him before.

Narelle:

Daniel went with him in the beginning. He is 14 now. He can choose for himself.

Steve:

Daniel knows what Sav has done. And Sav ditched him when he took Benji. It won't reflect on Monica.

Rekonnect:

Sorry Monica, just to check, will Benji and Daniel both be attending these

visits?
Monica:
Can I ask Daniel after school?
Rekonnect:
Absolutely. Just let me know and I will keep the supervisor updated. I have also asked Sav to provide food and drink for this visit, so you will not need to pack that. Just hats.
Monica:
Ok. Thank you.

On Tuesday from Rekonnect:
Hi Monica. Sav has advised that at this stage he cannot afford the visits. I will keep you informed if he gets back in touch.

Monica posts the Rekonnect message.
Monica:
That didn't last long.
Georgia:
Oh dear. He's the one that chose to go down this path.
Monica:
Exactly. No sympathy.
Georgia:
That's right. It's all manipulation. That's what he is trying to do. Or he wouldn't have requested then cancelled.
Monica:
Looks like he can't afford to be a parent.

There is a push to give doctors and teachers more training and support, according to an article published by Rosie King in *The Guardian* (September 17, 2024). Family violence education accounts for just three hours of a trainee doctor's study. Doctors see victims alone over a long period of time, putting them in a unique position. Research has found one in two to one in three Australian children are growing up in violent homes (ABC news, September18, 2024).

Dr Simonis, the Australia Medical Association general practice representative: 'I don't think general practitioners on the whole feel confident identifying the subtle signs of family violence because very few people will come in presenting with physical evidence of harm.'

Sienna to Monica:

Marco went to the house because Dad wasn't answering his phone and he wanted to grab some of his stuff. Dad went off at him, blamed me for everything that's happened. He's not accepting accountability and blames me for everything, including Benji being taken from him. Nonno and Nonna don't agree with what I've done. They think I should stay loyal to Dad. Gabby and Henry are minding their business and so are Kerrel and Salvador. Elena is confused.

Monica to Sienna:

That's horrible. Not your fault, as you know. Benji has been taken away because of Sav's own behaviour.

Narelle:

It's always someone else's fault with him.

Georgia:

Of course. Poor girl. What is Elena confused about?

Narelle:

Sav won't have told any of his family the truth.

Georgia:

Of course not. Only way he can live with himself, I suppose.

Monica to Sienna:

The truth will come out eventually.

Sienna:

I know that. But what hurts is his lack of awareness and ability to take responsibility. I don't think he'll ever learn in his lifetime from his actions, nor realise that his daughter is not to blame. So, I don't think I'll reconcile with that side of the family because of complicity, silence, and inaction. Not once have they checked up on us.

Monica:

Their inaction speaks volumes.

Georgia:

Sienna's smart. But it would be extremely hard.

Steve:

The Savingtons (all of them) know what Sav did to his previous wife, and they definitely know about what has gone on this time. They empower him by not calling out his criminal behaviour. They are all immoral and spineless. Apart from Sienna.

DAY 61– SELL-OFF

Benji is gradually settling back into normal life. He still has his moments, as he always did, but they refuse to let him get away with rude behaviour. For Monica, it is harder. Relieved to finally have him back, she is more lenient than she once was. That balance will return over time; what matters most now is that the bond between mother and child remains as strong as ever. Sav's attempts to destroy that relationship have failed.

To keep the boys off their devices and ensure they don't stay up too late, Monica has adopted a simple strategy: switch off the internet.

Meanwhile, Sav is selling more of the family's belongings on Facebook – a mattress, grinder, large fish tank, and drop saw. Mediation is scheduled in five days' time, on Friday, to reach an agreement over the property settlement.

- **Family Dispute Resolution (FDR)** is a special type of mediation for helping separating families to come to their own agreements. During FDR, families will discuss the issues, consider options, with the focus being on the needs of the children.

Robert Condos was put forward by Lisa to mediate, and Sav's solicitor has agreed.

Georgia:
If he's selling off your stuff to pay the mortgage, then his argument that he should get more to pay the mortgage is gone. You should keep a record for mediation.
Monica:
True.
Georgia:
I think in mediation you have to play up to his need to be seen as the good guy.
Monica:
How do I do that?

Georgia:

Maybe say, 'Look, I know you've sold a lot of my things and that's ok, I don't care about my things in this. I want the kid to be looked after… and I'm sure you do too. So let focus on them by giving me the money.'

Monica:

When I spoke with the mediator, he said I need to make him think he's winning.

Steve:

I can't see anything being resolved at mediation. BS won't agree to anything reasonable. It will end up in court. More $$$ unfortunately.

DAY 62 – BLAME BENJI

Monica:

I just had a call from the police asking if I would be willing to drop the tyre slashing charges as Sav's solicitor has requested this. I said I don't want the charges dropped. It's up to his boss to decide now. If it gets dropped, I might not have to worry about court in November. I think it needs to be on the record that I don't agree with dropping charges. With the phone calls, Sav is now saying it was Benji. He shouldn't get away with blaming Benji.

Georgia:

God, first Leonardo now Benji. What a joke! Didn't his affidavit say Leonardo made the calls?

Monica:

Pretty sure it did.

Georgia:

Tell them that.

Monica:

I just sent the police officer a message explaining.

Narelle:

He lied on his affidavit and now Leonardo won't go to the court, so he blames Benji. Really! Let Lisa know.

Georgia:

Leonardo lied too, so they should both be charged with making false

affidavits.
Monica:
Hopefully, we can talk to the prosecutor today.
Steve:
First Sav denied making phone calls. Then he claimed Leonardo made the calls. That is on his affidavit, so it's likely he told the police the same story. Now he's saying it was Benji.

Monica and Narelle attend a community meeting hosted by the Newcastle Women's Domestic Violence Court Advocacy Service. Court protocol and legal processes are explained, and a police prosecutor briefs potential witnesses on what to expect if called to testify. If Sav continues to plead not guilty to making the two phone calls, Monica will likely be cross-examined by his barrister. She picks up some useful pointers. Afterwards, she and Narelle take the opportunity to speak one-on-one with the police prosecutor. He is already familiar with the case and advises Monica to press ahead – not to let Sav off the hook. In his experience with men like Sav, the calls will start up again if he thinks he has gotten away with it.

The next day, Sav's breaches of his DVO bond are due before court. Narelle and Steve drive into town and manage to find a park in a two-hour zone near the courthouse. When they get up to the second floor, they spot Sav's solicitor waiting in the foyer, but Sav himself is not in attendance. When the matter is called, Sav's solicitor enters a plea of guilty to phoning Monica to wish her happy birthday, but not guilty to making the two no-ID calls. He applies successfully to have all Sav's matters adjourned until November.

Police have told Monica that Sav's phone was pinged in the Hamilton area the night she saw his car – the same night her tyres were slashed. But there isn't enough proof for charges over the slashing. Another matter listed for November is Sav contacting Monica's friend. He is pleading not guilty.

Steve:
All postponed until November.
Monica:
Bugger.

Georgia:
God why? What a waste of everyone's time!

DAY 66 – A WALK IN THE PARK

It's another overcast day. Intermittent showers and occasional patches of blue. The Family Dispute Resolution hearing between Sav and Monica is to be heard today. It will occur by video link. Monica travels to Lisa's office.

Steve:
I don't want to be negative, but he won't agree to any reasonable proposal.
Monica:
Lisa is going for Sav to pay my legal fees. I wouldn't have needed to pay so much if he hadn't taken off with Benji.
Narelle:
That's great.
Georgia:
That's great, and true.
Monica:
The mediator was saying this may be an emotional day and nerve racking going to court on zoom. Lisa said I have done thirteen child custody court hearings, so this is a walk in the park.
Georgia:
It's true.
Monica:
They are meeting with the mediator and solicitors. I'm not sure we'll get far today. Sav hasn't disclosed all the documentation.
Georgia:
Of course.
Narelle:
Delay, delay, delay. What a joke!
Monica:
Hopefully, all at his expense.
Georgia:
Did they say why Sav hasn't done all his stuff.
Monica:
Lisa is finding all these accounts and heaps of loans Sav has set up.
Narelle:
Wow… he's in real trouble.

Monica:

He's had a quote for a new engine for the Ford, saying the car isn't worth much because it needs all this work. The quote is from his mate's workplace.

Narelle:

Georgia:

Monica:

Still hasn't declared the Ute. We found in his bank statement where he paid for the Ute.

Narelle:

Georgia:

Narelle:

Did you show Lisa all the things he's selling?

Monica:

Yes, I did.

Steve:

Nothing's simple with him.

Monica:

Lisa said she has referred some of her clients to the Activity Centre.

Narelle:

Georgia:

Ha, ha, ha. Has anything else happened?

Monica:

Still going back and forth.

Five minutes passes.

Monica:

The best Sav would agree to was fifty-fifty.

Georgia:

If he has all this debt, is it your problem?

Monica:

Lisa thinks I should get 60/40. Debt is his problem. He wanted us to share debt because he has run up so much. Lisa won't let it happen.

Georgia:

Yeah, definitely. Ok. Good.

Monica:

We've agreed to sell the house and have the money sitting in a trust until we come to an agreement.

Georgia:

That's good. Least he'll have to move. Hopefully.

Monica:

They've asked for $40,000 from each of us after sale. To pay his legal fees. Lisa is negotiating.

Georgia:

That's his problem.

Monica:

Lisa doesn't want him to get more than his legal fees.

Georgia:

He can pay yours and his.

Monica:

Sav had tried to say he spent $14,000 on my engagement and wedding rings. And that he spent $4,000 on Roxie.

Georgia:

Oh wow!

Monica:

He's a liar.

Georgia:

Does he have evidence?

Monica:

Yeah… how could he, lol? Lisa agreed for $40,000 to go to his solicitor. I can pay back Mum and Dad when I get my money.

After the mediation wraps up, Monica asks Lisa about applying to have Steve's Family Court order removed. It's been a long day. When Monica says she wants everyone together by Christmas, Lisa gives her a questioning look. Monica realises Lisa thinks by 'together' she means together with Sav.

'I mean my dad,' Monica snaps, shocked that Lisa would think that for even a second.

Lisa would have seen clients change their minds mid-proceedings and drift back to abusive partners. It's probably one reason why many solicitors, including Lisa, insist on a deposit before starting work. Others – like Sav's solicitor – will take a client if they know there's real estate to secure fees against.

Lisa outlines a plan for Steve's order and for the unworkable supervision conditions the senior registrar imposed on Narelle. She'll wait until after Sav's November court date, then approach the ICL and, hopefully, with her support, file to have the orders affecting Steve and Narelle removed. By then Steve's DVO will have dissolved.

DAY 67 – A WEIRD POST

Percy Street is sold. Contracts have been exchanged, so there's no turning back. Narelle and Steve go house hunting. They need a dwelling that is both affordable and can be divided into two separate living areas. Last week they inspected a property that suited their needs, but it was overpriced and the vendor refused to negotiate. They are now looking at another one, with a similar floor plan, that has captured their interest. By coincidence, it is being sold by Myra, the real estate agent who handled the sale of their Hamilton house. Monica and the boys also like it, so they put in an offer.

From his reaction at the mediation hearing last Friday, Sav was annoyed that Monica knew – and had evidence – of him selling off their assets. One of Georgia's friends has been monitoring his Facebook posts. He retaliates, as he always does, by posting something weird and intimidating.

His post is titled 'Beyond Sausage' and depicts a sausage shaped like a penis. The accompanying text reads: Putana, $1.
With his name listed as the seller, he describes what he is selling in Italian:
Una bitch Narelle con la sua filia la merda come SK.
Translated from Italian it reads:
A bitch Narelle with her filia the shit like SK.
In Hinduism, Putuna, the killer of infants was sent by Krishna's evil uncle Kamsa to kill Krisna.
Georgia:
Matt thinks it says, 'Narelle is a bitch, your daughter is a bitch, like SK (Steve Kelty).' I can't believe he's, like, nearly 50 years old.
Steve:
Childish messages, calling people bitches. It's something an irate, immature

teenager might do.

Sav posts again under the picture of an animal enclosure:
Dear stalker NK. This fish tank belongs to my son. $150. Run along and mind your own business.

Narelle and Monica have been warned by workers in the field that it is a dangerous time. With the impending court case in November, Sav could feel trapped and desperate. Targeting Narelle is a change of tactic, and he has done it publicly.

Lisa has no doubt about his intentions:
Dear Monica,
Go to the police and report them. This is harassment and intimidation.

A few days later, Leonardo surprises Sienna by turning up at her house. He drops off several boxes containing Benji's clothes. Marco has come with him but waits outside in the car. That Marco told him where Sienna lives is a betrayal of trust. It puts Sienna in the firing line. Leonardo wants to know why Sienna retracted her statements backing Sav's lies. Her reply is simple: she wants to be a high school teacher, and perjuring herself will disqualify her. Leonardo replies that he won't lie in court, either. It's an interesting comment, considering he has already lied in an affidavit. One of his lies was claiming it was he who made the phone calls to Monica from Sav's phone. It is likely though that he has told his father he won't support him in court, and that was why Sav changed his story, claiming it was Benji who made the phone calls.

It's a week and a half later that Sav has his first two-hour supervised visit with Benji at Charlestown Square. Nearly three months have passed since he was permitted fortnightly visits. He asks the ReKonnect supervisor if he can give Benji a Lego set. The supervisor explains that any gift cannot be extravagant and must first be approved by Monica. That his choice of present needs Monica's approval will grate on him. So too will his new reality: Sav is not allowed to be alone with his son. Back home, Benji doesn't say anything about what transpired.

Lisa phones Steve a few days later to let him know his DVO dissolved the previous week. As explained earlier, he is fortunate to be part of a new system being trialled in Newcastle, where DVOs are withdrawn (dissolve) after three months if there isn't a breech. Otherwise, it would still be rolling through the courts costing thousands, as is the case with Monica's DVO which was issued at another precinct.

Narelle's bid on the house is accepted. They organise a deposit. Change is afoot. They will be moving in December or January if all goes according to plan.

DAY 85 – SAV FEELS THE HEAT

A heat wave warning has been issued by the BOM for most of the country. Things are also heating up for Sav, who faces local court for breaching his good behaviour bond.

Sav has already passed through security when Monica, Steve and Beth arrive at the courthouse. He tries to make eye contact, but they slip quickly into the reception enclave to avoid him. Steve is quietly pleased Sav saw them arrive. Now he knows Monica and Beth are prepared to take the stand and give evidence. Sav had originally denied phoning Monica's friend Beth. When he finally admitted it, he claimed it was only to be paid for a plumbing job. If he pleads not guilty, Beth will have to testify.

Monica and Beth make their way to the safe room on level two. Steve leaves the building to meet Narelle, who is on her way into town after dropping the boys at school. They meet up and grab a bite to eat before walking back across to the courthouse for what could be a long day. Taking the elevator to level two, they see Sav in a conference room with his sister Gabby. Steve chooses a seat directly opposite, ensuring Sav and his sister see him. After they are noticed, he and Narelle move away so Sav cannot accuse them of intimidation.

When proceedings begin, other cases are prioritised ahead of theirs. Narelle and Steve join Monica and Beth in the safe room, where they hope to hear more about what will happen. Steve is allowed inside because Monica is the only woman using the facility. Constable Blackwell, the officer who pushed the matter forward, is speaking with Monica. He has spoken to the prosecutor and tells them the magistrate is considering a suitable punishment for Sav, without anyone having to give evidence.

Narelle, then Monica, thank Blackwell for his persistence. Steve does the same, and the officer looks genuinely surprised. Police rarely receive thanks. But it is deserved. Monica was brushed off and wrongly accused many times, but once Blackwell saw through Sav's tactics, he went into bat for her, tracing the no-ID calls, and pursuing Sav's repeated breaches.

Shortly afterwards, Blackwell takes a call. Sav has finally pleaded guilty to the breaches, including the no-ID calls. Did he really have a choice after changing his story three times? Sentencing is set for six weeks' time.

They leave the courthouse and head home. Half an hour later, Monica's phone rings.

Monica:
The police prosecutor rang. They did sentence him today. Sav needs to pay a $500 bond. He is on a good behaviour bond for 15 months. He needs to report regularly at police corrections. He'll be reporting to them about doing a men's behaviour course and other things. His initial appointment is within 7 days. DVO against him remains in place. The magistrate who sentenced Sav has sent people to prison in the past for breaching bonds. Sav was promised gaol time if further breaches occur. If he does breach and pleads not guilty, he will be held in custody until a magistrate becomes available. If he pleads guilty, he will go to gaol.
Georgia:
How do you feel about that?
Monica:
Ok.
Georgia:
Oh well. He didn't get away with any of it.
Narelle:
That's right. It was a win for us.
Georgia:
He'll be livid tonight. Usually that's when he does something. After he's been pulled up.
Monica:
That's what Sienna thought. That he'll be angry. She's worried he'll go to her place.

Georgia:
Yeah. I would be worried too. Seeing he's blaming her and now he knows where she lives. Can she go somewhere else?
Monica:
She thinks he's more likely to do something to her car.

Monica's neighbour Sarah phones, wanting to know what happened in court. She says Sav revved his car up and spun his wheels when he left for court that morning. When Monica tells Steve about his antics, they laugh at his immaturity. 'Temper, temper, Constable Larry,' Steve says. 'That sort of behaviour will get you locked up. It'll be interesting to see if he can control his impulses and keep out of trouble for the next fifteen months.'

Sarah:
For Sale sign is on your house and Sav doesn't appear to be there.
Monica:
Yep. The house is now on the market. I wonder where he's gone.
Sarah:
He's definitely gone. I had a good look, nothing in the living area except bench stools. Hopefully, he's gone far away. Towel still on the window in the laundry though.

Despite being told not to remove anything else from the house, Sav has done so. Monica contacts the real estate agent, who has been there recently. She confirms that everything is gone from inside but doesn't know what's in the garage.

Monica:
Hi Lisa and Adele, please see below email from real estate with photos of the property. Sav has taken everything out of the house. It's empty. Are we able to ask where everything has gone?
Regards Monica

DAY 132 – CHRISTMAS

As Christmas approaches Monica, Narelle, Benji, Daniel and Roxie have moved into their new house. There are numerous boxes still to unpack, and flatpacks to assemble. Luca Savington hasn't attempted to see his son, apart from the one visit.

Monica receives Benji's school report. Again, his grades are fine, but he has been involved in conflicts with some of his classmates – mostly in the playground. Despite this, Benji insists on putting together a small Christmas present for everyone in his class.

The extent to which the months of solitude have affected him is difficult to gauge. According to his counsellor, he won't talk about his father, and at home nobody mentions him. Benji still wants to be near his mother most of the time. If he is in his room, he constantly checks that Monica or Narelle are within earshot. 'Are you still there?' he calls out.

Monica sets up a soccer net in the yard. Benji goes out there often, kicking the ball, playing with whoever is available. He has taught Roxie to dribble and make a play for the ball. If there were a national canine team, Roxie would be selected.

Daniel and Benji sometimes play together, doing stunts on their scooters in the backyard. It is a step forward. Daniel's resentment towards his brother is diminishing. He has been told by a few people that he shouldn't blame Benji – that Sav coerced both Sienna and Leonardo into lying to the authorities, and they are adults. Poor Benji was an 8-year-old child with no option but to do as his father demanded.

Georgia, Matt, and Emma come and stay for Christmas. Georgia and Matt find it strange without Steve there. On Christmas Day, Narelle drives to Chantel's place to have dinner with Steve. She is exhausted and not feeling her best. Events of the past year – and the supervisory role imposed by the Family Court, have affected her health. The restrictions on Monica and Steve are baffling to everyone who knows them.

In three weeks, the court interviews that precede final orders will take place. As with interim orders, they will be used by both the ICL and the registrar to form their views on the case. Monica, Benji, Narelle and Sav are listed to be interviewed. Originally, Sienna and Leonardo were included, but that is no longer the case. No reason is given.

Lisa is no longer returning calls. Monica hears that she is overwhelmed with work. She had promised to contact the ICL and push for Steve's restrictions to be lifted, but they have heard nothing. If it continues, they may need another solicitor. They also want Monica's DVO revoked. It is listed for mention in March 2025. Steve researches online, and finds on the NSW Legal Aid site, that provisional orders can be withdrawn by the officer who issued them. The advice is to contact the Local Area Command (LAC) that made the order.

DAY 146 – PROACTIVE

Steve sends a fax – as no email address is available – to the officer in charge of the rural police station that issued Monica's DVO. He argues that Monica is the victim and Sav the abuser, noting that the two children named on the order as needing protection live with Monica. He includes details of Sav's DVO, the harassment that led to it, his subsequent breaches and fifteen-month bond, his history of coercive control, harassment and violence, and the blatant fabrications exposed by the Family Court. Case file numbers and court orders are attached.

After the Christmas break, Monica returns to work. Narelle takes care of Benji and, to a lesser extent, Daniel, who received a gaming computer for Christmas. Daniel is content to spend hours playing online with his friends – all day and night if allowed. Benji enjoys games too but prefers being outdoors. In the new neighbourhood, he is fortunate to have friends living close by.

Monica:
Today, Benji's friend Callen was allowed to ride his bike to our place, two blocks from his house. Then we let Benji ride back to Callen's. The boys felt so grown up. They went back and forth ten times. Good the bike is back in

action.

Georgia:

When Dad's back, all the bikes will be back in use! Daniel won't be able to keep up with Benji.

Monica:

Benji said the last time he rode was with Pop. I feel like that was a breakthrough.

Georgia:

That he mentioned Dad?

Monica:

Yeah.

Steve:

That's positive. So good he has a friend nearby to play with.

Monica:

Yeah, he's loving that.

Georgia:

Emma is eighteen months old today.

Steve:

What a year and a half it's been. First with Emma's issues, then Battered Sav.

Monica posts on Facebook Messenger that Lisa wants to know Sav's new address.

Georgia:

How would you know his new address?

Monica:

I keep asking Lisa to find out his new address so I can avoid it, lol.

The following points are drawn from an article titled 'How the housing crisis is pushing domestic violence victims back to perpetrators,' posted on Jan 5, 2025, by ABC news reporter Leonne Thorne. Demand at homeless services is increasing due to the housing crisis, high rents, and longer queues for social housing, leaving those escaping domestic violence with fewer options.

A homeless centre might have one bed free and several in need. It is an invidious choice for staff, as most people seeking accommodation at homeless centres are women and children fleeing domestic violence. Some who cannot get into a refuge will be placed in hotels instead. When this happens, they are more likely to return to the perpetrator.

Consultancy firm Equity Economics estimates 18,700 people – mostly women and children – became homeless in 2024, nearly double its 2021 estimate.

There were 78 women killed by gender-based violence in 2024 according to the organisation Counting Dead Women.

DAY 148 – STEVE'S PLIGHT

Monica emails Lisa asking her if she has contacted the ICL regarding Steve's Family Court orders.

Lisa replies to Monica:
I won't be contacting the ICL until after your interviews on Monday. I'm hopeful that you will receive some positive feedback for you and Benji, so I can then take that to the ICL. Having said this, I believe that the ICL will be relucent to do anything until your DVO is finalised. She is just taking a cautious approach.

Narelle:
I wish she had told us that before.
Monica:
Yeah, hopefully the police drop my DVO soon after receiving Dad's complaint.
Georgia:
Why isn't Lisa working to have the DVO dropped?
Monica:
She sort of has been. She wrote out a thing for the prosecutor. But it wasn't as detailed as what Dad wrote.

Monica to Lisa:
Hi Lisa,
I've appreciated all your support and assistance with my legal issues so far. We need to move on changing the orders – particularly so that my dad, Steve, can return to his family. There is no longer a DVO between him and Benji. Both the police and the DCJ investigated allegations made against Dad and cleared him of any wrongdoing. It is very clear Sav forced Benji into lying to

try to get full custody of Benji in the Family Court. Daniel, and Benji both need their Pop back in their lives. We're in our new house now and missing him terribly. My dad is into his 70s and this current situation is having an enormous impact on his health, both physically and mentally. My mum's health has also been affected. Please consider the above information and advise us what we can do to progress forward and get my dad home asap.
Regards,
Monica Savington.

Steve:
That's good Monica. Lisa hasn't done what she originally said she would.

The next day, Narelle sends an email to the convener of the family report interview team, requesting Steve and Daniel be included. Later in the day, she receives an email granting her request. Narelle, and Steve are pleased, although Daniel isn't keen to be interviewed. Once he is told it will help his mum and might hasten Poppy's return, he is more compliant.

Georgia:
Sav has a girlfriend.
Monica:
That's good.
Georgia:
Not for her. Poor girl. We know where that ends up. Maybe I'll invite her to the final hearing.

Monica is notified by the Family Court that a safety room has been organised for the interviews. They will be staggered to minimise the risk of encountering the other party. It seems to indicate Sav is attending, which is surprising considering he has only seen Benji once since he was placed in Monica's care.

DAY 150 – A COWARD'S RETREAT

Lisa Jones to Monica:
I have just read this email from Sav's solicitor. Was in a long interview when it came in. If possible, can you ring me. If you can't get through, you must continue with the interviews for you and Benji next week.

Lisa forwards the email. The attachment contains four pages. It is a notice of discontinuance. Applicant: Luca Savington. It is stamped by the Federal Circuit and Family Court.

- Discontinuance: Filing a Notice of Discontinuance is formally informing the court of your intention to terminate your part in proceedings. It is a unilateral decision made by one party.

Monica:
Looks like he is pulling out of everything.
Narelle:
Says all areas.
Georgia:
Amazing.
Monica:
Lisa doesn't seem to think it's great news. Now we need to urgently file for final orders. I have to see Lisa after court on Monday. Lisa told George that Sav better not think he can go get Benji with nothing in place. Sav's solicitor said he talked to Sav about it. I'm confused. Surely the orders are still in place.
Narelle:
I'm sure they are. I think she means Sav should know it doesn't stop the orders.
Steve:
From what I could find out, interim orders are still in place. Don't forget his DVO. Now he's pulled out, I think it's even more likely he will be billed for costs. He instigated proceedings and he bailed.
Monica:
Sarah said someone has been in the house. The curtains are drawn again.

DAY 154 – INTERVIEWS

The Family Court interviews take several hours. Melissa, the social worker conducting the sessions, is astute and empathetic. She did the interviews for the interim hearing and is already familiar with the background of the case. To observe how Monica, Narelle, Daniel and Benji interact, she asks them to play Uno together. It is clear Benji feels at ease with everyone.

Monica's interview centres around her relationship with Benji and is the most thorough. Narelle reiterates her concerns – that Sav is a flight risk if given unsupervised access to Benji. His despicable character is already on record, so little more needs to be said. Daniel is clear that he wants nothing to do with Sav. He tells Melissa that Sav lied about his mother and was always angry. He says he is happy in his new home. When Melissa interviews Benji, she asks him if he has any worries about his mum. Benji replies, 'I'm worried she can't run.'

Steve explains to Melissa how Sav manipulated the police to secure two DVOs against Monica and forced Benji to lie to the Sexual Abuse Squad. At one point, Steve becomes emotional. Melissa tells him Benji said he misses his Pop but feels anxious about seeing him. She asks Steve's opinion on how to reintroduce contact. They agree it should be gradual.

Luca Savington does not attend. Melissa says her report will be ready in a few weeks.

It is now nearly a year since Benji has had contact with his Pop. The Registrar's orders have been in place for nearly six months.

Later in the day, Lisa sends a message to Monica:
Will advise when I know the court date.
Monica:
Is it going to court for the house or family?
Lisa:
For the Property Recovery Order.

- **A Property Recovery Order (PRO)** is a court order that allows a person to retrieve their belongings from premises where they lived or where their property is. It's a legal tool, designed to help a person safely reclaim their possessions, reducing the risk of conflict or further harm.

The property settlement date is in two weeks, and Monica still hasn't had the opportunity to see what items are left at the house.

Georgia:
I'm confused.
Monica:
Lisa says she now wants to wait for the Court report before contacting the ICL about Dad's restrictions. We should get moving, knowing we'll have the report in a few weeks.
Georgia:
Maybe she needs to see what's in the report, so she knows how to approach it.
Monica:
Yeah... Lisa says she needs to have access to the report and then speak with the ICL.
Georgia:
But seeing he's given up – it should be pretty clear.
Monica:
Lisa said that to lodge for the final hearing now, a fee must be paid. She is trying to work out a way of me not paying, but we can still lodge it. Surely, we're almost there.
Steve:
Ok... patience. Almost there.

DAY 155 – RUBBISH

Monica's real estate agent contacts her. Sav has handed in his keys, saying he wants nothing more to do with the property. The agent asks who will clear the rubbish once Monica has taken what she wants. There is still no news on the Property Recovery Order, and Monica grows anxious as the property settlement date approaches. She knows most of what Sav has left will have to be thrown out. When she contacts council to arrange a roadside collection, she discovers Sav has already used the two allocated pick-ups.

Monica:
Surely, I don't have to remove the rubbish. I don't even have a key.
Georgia:
Well, considering he insisted on staying on at the house, it's his responsibility to clean it. Idiot!
Monica:
He's saying he's moved far away.
Georgia:
Say the neighbours have seen him coming and going. He's just lazy.
Monica:
It was the real estate agent who closed the curtains. She said she's been checking the house to make sure it hasn't been broken into or water damaged.
Georgia:
That's nice of her.
Monica:
Real estate also said the new owners wanted early access to clean the kitchen and bathroom as Sav has left them filthy.
Georgia:
Bloody hell. He's such a shit person. Honestly!
Monica:
Lisa said no to early access. She doesn't want him to have any excuses for things not being in house.

DAY 156 – A GAMBLE

Georgia posts a picture of an Oz Lotto entry form.

Monica:

50 mil sounds good.

Georgia:

Yeah. Do you think we should increase it to double the week after?

Monica:

How much will I transfer? We should play weekly.

Georgia:

Well, do Mum and Dad want to join? We can do lower amounts.

Monica:

Sounds good. Benji cleaned his room today. He's so proud. Won't stop talking about it. I can hear him telling his friend, 'This took me so long to do.'

Georgia:

It's $4.95 a week each.

Narelle:

I'll put $5:00 a week in.

Steve:

Am I in?

Georgia:

Yes, if you want to. You have to send money though. And we know how hard that will be.

Steve:

I might do my own with that attitude.

Georgia:

Hahahaha. $257 investment for the year.

Monica:

I'll transfer $5:00.

Georgia:

If you send $5 and we win, you can't claim an extra 0.01%.

Narelle:

Should we save it?

Georgia:

I'm kidding!

DAY 157 – CONFUSED

Monica:

Benji's counsellor said he was getting upset talking about Monday's interview. He was crying about his dad. I think he was emotional because he was tired from having his friend stay over last night. I talked to him about it. Said I had no idea why his dad isn't doing the fortnightly visits.

Georgia:

Yeah. It's good if he's talking about it.

Monica:

Feel like reminding him how horrible his dad is, but I don't think that will be helpful. We got some snacks and are going to have a movie night.

Georgia:

That's a good idea. Just tell him he can ask questions, and you'll answer them as best you can. That Sav hasn't tried to see Daniel either.

Monica:

Yes, I did. I said Sienna too, but he said, 'No, Sienna left.'

Georgia:

It would be confusing because one minute his father is saying he wants to keep him, and the next he doesn't even try to see him.

Monica:

Yes, it's rough.

DAY 160 – PUZZLING

The police and Monica's solicitor have advised her against going near the property, even to find out what's left of her and the children's belongings. In view of Sav's past behaviours, and the fact he has a DVO out against her, this makes perfect sense. Which makes the email Monica receives from Lisa even more puzzling.

Lisa to Monica:
Good morning, Monica,
The registrar has refused to list the Property Recovery Order, because they are
of the view that you can go to the house. Please contact the agent and get the
keys to collect your belongings. Make sure you are in the company of your
mum and another family member. If Sav turns up, leave immediately and
contact me.

Lisa schedules a meeting with Monica for the following Friday, at 4 pm. Monica
contacts the real estate agent to organise a key. Sav has insisted on being told
when Monica will be going to the house. The agent has no intention of doing
so; she leaves a key for Monica in a locked box, chained to the rail on the
veranda. Monica decides to hire a skip to dispose of the items she doesn't want.

The police have not responded to Steve's attempt to have Monica's DVO
withdrawn. The clerk at the post office assured him the fax was received.
Enough time has passed without a reply, so he posts the information directly
to NSW Commissioner of Police, Karen Webb. He includes a cover note stating
clearly that the complaint relates to domestic violence.

Karen Webb has made public statements about her commitment to tackling the
issue. She has said that all governments and non-government agencies must
'work in partnership' to identify and support victims of domestic violence so
police can 'hold offenders to account' (ABC Stateline, October 10, 2024).

That Monica was initially wrongly identified as the perpetrator by the police,
and Luca Savington was able to convince police he was the victim, should be
of concern to the Police Commissioner's team. As was highlighted earlier, the
problem is widespread. Recently (ABC News, Dec14, 2024) Rhiannon Hobbins
and Gemma Breen reported on statistics from the NSW Bureau of Crime
Statistics and Research (BOCSAR). These figures indicate 64% of women
brought before the courts on DV charges between July 2022 and June 2023
were previously known to be victims of DV assault. For Indigenous women,
the figure is a staggering 85%. In 2021, Victoria's Reform Implementation
Monitor found misidentification ranged from 10-58.7% of DV cases.
According to more than thirty frontline services, experts and advocates
contacted by the ABC, this issue is widespread and in urgent need of attention.

The evidence shows the present system is miserably failing victims of domestic violence. According to the police, nearly half their time is spent dealing with domestic violence issues. The New South Wales Police Force is committed to officers receiving 'extensive foundational training' in domestic violence while training and receiving 'a range of mandatory domestic and family violence related training' throughout their careers (*parliament.nsw.gov.au*).

Despite the training, the statistics show, misidentification by the police is common. Police often cannot distinguish the victim from the perpetrator. According to her DVO, Monica is presently classified as a perpetrator of domestic violence, yet irrefutable evidence indicates the person named as needing protection (Luca Savington) is the abuser. It's a massive failure of the police and justice system, and an egregious waste or resources. If domestic and family violence work was done by highly trained teams (including police and detectives) with insight, expertise and knowledge, the savings in productivity alone would be enormous.

In 2024 over two in five recorded murders in NSW were related to family and domestic violence (ABS 2024); 77% of these involved a male killing a current or former female partner.

DAY 162 – THE CLEAN UP

Monica:
Sarah saw Sav at the house yesterday. Going into the house and garage.
Georgia:
I thought he couldn't access the house. Too far away. Handed his keys in.
Monica:
Real estate agent said the garage looks the same.

Monica, Narelle and Steve meet at the house at 2 p.m. The skip Monica has hired arrives just after they do. The heat is oppressive – thirty-six degrees outside, hotter still inside the shed. The lack of a formal Property Recovery Order puts Monica in a precarious position. Technically, until settlement, it is still Sav's address. They know he has been back to the house and lied about handing in his key. The thought makes them uneasy, and they work quickly in the sweltering heat.

The neighbour, Darren, and his son Stu come over to lend a hand. As Monica expected, most of what Sav left behind is worthless: broken appliances, battered wardrobes, outmoded tables and chairs, bags of outgrown clothes that once belonged to Daniel and Benji, and two old mattresses. A few pieces – a couple of chairs and a chest of drawers in decent condition – are left on the kerb with a 'For Free' sign. After a few hours, the job is done. Luca Savington doesn't appear.

When Steve gets home, he checks on the progress of the letter he posted to the Police Commissioner. He sees it was delivered to the Paramatta address earlier in the day.

Kon Karapanagiotidis, founder of the Asylum Centre Resource Centre, posted the following comments on Bluesky Social:
5 women killed in the last 8 days due to male violence in Australia and yet neither Albo nor Dutton have uttered a word in 2025 about safety of women. They are not part of emergency cabinets, social cohesion or community safety pledges, or speeches they've made this year. How is the safety of women from violence not the top social cohesion and community safety issue for our so-called leaders?
To put the above comments in context, there has been a rise in hate crimes against the Jewish community. Following an arson attack on a childcare centre near the Maroubra synagogue in Sydney, Prime Minister Albanese has convened a national cabinet on antisemitism.

DAY 163 – ON THE PROWL

Monica to the real estate agent:
Hi… did Sav get the keys off you? He was just at the house throwing stuff into the skip bin. He has overloaded the bin, which could be an issue when it is picked up.
Real estate agent:
Hey, no. I have the full set in my office. Definitely haven't given any out. That's strange, because he assured me yesterday that I had all the keys and

he was out of the area. Neighbour on LHS said she hadn't seen anyone around for the past few days. Very strange.

Monica:

Yes, other neighbours saw him, and they have video cameras. He put surfboards and other items in the bin.

Monica exchanges texts with Narelle and Georgia:

Darren saw Sav driving around the area. He's prowling again.

Narelle:

Looking to see where you are.

Georgia:

At least you have a camera. Does it show the street?

Monica:

Yes. It shows the street.

DAY 164 – THE DVO

While out shopping, Monica runs into two former neighbours from across the road. After asking how Benji is, they tell her that the previous day, Sav had been out the front causing a commotion, yelling, and throwing things around. The likely trigger for his angst was that Monica had been to the house without his knowledge. They add that Sav had a young boy with him, which unsettles Monica, given how he treated his own son.

Later that afternoon, Monica and Steve meet with Lisa. She is upbeat about their prospects and suggests that, because of Sav's behaviour throughout proceedings – and the fact that he both instigated and then withdrew from them – it is increasingly likely he will be ordered to pay costs for the Family Court hearings, including the ICL's fees. Monica and Steve temper their expectations, but it is encouraging to hear.

Lisa explains that the reason she has been unable to contact the ICL is that she is still on vacation. Many in the legal profession take time off at this time of year, some courts even close. The Supreme Court, for instance, shuts before Christmas and does not reopen until February 3. Lisa also mentions a possible

Family Court date for the final hearing, though it is still nearly two months away.

According to Lisa, the officer who issued Monica's DVO and the police prosecutor both want it dropped, but procedure prevents DVOs being withdrawn once they are issued. The same thing happened with Steve's DVO – Detective Bauer wanted it revoked once she knew the truth, but her superior refused. Steve is confused. This information doesn't align with what he was previously told by police, nor with the information on the Legal Aid NSW website, which states you can apply to vary or revoke a provisional order by contacting the Local Area Command (LAC) of the police who applied.

'But they dropped Monica's other DVO,' says Steve.

'That's because they still have another one in place,' replies Lisa.

Which raises the question: why did police issue two DVOs in the first place?

'I've put in a complaint to the NSW Police Commissioner about Monica's DVO,' says Steve.

'That can only help. But they'll only intervene if there was a procedural error,' Lisa replies.

The fabricated DVO continues to cause immense problems. It influenced the ICL's recommendations to the Family Court and, because of her power, led to the senior registrar's ruling that prevents Benji from being alone with his perfectly capable mother. According to Lisa, it is unlikely the ICL will move to have the Family Court order lifted while the DVO remains in place. Yet police have been aware of Luca Savington's lies for well over six months. They know Monica is the innocent victim.

As previously mentioned, misidentification is a serious problem. Numerous victims of domestic violence have suffered similar fates to Monica.

The point was made earlier that many women leaving abusive relationships cannot afford a solicitor and are forced to rely on Legal Aid. In Monica's case, the $15,000 cap for a Legal Aid matter would have made it impossible for her to keep pace with Sav and stay in the fight for Benji. By this stage, her legal fees are three to four times the Legal Aid limit. In any case, she would have been unlikely to qualify.

Katherine McKernan, Executive Director of National Legal Aid, noted in an interview on ABC Radio National Breakfast (Jan 23, 2025) that receiving help from Legal Aid is far from guaranteed. Only 8% of Australian families qualify – excluding many women who live below the poverty line. These women are left with a bleak choice: defend themselves in court or do nothing at all.

Luca Savington's first wife did nothing, and she became a sitting duck for Sav's spurious accusations. Katherine McKernan identified another problem facing women wanting to leave abusive relationships: solicitors are not always available in Indigenous and rural communities.

DAY 166 – POOR SAV

There is a picture of Luca Savington on Instagram. He is wearing a white gown and lying in a hospital bed, with standard cardiac monitoring tubes attached to his chest. Below the post, uploaded from somewhere on the Gold Coast, is a cloying plea to Leonardo and Marco – a nostalgic lament for their childhood and the passing of time. Sav humbly praises his sons, claiming they taught him invaluable lessons about life.

Leonardo and Marco will recognise this strategy – drawing sympathy, feigning remorse, expressing gratitude, heaping praise – all designed to lure the target back into his orbit for another spin on the emotional rollercoaster.

Monica:
He's pretending to be in Queensland.
Narelle
What!
Georgia:
That says five days ago.
Monica:
He was hanging around here five days ago.
Steve:
BS's photo looks familiar. I'm sure it is the same one he posted last January, from a hospital bed in Newcastle, when he tried to get Monica to go back to him.

Steve sends a fax to the police prosecutor who'll be prosecuting Sav's case against Monica, asking for the DVO to be revoked. It contains the same information that was posted to The Police Commissioner's Office, faxed to the police station in western NSW that instigated proceedings against Monica. It can't do any harm. At worse it will be ignored.

DAY 178 – ROSES

It's Rose Day when lovers exchange roses as a symbol of love. The Family Impact Report has been released, and the findings are anything but rosy for Luca Savington. Sav's involvement in Benji's upbringing is seen as problematic due to his history of coercive control and willingness to use Benji to attain revenge. It is deemed likely he will continue in his attempts to turn Benji against Monica and her family to the detriment of the child.

It is recommended Monica have full responsibility for Benji. If Sav is to have any contact, it should be minimal. The possibility of Sav being allowed two-hour supervised monthly visits is mentioned. It is recommended that the order placing Narelle in a supervisory parenting role be lifted as the evidence points to Monica being a capable parent. Sav's attempts to demonise her are noted. As are Sav's accusations against Steve. If Steve is cleared of wrongdoings (which has already happened), it is advised that he and Benji be reacquainted gradually, with the support of a counsellor.

A few days later, a letter arrives for Steve at Irene's house in New Lambton. When he is told it is from the police, he grows apprehensive, bracing for the possibility that Luca Savington has concocted new allegations. He asks Irene to open it. His fears ease as she reads it aloud. The letter is a reply from the NSW Police Commissioner's Office, acknowledging receipt of his complaint and confirming it has been forwarded to the relevant command within the NSW Police Force for 'appropriate attention.'

DAY 195 – TORTILLA CHIPS

It is National Tortilla Chip Day. That such a day exists to celebrate a corn chip seems almost comical. Steve accompanies Monica to her solicitor's appointment. Lisa welcomes them into her office, mentioning she'd run into Sav's solicitor the previous Friday at the fish and chip shop near her office. Although Sav has withdrawn from Family Court proceedings, his solicitor is still handling the property settlement and criminal court matters. As she was leaving the shop, Lisa asked him to send through details of Sav's upcoming court appearance.

Monica and Steve are frustrated that Lisa still hasn't spoken with the ICL, as she had promised at the last appointment. When Monica pushes the issue, Lisa says it might be possible to have Steve's restrictions lifted before the final hearing – but the ICL would not agree to lifting Monica's restrictions while the DVO against her remained in place.
'How is the boy?' asks Lisa. Her interest in Benji is genuine – she was visibly distressed when Sav was manipulating him.
'He'll be much better when his Pop comes home,' Monica replies.

Monica's DVO is listed for court in two weeks. Lisa now has Sav's police interview and the documentation that led to the order being issued. In his affidavits, and on the DVO, Sav asserted that he had a witness – first Sienna, then more recently Leonardo. When Leonardo came to her Sienna's house and spoke with her, he had said he also would not lie in court for his father. The police evidence reveals the reality: Sav doesn't have a witness to his claims. It is just his word. Lisa says she intends to file for costs against the police on the grounds they knew for some time that Sav's claims were false.

Monica:
I have to go to court in two weeks for the DVO hearing against me. The barrister is confident, but it means more time off work. Lisa heard back from Sav's solicitor, and his upcoming court date is for a DVO breech from last July. We are not certain but think it is to do with the lolly bags. If Sav pleads guilty, he will be breaching his good behaviour bond. If he pleads not guilty, it will go to court again. Lisa doesn't know how much money is in the trust. The

trust account is with Sav's solicitor. This is annoying because it is not what we agreed to at mediation.

Georgia:

Lisa is meant to have the trust account. Did you question that?

Monica:

Yes, I did. She said it doesn't matter who it's with because it can't be withdrawn without two signatures.

Georgia:

Hmm. I don't know why she says one thing and does another.

Monica:

Lisa said Sav's solicitor keeps emailing her about getting his money. We agreed at mediation to release $40,000 after the sale of the house, so Sav could pay his legal bill ($30,000 according to Lisa). But Lisa doesn't want the money dispersed until costs are decided. I got an email today saying we had overpaid $1260 when the mortgage was discharged. Sav tried to get the money put into his account. I rang ME banking and got it stopped. I contacted Lisa and Sav's solicitor (the conveyancer and trustee) and told them it had to go into the trust account.

Georgia:

The audacity. Especially when you're on the email too. What a fool!

Monica:

I sent Lisa an email saying I didn't think Sav's solicitor should be in control of the trust. That I wanted her to do it. And that we need to do something about bringing Dad home.

Steve's diary:

Mulling over events of the past year, the impact of Monica's DVO cannot be underestimated. It was instrumental in ensuring Benji remained in Luca Savington's clutches, even though the DCJ knew the child was being coerced and psychologically abused by the father. It seems incredulous a DVO was granted WITHOUT ONE SHRED OF EVIDENCE. Both DVOs served on Monica were based on what a jealous, abusive, deceitful, and manipulative ex-partner told the police, and as the statistics show, police regularly mistake perpetrators for victims.

If Sav has breached his DVO, why have the police taken until now to charge him over an incident that happened eight months earlier? Is it because of the faxes Steve sent to the police four weeks earlier? Maybe it is a result of his complaint to The Police Commissioner.

DAY 197 – TRUST

Monica still hasn't received any information from Sav's solicitors regarding the house settlement or the trust account. She has no idea how much money is in the trust. The previous day, she emailed McGuiness & Associates, requesting the property settlement and trust account details, but they have not responded. Frustrated, she decides to phone their office.

The woman who answers is adamant that no documentation will be sent until Monica signs for the release of $40,000 from the trust account, as agreed. Her tone is sharp and dismissive, scolding Monica for calling and warning her not to contact the office again. Monica stands her ground. She refuses to sign for the release of the money. Two days later, McGuiness & Associates relent, finally sending through the trust and property settlement details.

The behaviour of Luca Savington's solicitors has not gone unnoticed; that the firm supported him with his fabricated affidavits (supposedly punishable by imprisonment), apparently without him having to pay a cent, is morally wrong. The proposition that Monica could drink three or four bottles of wine a night and hold down a steady job, take children to school, social and sporting activities, is beyond the realms of reality. Yet they repeated the accusations after the follicle test came back negative, and after Monica's work record and a reference from her doctor had been filed. The solicitors will argue they are simply following their client's instructions, but unless they are sleepwalking, they are fully aware of the destructive lies and manipulations they have endorsed. On two occasions, McGuiness & Associates withheld information from the court. The ICL was livid when she discovered Sav had taken Benji to the police station, forcing Sienna to collect him while Sav spent the night behind bars. On the second occasion, when Sav was required to report to the police station, he left Benji at his sister's place for the night and Benji missed school the next day.

The headline in *The Guardian* on March 17, 2025, reads: 'Teachers are describing something different: the escalating culture of misogyny in Australian classrooms.' The article quotes Jess Hill's quarterly essay, and shows what teachers are up against:

On average, young people are thirteen when they get their first lessons in sex and intimacy from free online porn. Almost half find it accidentally, via online searches or pop-ups. In much of this porn, degrading and painful sex acts are unremarkable, as are explicit racism and misogyny. In the majority of these clips, not only do women go along with degrading treatment, but are almost always grateful for it.

The Guardian article highlights the problem facing teachers:
Teachers — more than 70 % of whom are female — are coming up against what Monash researchers Stephaie Wescott and Stephen Roberts have termed a resurgent male supremacy. While sexual harassment in schools isn't a new problem, Teachers are now describing something different: an escalating culture not only of sexual harassment, but of language and behaviours expressing belief in male superiority and other misogynistic views.

Benji is regaining his confidence, and happily plays with friends and attends school but, understandably, he wants to be with his mother at night. He has attempted to sleep over at his friend's place a couple of times but on both occasions, Monica has been called to collect him in the middle of the night. Which means, according to the Family Court ruling, Narelle must always be at the house. The court order is placing an insurmountable pressure on everybody. Steve has been isolated, separated from his family for nine months. He has had a place to stay, but for many men that would not be the case. Considering Steve's DVO dissolved months earlier, the Family Court orders become more absurd the longer they are in place.

DAY 212 – DAVID VS GOLIATH

It is National Good Samaritan Day. Perhaps it is an omen and Monica's DVO will be dropped. Monica and Steve meet with Monica's barrister in Lisa's office before court. As they thought, Sav's upcoming court appearance is regarding the paper bag incident. He has been charged, and the barrister plans to use it to highlight Sav's reputation as a troublemaker – to show his disregard and disrespect for the law. He hasn't yet entered a plea.

The barrister expects that today the magistrate will rule in Monica's favour once Sav's history of DVO breaches is laid out. After a brief discussion with Lisa about the magistrate who will be hearing the case, he adds a now-familiar caution, there are no guarantees.'

Steve discusses the DVO system with the barrister, and he reiterates what Lisa said previously: the police are unwilling to withdraw DVOs once they are in place. The problem, according to the barrister, is that the police crime officers (it is not just an issue with this command) will not budge once a DVO is issued because they will be in the firing line if a mistake is made. The barrister makes a derisory quip about crime officers not being solicitors, but police who have risen through the ranks.

Narelle arrives as they are finishing up, and they all make their way across to the courthouse. It is only five minutes away. The building is dilapidated, its wooden frame crying out for renovation – even a lick of paint would help. The sheriff, gruff in appearance and manner, could have stepped straight off the set of a Mad Max movie. There is no X-ray machine, so he checks everyone manually with a hand-scanner. Steve goes first and strolls down the corridor where he spots Luca Savington sitting alone in a small waiting area. Steve quickly returns to the sheriff, asking if there is a safe room for Monica. A middle-aged woman soon arrives and escorts her into another part of the maze-like structure. Steve waits for Narelle to clear security, and together they walk past a poker-faced Sav, taking a seat in another room.
Monica's barrister approaches them after ten minutes or so, and they enter the court room.

The barrister is running a 'show to cause' hearing, meaning it must be shown beyond a reasonable doubt that Sav is fearful for his safety. He has tendered the filed statements and Family Court orders to the magistrate and the police prosecutor, who are aware that Luca Savington is still before the courts for breaching his DVO.

After the current case ends, the barrister, knowing the magistrate has a 'partially heard' trial to attend to next, approaches the court and asks if Monica's case can be heard after lunch. This is agreed to by the magistrate.
'It's better than waiting around all day. Come back at two o'clock,' says the barrister, adding, 'Just make sure you don't go too far away, in case we get called earlier.'

They return to the courthouse at 1:50 pm, only to find it locked, with nobody else in sight. Moments later, Luca Savington appears. When he sees them, he stops in his tracts, then quietly takes a seat around the corner, out of view. Just before two, Monica's barrister saunters into the grounds, his face unreadable as usual. Maybe years in the job have made him detached; his demeanour never changing, no matter the news he carries.

This time, his words are honey to their ears, 'I've spoken with the police prosecutor. He's withdrawing Monica's DVO.'

For a moment, they simply stare at him, bewildered. For twelve long months Monica has lived under the shadow of the document, hanging over her like an executioner's axe. Finally, common sense has prevailed. Steve can hardly believe it. That very morning, they had been told police policy was to never withdraw a DVO.

'You can go,' says the barrister. 'I'll stay and sign a few papers, but there's no need for you to be here.'

They thank him vociferously, their elation on full display. On the matter of costs, however, his view differs from Lisa's. Only in extreme circumstances, he says, will magistrates rule against the police and, in his experience, that has happened just twice.

Monica, Narelle, and Steve leave through the side gate, glimpsing the dour face of Luca Savington sitting alone, head down. He has been at the courthouse all morning, waiting for his chance to watch Monica suffer.
'He has no idea what's going on,' Steve quips. 'I'd love to see his face when he finds out.'

With the last of the DVOs gone, the relief is palpable. The path is now clear for the Family Court to lift its restrictive orders. The barrister's fee for the day: $2,200. Lisa's preparation fee will be similar. Defending the two DVOs has cost Monica near on $20,000. And that's just the financial cost.

For the police officers who issued and authorised the two DVOs against Monica, there will be no consequences. It is unlikely they will ever acknowledge that their decisions empowered an abuser, kept a capable mother from her son for over seven months, and caused immense grief. Nor will they ever have to face the fact that their actions were complicit in inflicting psychological damage on a ten-year-old boy, or that, according to domestic violence experts, they had placed his life at risk.

A week later, Narelle is perusing the court lists when she comes across Monica's DVO – supposedly withdrawn the previous week. The discovery triggers a wave of anxiety leading up to the Family Court hearing. Monica contacts Lisa, who reassures her it is a clerical error – the police had confirmed the withdrawal to her the week before.

There is a brief compliance and readiness hearing to prepare for the final hearing which the solicitors attend. Lisa has spoken with the ICL, who agrees to the restrictive orders being lifted and that Monica be granted sole care of Benji. But that won't take effect until the final hearing, which is still six weeks away. Ordinarily the wait would be far longer, but Lisa already has a matter listed that will not require its full three-day allocation and she manages to have Monica's case slotted into that space.

DAY 267 – PENULTIMATE FINAL HEARING

One might expect that an uncontested final hearing would be a straightforward matter.

The ICL, the NSW Department of Communities and Justice (DCJ), and the court report all recommend Monica be given sole parenting rights and that the restrictive orders imposed at the interim hearing be excluded from the final orders. A ruling on costs will, hopefully, be decided in Monica's favour, considering Sav and his solicitors have repeatedly misled and lied to the court. But as the Kelty family has come to realise, when dealing with the Family Law Court, expectations count for little. For predicting the outcome, Murphy's Law, 'If anything can go wrong it will,' is the relevant legal precedent.

When proceedings begin, the senior registrar asks for Luca Savington's address. Both the ICL – appearing by video link – and Lisa explain that the father's solicitor refuses to disclose it, and that all correspondence has been sent to Sav's email account. The senior registrar is displeased, though she offers no solution. She then expresses her annoyance that the ICL is not attending the hearing in person, despite knowing this would be the case.

To an outsider, it appears the senior registrar is stalling – an impression reinforced when she blames Lisa for not providing sufficient proof that Monica's DVO has been withdrawn. Lisa responds that all documentation supplied by the police has already been forwarded to the court. She doesn't press the issue, not wanting to get the senior registrar offside. If it was insufficient, why wasn't Lisa informed earlier?

10:15 am, Georgia:
Have you gone in?
Narelle:
Yes. Just adjourned while the magistrate reads the appropriate parts.

During the break in proceedings, Lisa is given permission to access police records. She uncovers more details of Luca Savington's sordid past. Along with earlier allegations of assault and suspected larceny, there are AVOs taken out by Luca Savington himself – most likely his early attempts at playing the victim.

Also on file is a statement from Detective Bauer, who investigated the sexual abuse allegations against Steve. Bauer admits to being initially 'duped' by Sav. This was on police record back in early June before the interim hearing even commenced. Bauer further notes that the father is likely to react in a hostile manner if the Family Court decision goes against him – putting both mother and child in danger.

On record, too, is a statement from Sienna, declaring that Sav fabricated the allegations against Steve. Yet Steve's DVO remained in place. When Bauer's comments are combined with the court report and the extensive DCJ files warning that the child is at serious risk of harm, the questions loom large: Why wasn't something done to protect Benji? Why was a child left in the care of a man with a history of violence for so long?

Two hours pass.
12:15 pm, Georgia:
Has the registrar read it yet?

Monica:

No. It's likely to be adjourned to another day. From what Lisa is saying, six weeks at least.

Georgia:

What! Six weeks to read a file? Hopefully, they pull a rabbit out of the bag. The interim hearing looked like this too.

Monica:

June 25.

Georgia:

Omg. Whyyyy?

Monica:

There was an earlier date available, in four weeks, but Benji's solicitor (the ICL) wasn't available.

Georgia:

Gosh, this is a joke. Are they saying why they aren't doing it today?

Monica:

Magistrate not ready.

Georgia:

God! Why not? Will the magistrate cover the costs?

Narelle:

Sav withdrew from proceedings four months earlier. The senior register was assigned the case eight weeks ago, back when the interim hearing ended. Now she needs time to read the documents. Really!

The official transcript reads the hearing was vacated because there was 'no appearance by or on behalf of the Respondent Father when the matter was called at 10:14 am.' That there was 'insufficient evidence as to service on the Applicant Father and the Respondent Mother also sought further time to file evidence as to the outcome of the Local Court DVO proceedings.' The registrar now insists the ICL attend court in person.

Steve:

Regardless of what the official transcript says, for those sitting in the courtroom, the ineptitude of the Family Court is obvious. The sedated 88-armed octopus kept everyone at the courthouse well into the afternoon, waiting for something to happen. Nothing did. More legal costs (thankfully Monica has not hired a barrister), unpaid leave from work, and a day wasted for all in attendance.

The Family Court has proven to be inadequate at every turn. Over a year ago, the allocated registrar was replaced with a junior one. Benji – despite being assessed by the DCJ as being at risk – was left with an unhinged father, while Monica was forced to accept two-hour fortnightly visits. Then came the long-anticipated interim hearing, where the senior registrar took two months to deliver a decision – despite the DCJ, the court report, and the ICL having all declared that Benji was at serious risk of harm with his father and subject to ongoing psychological abuse.

The latest inaction means the unworkable, unjust, and unnecessary restrictions – which continue to have a negative impact on the lives of Benji, Monica, Narelle, and Steve – remain in place. The Family Court has not acted in the best interests of the child. If Monica's case is any indication, the Family Court has become a detached, haughty institution, seemingly oblivious to the impact of its actions on the lives of the people it was created to serve and protect.

Monica's legal costs to this point – with the final hearing and property distribution (likely to end up in court) still ahead of her – total $71,495.50.

DAY 316 – THE FINAL HEARING

The wind howls through the streets of the city as Monica and Steve make their way from the carpark and into the Family Court building for what they hope will be the last time. Narelle is expected in half an hour, after dropping the boys at school. Chantel and Phillip will meet them inside the courthouse.

Monica and Steve pass through security and take the lift to the fourth floor. They check the court listings and discover their case is up second. When Lisa arrives, they retreat to a private room. She grumbles about the extensive roadworks she encountered on the drive into town, pulling two massive bundles of paper from her bag.
'A rainforest of paper,' Monica jokes, easing the tension.

Today's hearing might feel like a fait accompli, but they all know anything is possible. They engage in light conversation while Lisa organises her files.

Narelle arrives, followed shortly by Chantel and Phillip. Soon it is time to move to the courtroom. Their group takes up most of the public seating. The ICL enters and positions herself next to Lisa. Her stack of papers rivals Lisa's – a stark reminder of the countless hours spent deciding Benji's fate.

The first case is deferred after a brief exchange between the senior registrar and an extensively bearded solicitor. There is a pause while the senior registrar makes notes, then she addresses Lisa and the ICL. The ICL, clearly miffed at having to appear in person, makes a quip about the registrar postponing the previous hearing – adding that it was unfair on Benji, Monica, and her family, who 'have been put through enough already.'

The solicitors make their final presentations. Lisa mentions Sav's recently discovered criminal history and his upcoming court case for the DVO breach. The ICL reiterates points from the interim hearing, which paint Sav as an unsavoury, despicable character. When the ICL finishes, the senior registrar adjourns to deliberate.

Fifteen minutes later, Steve is at the coffee shop down the road when his phone buzzes. A text, alerting him that the court is reconvening. He dashes back, leaving Chantel and Phillip to collect the order. As he re-enters the courtroom, the senior registrar is already delivering her findings. From the back pew, it is difficult to hear clearly – her hushed tones appear aimed at the recording device. The summation lasts thirty to forty minutes.

The Family Court of Australia orders on a final basis that:
– All previous orders are discharged (Steve, Narelle and Monica's restrictions are lifted).
– The child is to live with the mother.
– The mother has sole decision-making authority.
– The mother may obtain a passport for the child without the father's consent.
– It is noted that the applicant father has not appeared.

Joy erupts in the courtroom. They move the celebration to one of the meeting rooms. It has been seventeen months since Steve has been allowed to see Benji. Ten months since the interim hearing and the imposition of the restrictive orders. Their jubilation continues as they inform family and friends of the registrar's decision.

Lisa declares, 'We've won round one.' Round one? Feels more like a thirty rounder! Over the past eighteen months, Monica's solicitors (Adele, Lisa, and the ICL) have been required to attend thirteen sessions before court; the reason it has been so costly. Lisa also had to respond to the affidavits and numerous allegations she received from Sav via his solicitor.

Steve waits until an opportune moment, to discuss the elephant in the room. The senior registrar did not make a ruling on costs.

The non-decision on costs came about because the ICL filed for the court to pay her legal fees, capped at $16,000 – a modest amount considering the work she has done. The reasoning was that not only was Luca Savington unlikely to contribute, but if a ruling on costs went against Luca Savington, he may react aggressively, endangering both mother and child. This was a concern expressed by Detective Bauer and supported by the court report. The senior registrar accepted the ICLs argument, and it put Lisa in a difficult position. If she filed for costs against Sav, it would appear as though she was not acting in the best interests of the child. After a brief exchange with a not-too-impressed Monica, Lisa chose not to file for costs against Luca Savington.

While Steve expresses his disappointment at the court's handling of the cost issue, Lisa's reply gives them reason for hope. After reiterating what she had told Monica – that her hand was forced by the ICL and senior registrar – she tells them she intends trying to 'claw back costs' from Sav's share of the asset distribution. How this works out in practice will be interesting. Unless there is a 'conversion on the way to Damascus,' it is unlikely Sav will agree to paying a share of Monica's legal bill, nor to the assets being split in favour of Monica.

Steve Kelty:
As Sav initiated proceedings, caused the delays, and ultimately withdrew from proceedings when he knew he couldn't win, it seems only right that he be made to pay at least a share of Monica's expenses. From my perspective, I witnessed three females (the senior registrar and two solicitors) caving in to a recalcitrant male – because of what he might do. Isn't that giving in to the abuser? Using the same logic, Luca Savington should get everything he wants when the assets are divided in case he reacts angrily. It felt like a massive cop out. Isn't it in the child's interest that the mother has sufficient money to provide for herself and the child? On the positive side, the senior registrar ruled that the ICL's legal fees be paid by the Commonwealth, which means Monica will not be out of pocket for her share.

A DAY LATER – REUNION

When Monica tells Benji that Steve will be moving into the house, Benji doesn't react. But he must be wondering how his Pop will treat him. They decide the best way for Benji and Steve to reconnect is at a family picnic. At Lambton Park, Monica and Narelle prepare lunch while Benji kicks a ball with Daniel. When Steve arrives, he greets Daniel first, then turns to Benji, asking how his soccer is going. Benji proudly says he scored two goals the previous day. Sensing the need to ease in gently, Steve gives him space.

Ten minutes later, as they eat chicken and salad rolls together, Steve asks if Benji is still riding his bike. Benji jumps in, asking if they can ride the following afternoon after school. He wants to ride to the 7-Eleven – a trip he hasn't been allowed to make on his own. He has an ulterior motive: to buy a slushy and try a new savoury snack that has just come out. 'I have the money,' he says, explaining that Nana paid him for a job around the house.

Steve tells him he can't just yet – his bike is still at his sister's place – but the message is clear. Benji feels comfortable with his Pop and is more than happy to be alone with him. He knows now that his Pop, like the rest of Monica's family, does not resent him, despite what his father might have told him. Benji is young, resilient, and strong-minded. The separation from Monica and his virtual imprisonment must have been traumatic, and it may haunt him at times, but he will recover.

PROSECUTION – LACKLUSTRE

As the day approaches for Luca Savington to appear in court for breaching his DVO, police contact Monica. Sav is pleading not guilty to delivering two paper bags containing sweets to Monica and Daniel in the McDonald's car park in 2024, which means Monica must attend court as a witness. If convicted, Lisa believes Sav may face gaol time, but the best outcome for Monica will be an extension of the DVO.

Steve and Monica arrive at the courthouse at the same time as Phillip and Chantel. Monica and Chantel retreat into the safe room. Once again, Narelle comes after dropping Daniel and Benji at school. Sav's breach is heard around 11 am.

The police officer testifies first. The defence lawyer asks whether there is photographic evidence from the McDonald's car park. She answers no. Does she have the actual paper bags? No. Have they been fingerprinted? No. Has the handwriting been checked by experts? No.

Monica is questioned in a closed courtroom. As expected, Luca Savington lies, claiming she concocted the evidence. Sav's barrister also accuses her of lying and fabricating the paper bag story to gain advantage in the Family Court. This isn't challenged by the prosecutor. The prosecutor's cross-examination is lacklustre. Sav simply denies the handwriting on the paper bags is his. The police didn't bother taking statements from Narelle or Sienna, both of whom would have corroborated Monica's account.

In his summing up, the magistrate quotes several similar cases and concludes that both Monica's and Sav's accounts are believable. He states that he can only judge the matter on what is presented to him. On that basis, he finds insufficient evidence to convict. 'Beyond reasonable doubt' is the required standard of proof, and the magistrate rules that threshold has not been met.

Phillip:
From the moment the defence lawyer commenced cross-examination of the police constable, it was clear the prosecution case was poorly prepared, and a guilty verdict was unlikely. Many simple but key aspects of the police investigation had not been done. A significant miss was

they failed to contact the maternal grandmother and have her appear as a witness. This alone could have resulted in a guilty finding. To say the prosecution was poorly prepared would be generous. They were abysmal.

Steve:
Sitting in the courtroom and witnessing the ill-prepared crown case, to me it seemed the police prosecutor was just going through the motions. Maybe taking on this twelve-month-old breach was a response to my complaint to the Police Commissioner, just ticking the box. Monica had to face accusations from Sav's solicitor, and the prosecution did not have a comeback. The court support worker who assisted Monica said many abused women do not turn up to court. After witnessing Sav and his solicitor attack Monica with unchallenged malicious lies, why would an abused woman put herself through it? At least Sav knows we won't back down. That he will be held to account.

According to Lisa, a conviction against Sav would have counted against him if the property settlement went to court, adding to his profile as a law-breaking unsavoury type, unwilling to abide by court rulings or to contribute to his son's ongoing care. But surely this is the case already, with the damning Family Court edict and his criminal history, including the recently discovered convictions of assault and suspected larceny.

MEDIATION – THE BULLDOG

The mediation takes place by video hook-up, with each party in the company of their solicitor. Sav's initial ask is 46%, with each to keep the assets they already hold. Lisa is in her element, putting Luca Savington's solicitor on the back foot by demanding 100% of the remaining trust funds. Lisa argues that if the matter goes to court, given Sav's police record, the fact he illegally sold off assets, his behaviour in the Family Court and that it is deemed unlikely he will contribute to his son's upbringing, Monica will almost certainly get the lot. Monica said Lisa was formidable, with Sav's inexperienced solicitor clearly out of his depth.

Sav's solicitor counters with an offer of 44.5%, but Lisa refuses to negotiate unless they 'get serious.' Monica then agrees to give Sav $15,000 of the remaining trust funds but holds firm beyond that. Hours drag by, neither side budging, until Monica – weighing the likely cost of a court hearing – makes a final offer of $30,000. This means Sav walks away with $70,000, after taking into account the $40,000 he has already been given from the trust.

The mediator spends most of his time with Sav and his solicitor. What is said remains unknown, but it is likely Sav is reminded of points Lisa made and that he runs the risk of ending up with nothing and could even lose his precious car. Whatever is said, Sav capitulates, to everyone's surprise.

Afterwards, Monica feels an enormous sense of relief. A weight begins to lift – not just the burden of the past eighteen months, but the strain carried throughout her twelve-year marriage to Luca Savington. Apart from the divorce, which is a formality, it is over.

When the calculations are done – factoring in the assets Sav sold off or still possesses – the final division is close to 70-30%. It is a far better outcome for Monica than the 60-40% split Lisa offered Sav at the first mediation months earlier, before the house was sold.

SUMMATION – SOMETHING IS SERIOUSLY WRONG

At the time of writing, there is no indication Luca Savington will be held to account for his actions.

The ICL, Lisa, the DCJ, the NSW Child Abuse Squad and the Family Court are aware
that Luca Savington coached Benji to frame Steve Kelty. The ICL submitted files to the Family Court from Benji's Child Abuse Squad interview showing phrases he used were identical to those Sav's son Leonardo used, in a case against his uncle years earlier.

Something is seriously wrong with a justice system that allows a person to manipulate a child and make false allegations of sexual abuse with impunity.

Something is seriously wrong with a justice system that allows a person to instigate proceedings by making numerous false allegations, only to withdraw when those fabrications are exposed – leaving the victim burdened with a massive legal bill and a damaged reputation.

The Family Court is aware that Luca Savington's affidavits contained blatant lies.
They have the power to act.

- **Power of Referral (Dorter Family Lawyers and Mediators)**
  Despite the protection offered by Section128 (Family Law Act), the Court retains powers to refer matters to appropriate agencies or departments, where it considers an investigation is warranted (including the Director of Public Prosecutions).

There is something seriously wrong with a justice system that permits an individual to fabricate death threats against themselves – for the purpose of falsely incriminating another – without consequence.

There is something seriously wrong when a person with Sav's documented history can make false allegations to the police, claim victim status – bearing in mind that perpetrators of domestic violence are predominantly male – and be granted two DVOs against a woman who is a respected member of the community.

As discussed earlier, statistics show it is not uncommon for DVOs to be granted on false grounds – in favour of the abuser. Something is seriously wrong when these orders significantly influence Family Court decisions.

Something is seriously wrong with a child protection system that allows an 8-year-old child – deemed by experts to be at serious risk of harm – to be left in the care of a mentally unstable father with a history of violence.

Each month in Newcastle, leading support workers in the field of domestic and family violence meet with NSW police. Cases are reviewed, and police are provided with a prioritised list of women considered at risk of serious harm from their ex-partners. Yet, while Monica sat at the very top of this list, she was persistently harassed by police – carrying out the bidding of Luca Savington, her abuser. Something is seriously wrong when police relentlessly pursue a woman who has been assessed by experts to be the victim, and as someone in grave danger.

Something is seriously wrong with a law enforcement system that denies a woman protection because her abuser – a man with a history of violence – downplays an incident as a 'normal argument between husband and wife.' To reiterate, had a DVO been granted to Monica when she first left Luca Savington and reported his abuse, it would have restricted his capacity to wreak havoc on the lives of Monica, Benji, Steve, Narelle, and their family. It would have saved Monica seventy thousand dollars in legal expenses and prevented the egregious waste of police, court, and community resources.

These events occurred in 2024-25, at a time when deaths from domestic violence were at record levels and attracting widespread political and media scrutiny.

SOMETHING IS SERIOUSLY WRONG.

ACKNOWLEDGEMENTS:

Thank you for reading *SOMETHING IS SERIOUSLY WRONG.*

Monica and her family extend their sincere thanks to the friends and relatives whose unwavering support sustained them through the dark days. They also acknowledge the Newcastle domestic violence support network and the staff of the Mater Hospital for their understanding, insight and professionalism.

A special thanks to Janet for her astute insights and on-going support. Thank you Vicki for providing much needed advice. Thanks Jinny for your invaluable expertise. I'd also like to express my gratitude to Jill, Sharon and Steven.